WOMEN

THE·LONGEST
·REVOLUTION·

JULIET MITCHELL

WOMEN

THE·LONGEST ·REVOLUTION·

PANTHEON BOOKS, NEW YORK

All rights reserved under International and Pan-American
Copyright Conventions. Published in the United States by
Pantheon Books, a division of Random House, Inc., New
York, and simultaneously in Canada by Random House of
Canada Limited, Toronto.
Originally published in Great Britain in 1984 by Virago
Press, Ltd.

Library of Congress Cataloging in Publication Data

Mitchell, Juliet, 1940–
Women, the longest revolution.
Bibliography: p.
Includes index.
1. Feminism—Addresses, essays, lectures. 2. Women in
literature—Addresses, essays, lectures. 3. Psychoanalysis—
Addresses, essays, lectures. 4. Femininity (Psychology)—Ad-
dresses, essays, lectures. I. Title.
HQ1154.M542 1984   305.4'2   83-43144
ISBN 0-394-72574-3

Manufactured in the United States of America

First American Edition

For Martin and Polly

Contents

8

Preface

I have arranged this selection of essays in three parts: essays and lectures on politics, literature and psychoanalysis. To maintain the theme I have occasionally broken the chronological order by a few months. And although I have situated each piece briefly in time and place, I have not attempted any self-criticism for that would be another book.

I took my degree in English Literature and for ten years taught literature to university students. During this period – the 1960s – I was actively involved in politics, first in Marxist politics around the *New Left Review* and then in the feminism of the Women's Liberation Movement. I wrote both literary and political articles. At the time I thought of my work as going along separate but parallel lines. When I came to make this selection, I could see retrospectively their points of connection in myself.

Not very consciously, as a child and as an adult, I had always been held by a feeling that for the last three hundred years – in English culture at least – our determining sensibility had been about growing up, our relationship to ourselves in time. How do we become ourselves – men or women? This preoccupation took in the question of femininity, of sexual difference.

My first political interests were influenced by the Sartre who claimed that since Freud, novel-writing was almost

9

impossible: to explain character we needed to comprehend the entire determining effect of childhood. I was able to focus a wish to understand something of the position of women around an Althusserian concept of ideology. Ideology was not a plus on top of our social and economic lives; it was the very way we lived ourselves. When I started to write a literary thesis on childhood in the nineteenth-century novel, I used concepts imported from Sartrean phenomenology into psychology by R. D. Laing and David Cooper.

In 1970 I gave up my university post. I wrote *Woman's Estate* (Harmondsworth, 1972) and lectured freelance, mainly abroad, on literature and the politics of feminism. The parallel lines started to come together and the underlying concern in literature and politics met in my growing interest in psychoanalysis. Freud had said: 'We cannot say what a woman is . . . only *how she comes into being* from a child with a bisexual disposition.' I wrote *Psychoanalysis and Feminism* (Harmondsworth, 1974). Then I trained as a psychoanalyst. Today I am a practising psychoanalyst, lecturing in politics, literature and psychoanalysis. I write. In very different ways, the same problems surface in the literary as in the political and psychoanalytic pieces where they emerge as the dominant obsession.

But being a writer is not for me an identity. It is a struggle. Something I delay as long as possible; it mainly has to do with a need to understand what I cannot grasp. Whenever I feel confronted with something that interests but baffles me, I decide to write about it. It could be a novel, a poem, an intellectual problem that perplexes me. My writing is characterised by a sense of solution – always necessarily false, or at best temporary. When I finish something, the experience of relief outweighs the difficulty of the struggle. It is as though something is solved – for the time being. I know the solution is incomplete, fragmentary, will be found wrong, awaits revision, continuation. But for the time being, it is done and I can forget it. The long day's night temporarily is passed. A successful lecture can leave me feeling high. I have included some lectures here. I lecture nearly always from the beginning of a problem; though the lecture may sound rounded and complete in structure, it never is – it consists of some throw-out thoughts that may or may not lead to a task that I shall then have to write about. By the time I write, it is a task. Enough said.

My study of childhood in the English nineteenth-century novel was not of children, but of growth, and how this novel form was organised around central characters who grew up – they did not arrive, as in the French novel, as ready-made adults. An avid novel reader since childhood, I share the preoccupation with the novelists I studied. It is, after all, what Freud's psychoanalysis is about: the child is father or mother to the man or woman.

London, 1983

Acknowledgements

'Aspects of Feminism' is published here by kind permission of the Australian Broadcasting Company; 'On Freud and the Distinction Between the Sexes' appeared originally in *Women and Analysis* edited by Jean Strouse, copyright © 1974 by Jean Strouse, published by Grossman Publishers, a division of Viking Penguin; 'Freud and Lacan: Psychoanalytic Theories of Sexual Difference' is published by kind permission of The Macmillan Press; 'What Maisie Knew: Portrait of the Artist as a Young Girl' first appeared in *Air of Reality: New Essays on Henry James*, and is published by kind permission of Methuen Ltd; 'Women: The Longest Revolution' and 'Psychoanalysis and Child Development' are published by kind permission of *New Left Review*; 'Moll Flanders: The Rise of Capitalist Woman' is published by kind permission of Penguin Books Ltd; 'The Ordeal of Richard Feverel: A Sentimental Education' was first published in *Meredith Now* edited by I. Fletcher (Routledge & Kegan Paul, London, 1971).

I should like to thank Rosalind Delmar and Margaret Walters.

Part I

Feminism and the Question of Women

Women: The Longest Revolution

¶ 'Women: The Longest Revolution'
was published in *New Left Review* in 1966. It was taken up
subsequently by the Women's Movement and appeared
(pirated) frequently as a pamphlet and in anthologies.
Written before there was a women's movement in Britain
and before I was aware of feminist stirrings in the United
States following Betty Friedan's *The Feminine Mystique*, I
found it satisfying that feminists thus made it retrospectively
their own. It was widely translated.

My interest in women arose negatively. As a student I had
read Simone de Beauvoir's *The Second Sex* and thought it
brilliant but somehow applicable only to some inexplicable
predicament of French women. I was active in the New Left,
where we were then preoccupied with the countries of the
Third World. It was Frantz Fanon's argument from his Algerian
experience that women – a conservative force – should be
emancipated only after a revolution that provoked my
indignation and tied in with my personal experience. I
lectured in a well-established department of English
Literature (Leeds). In the Marxist meetings on the politics of
the Third World, in the University common rooms I
frequented, where were the women? Absent in the practices
and in the theories. Why this sort of common experience led

so many of us to feminism at that particular time, though I can think of many explanations, I do not really know. Anyway, in 1962 I started a book that I never completed on the position of women in Britain; finally, I wrote 'Women: The Longest Revolution' – very much for my New Left friends and colleagues.

It arose out of my involvement with Marxism and my dissatisfaction with any economist understanding of the position of women. The partially buried framework made use of Louis Althusser's work, particularly his then recently published essay: 'Contradiction and Over-determination'. It was Althusser's emphasis on the importance of ideology that I found most useful. His definition of it as 'the way we live ourselves in the world' seemed to me an insistent dimension in any analysis of women. It was one strand that led me forward to my subsequent interest in psychoanalysis.

The situation of women is different from that of any other social group. This is because they are not one of a number of isolable units, but half a totality: the human species. Women are essential and irreplaceable; they cannot therefore be exploited in the same way as other social groups can. They are fundamental to the human condition, yet in their economic, social and political roles, they are marginal. It is precisely this combination – fundamental and marginal at one and the same time – that has been fatal to them. Within the world of men their position is comparable to that of an oppressed minority: but they also exist outside the world of men. The one state justifies the other and precludes protest. In advanced industrial society, women's work is only marginal to the total economy. Yet it is through work that man changes natural conditions and thereby produces society. Until there is a revolution in production, the labour situation will prescribe women's situation within the world of men. But women are offered a universe of their own: the family. Like woman herself, the family appears as a natural object, but it is actually a cultural creation. There is nothing inevitable about the form or role of the family any more than there is about the character or role of women. It is the function of ideology to present these given social types as aspects of Nature itself. Both can be exalted paradoxically, as ideals. The 'true' woman and the 'true' family are images of peace and plenty: in actuality they may both be sites of violence and despair. The apparently natural condition can be made to appear more attractive than the arduous advance of human beings towards culture. But what Marx wrote about the bourgeois myths of the Golden Ancient World describes precisely women's realm: ' . . . in one way the child-like world of the ancients appears to be superior, and this is so, insofar as we seek for closed shape, form and established limitation. The ancients provide a narrow satisfaction, whereas the modern world leaves us unsatisfied or where it appears to be satisfied with itself is vulgar and mean.'

Women in Socialist Theory

The problem of the subordination of women and the need for their liberation was recognised by all the great socialist thinkers in the nineteenth century. It is part of the classical heritage of the revolutionary movement. Yet today, in the West, the problem has become a subsidiary, if not an invisible element in the preoccupations of socialists. Perhaps no other major issue has been so forgotten. In England, the cultural heritage of Puritanism, always strong on the Left, contributed to a widespread diffusion of essentially conservative beliefs among many who would otherwise count themselves as 'progressive'. A *locus classicus* of these attitudes is Peter Townsend's remarkable statement: 'Traditionally Socialists have ignored the family or they have openly tried to weaken it – alleging nepotism and the restrictions placed upon individual fulfilment by family ties. Extreme attempts to create societies on a basis other than the family have failed dismally. It is significant that a Socialist usually addresses a colleague as "brother" and a Communist uses the term "comrade". The chief means of fulfilment in life is to be a member of, and reproduce a family. There is nothing to be gained by concealing this truth.'[1]

How has this counter-revolution come about? Why has the problem of woman's condition become an area of silence within contemporary socialism? August Bebel, whose book *Woman in the Past, Present and Future* was one of the standard texts of the German Social-Democratic Party in the early years of this century, wrote: 'Every Socialist recognises the dependence of the workman on the capitalist, and cannot understand that others, and especially the capitalists themselves, should fail to recognise it also; but the same Socialist often does not recognise the dependence of women on men because the question touches his own dear self more or less nearly.'[2] But this genre of explanation – psychologistic and moralistic – is clearly inadequate. Much deeper and more structural causes have clearly been at work. To consider these would require a major historical study, impossible here. But it can be said with some certainty that part of the explanation for the decline in socialist debate on the subject lies not only in the real historical processes, but in the original weaknesses in the traditional discussion of the subject in the classics. For while the great studies of the last century all stressed the importance of the problem, they did not *solve* it theoretically. The limitations of their approach have never been subsequently transcended.

Fourier was the most ardent and voluminous advocate of women's liberation and of sexual freedom among the early socialists. In a well-known passage he wrote: 'The change in a historical epoch can always be determined by the progress of women towards freedom, because in the relation of woman to man, of the weak to the strong, the victory of human nature over brutality is most evident. The degree of emancipation of women is the natural measure of general emancipation.'[3] Marx quoted this formulation with approval in *The Holy*

Family. But characteristically in his early writings he gave it a more universal and philosophical meaning. The emancipation of women would not only be as Fourier, with his greater preoccupation with sexual liberation saw it, an index of humanisation in the civic sense of the victory of humaneness over brutality, but in the more fundamental sense of the progress of the human over the animal, the cultural over the natural: 'The relation of man to woman is the *most natural* relation of human being to human being. It indicates, therefore, how far man's *natural* behaviour has become human, and how far his *human* essence has become a *natural* essence for him, how far his *human nature* has become *nature* for him.'[4] This theme is typical of the early Marx.

Fourier's ideas remained at the level of utopian moral injunction. Marx used and transformed them, integrating them into a philosophical critique of human history. But he retained the abstraction of Fourier's conception of the position of women as an index of general social advance. This in effect makes it merely a symbol – it accords the problem a universal importance at the cost of depriving it of its specific substance. Symbols are allusions to or derivations of something else. In Marx's early writings woman becomes an anthropological entity, an ontological category, of a highly abstract kind. Contrarily, in his later work, where he is concerned with describing the family, Marx differentiates it as a phenomenon according to time and place: '. . . Marriage, property, the family remain unattacked, in theory, because they are the practical basis on which the bourgeoisie has erected its domination, and because in their bourgeois form they are the conditions which make the bourgeois a bourgeois . . . This attitude of the bourgeois to the conditions of his existence acquires one of its universal forms in bourgeois morality. One cannot, in general, speak of the family *as such.* Historically, the bourgeois gives the family the character of the bourgeois family, in which boredom and money are the binding link, and which also includes the bourgeois dissolution of the family, which does not prevent the family itself from always continuing to exist. Its dirty existence has its counterpart in the holy concept of it in official phraseology and universal hypocrisy. . . [Among the proletariat] the concept of the family does not exist at all . . . In the eighteenth century the concept of the family was abolished by the philosophers, because the actual family was already in process of dissolution at the highest pinnacles of civilisation. The internal family bond was dissolved, the separate components constituting the concept of the family were dissolved, for example, obedience, piety, fidelity in marriage, etc.; but the real body of the family, the property relation, the exclusive attitude in relation to other families, forced cohabitation – relations produced by the existence of children, the structure of modern towns, the formation of capital, etc. – all these were preserved, although with numerous violations because the existence of the family has been made necessary by its connection with the mode of production that exists independently of the will of bourgeois society.'[5] Or, later still, in *Capital*: 'It is, of course, just as absurd to hold the Teutonic-Christian form of the family to be absolute and final as it would be to apply that character to the ancient Roman, the ancient Greek, or the eastern forms which, moreover, taken together form a series in historic development.'[6] What is striking is that here the problem of women has been submerged in an analysis of the family. The difficulties of this approach can be seen in the somewhat apocalyptic note of Marx's comments on the fate of the bourgeois family here and elsewhere (for example, in the *Communist Manifesto*). There was little historical warrant for the idea that it was in effective dissolution, and indeed could no longer be seen in the working class. Marx thus moves from general philosophical formulations about women in the early writings to specific historical comments on the family in the later texts. There is a serious disjunction between the two. The common framework of both, of course, was his analysis of the economy, and of the evolution of property.

Engels

It was left to Engels to systematise these theses in *The Origin of the Family, Private Property and the State*, after Marx's death. Engels declared that the inequality of the sexes was one of the first antagonisms within the human species. The first class antagonism 'coincides with the development of the antagonism between man and woman in the monogamous marriage, and the first class oppression with that of the female sex by the male'.[7] Basing much of his theory on Morgan's inaccurate anthropological investigations, Engels nevertheless had some valuable insights. Inheritance, which is the key to his economist account, was first matrilineal, but with the increase of wealth became patrilineal. This was woman's greatest single setback. The wife's fidelity becomes essential and monogamy is irrevocably established. The wife in the communistic, patriarchal family is a public servant, with monogamy she becomes a private one. Engels effectively reduces the problem of woman to her capacity to work. He therefore gives her physiological weakness as a primary cause of her oppression. He locates the moment of her exploitation at the point of the transition from communal to private property. If inability to work is the cause of her inferior status, ability to work will bring her liberation: '. . . the emancipation of women and their equality with men are impossible and must remain so as long as women are excluded from socially productive work and restricted to housework, which is private. The emancipation of women becomes possible only when women are enabled to take part in production on a large, social, scale, and when domestic duties require their attention only to a minor degree.'[8] Or: 'The first premise for the emancipation of women is the reintroduction of the entire female sex into public industry . . . this . . . demands that the quality possessed by the individual family of being the economic unit of society be abolished.'[9] Engels thus finds a solution schematically appropriate to his analysis of the origin of feminine

oppression. The position of women, then, in the work of
Marx and Engels remains dissociated from, or subsidiary to, a
discussion of the family, which is in its turn subordinated as
merely a precondition of private property. Their solutions
retain this overly economist stress, or enter the realm of
dislocated speculation.

Bebel, Engels' disciple, attempted to provide a pro-
grammatic account of woman's oppression as such, not
simply as a by-product of the evolution of the family and of
private property: 'From the beginning of time oppression was
the common lot of woman and the labourer. . . . *Woman was
the first human being that tasted bondage*, woman was a slave
before the slave existed.'[10] He acknowledged, with Marx and
Engels, the importance of physical inferiority in accounting
for woman's subordination, but while stressing inheritance,
added that a biological element – her maternal function –
was one of the fundamental conditions that made her
economically dependent on the man. But Bebel, too, was
unable to do more than state that sexual equality was
impossible without socialism. His vision of the future was a
vague reverie, quite disconnected from his description of the
past. The absence of a strategic concern forced him into
voluntarist optimism divorced from reality. Lenin himself,
although he made a number of specific suggestions, inherited
a tradition of thought which simply pointed to the *a priori*
equation of socialism with feminine liberation without
showing concretely how it would transform woman's
condition: 'Unless women are brought to take an independent
part not only in political life generally, but also in daily and
universal public service, it is no use talking about full and
stable democracy, let alone socialism.'[11]

The liberation of women remains a normative ideal, an
adjunct to socialist theory, not structurally integrated into it.

The Second Sex
The contrary is true of De Beauvoir's massive work *The Second
Sex* – to this day the greatest single contribution on the

subject. Here the focus is the status of women through the ages. But socialism as such emerges as a curiously contingent solution at the end of the work, in a muffled epilogue. De Beauvoir's main theoretical innovation was to fuse the 'economic' and 'reproductive' explanations of women's subordination by a psychological interpretation of both. Man asserts himself as subject and free being by opposing other consciousnesses. He is distinct from animals precisely in that he creates and invents (not in that he reproduces himself), but he tries to escape the burden of his freedom by giving himself a spurious 'immortality' in his children. He dominates woman both to imprison another consciousness which reflects his own and to provide him with children that are securely his (his fear of illegitimacy). The notions obviously have a considerable force. But they are very atemporal: it is not easy to see why socialism should modify the basic 'ontological' desire for a thing-like freedom which De Beauvoir sees as the motor behind the fixation with inheritance in the property system, or the enslavement of women which derived from it. In fact she has since criticised this aspect of her book for idealism: 'I should take a more materialist position today in the first volume. I should base the notion of woman as *other* and the Manichean argument it entails not on an idealistic and *a priori* struggle of consciences, but on the facts of supply and demand. This modification would not necessitate any changes in the subsequent development of my argument.'[12] Concurrent, however, with the idealist psychological explanation, De Beauvoir uses an orthodox economist approach. This leads to a definite evolutionism in her treatment in Volume I, which becomes a retrospective narrative of the different forms of the feminine condition in different societies through time – mainly in terms of the property system and its effects on women. To this she adds various suprahistorical themes – myths of the eternal feminine, types of women through the ages, literary treatments of women – which do not modify the fundamental structure of her argument. The prospect for women's liberation at the end is quite divorced from any historical development.

Thus, the classical literature on the problem of woman's condition is predominantly economist in emphasis, stressing her simple subordination to the institutions of private property. Her biological status underpins both her weakness as a producer, in work relations, and her importance as a possession, in reproductive relations. The fullest and most recent interpretation gives both factors a psychological cast. The framework of discussion is an evolutionist one which nevertheless fails noticeably to project a convincing image of the future, beyond asserting that socialism will involve the liberation of women as one of its constituent 'moments'.

What is the solution to this impasse? It must lie in differentiating woman's condition, much more radically than in the past, into its separate structures; which together form a complex – not a simple – unity. This will mean rejecting the idea that woman's condition can be deduced derivatively from the economy or equated symbolically with society. Rather, it must be seen as a *specific* structure, which is a unity of different elements. The variations of woman's condition throughout history will be the result of different combinations of these elements – much as Marx's analysis of the economy in *Precapitalist Economic Formations* is an account of the different combinations of the factors of production, not a linear narrative of economic development. Because the unity of woman's condition at any one time is the product of several structures, it is always 'overdetermined'.[13] The key structures can be listed as follows: Production, Reproduction, Sex and Socialisation of Children. The concrete combination of these produces the 'complex unity' of her position; but each separate structure may have reached a different 'moment' at any given historical time. Each then must be examined separately in order to see what the present unity is and how it might be changed. The discussion that follows does not pretend to give a historical account of each sector. It is only concerned with some general reflections on the different roles of women and some of their interconnections.

Production

The biological differentiation of the sexes and the division of labour have, throughout history, seemed an interlocked necessity. Anatomically smaller and weaker, woman's physiology and her psycho-biological metabolism appear to render her a less useful member of a work-force. It is always stressed how, particularly in the early stages of social development, man's physical superiority gave him the means of conquest over nature which was denied to women. Once woman was accorded the menial tasks involved in maintenance whilst man undertook conquest and creation, she became an aspect of the things preserved: private property and children. All socialist writers on the subject mentioned earlier – Marx, Engels, Bebel, De Beauvoir – link the confirmation and continuation of woman's oppression after the establishment of her physical inferiority for hard manual work with the advent of private property.

But woman's physical weakness has never prevented her from performing work as such (quite apart from bringing up children), only specific types of work, in specific societies. In primitive, ancient, oriental, medieval and capitalist societies, the *volume* of work performed by women has always been considerable (it has usually been much more than this). It is only its form that is in question. Domestic labour, even today, is enormous if quantified in terms of productive labour.[14] In any case, women's physique has never permanently or even predominantly relegated them to menial domestic chores. In many peasant societies, women have worked in the fields as much as or more than men.

Physique and Coercion

The assumption behind most classical discussion is that the crucial factor starting the whole development of feminine subordination was women's lesser capacity for demanding physical work. But, in fact, this is a major oversimplification. Even within these terms, in history it has been woman's lesser capacity for violence as well as for work that has determined her subordination. In most societies woman has not only been less able than man to perform arduous kinds of work, she has also been less able to fight. Man not only has the strength to assert himself against nature, but also against his fellows. *Social coercion* has interplayed with the straightforward division of labour, based on biological capacity, to a much greater extent than generally admitted. Of course, it may not be actualised as direct aggression. In primitive societies women's physical unsuitability for the hunt is evident. In agricultural societies where women's inferiority is socially instituted, they are given the arduous task of tilling and cultivation. For this coercion is necessary. In developed civilisations and more complex societies woman's physical deficiencies again become relevant. Women are no use either for war or in the construction of cities. But with early industrialisation coercion once more becomes important. As Marx wrote: 'Insofar as machinery dispenses with muscular power, it becomes a means of employing labourers of slight muscular strength, and those whose bodily development is incomplete, but whose limbs are all the more supple. The labour of women and children was, therefore, the first thing sought for by capitalists who used machinery.'[15]

René Dumont points out that in many zones of tropical Africa today men are often idle, while women are forced to work all day.[16] This exploitation has no 'natural' source whatever. Women may perform their 'heavy' duties in contemporary African peasant societies not for fear of physical reprisal by their men, but because these duties are 'customary' and built into the role structures of the society. A further point is that coercion implies a different relationship from coercer to coerced than exploitation does. It is political rather than economic. In describing coercion, Marx said that the master treated the slave or serf as the 'inorganic and natural condition of its own reproduction'. That is to say, labour itself becomes like other natural things – cattle or soil: 'The original conditions of production appear as natural prerequisites, *natural conditions of the existence of the producer,* just as his living body, however reproduced and developed by him, is not originally established by himself, but appears as his *prerequisite.*'[17] This is preeminently woman's condition. For far from woman's physical weakness removing her from productive work, her social weakness has in these cases evidently made her the major slave of it.

This truth, elementary though it may seem, has nevertheless been constantly ignored by writers on the subject, with the result that an illegitimate optimism creeps into their predictions of the future. For if it is just the biological incapacity for the hardest physical work which has determined the subordination of women, then the prospect of an advanced machine technology, abolishing the need for strenuous physical exertion, would seem to promise, therefore, the liberation of women. For a moment industrialisation itself thus seems to herald women's liberation. Engels, for instance, wrote: 'The first premise for the emancipation of women is the reintroduction of the entire female sex into public industry . . . And this has become possible only as a result of modern large-scale industry, which not only permits of the participation of women in production in large numbers, but actually calls for it and, moreover strives to convert private domestic work also into a public industry.'[18] What Marx said of early industrialism is no less, but also *no more* true of an automated society: ' . . . it is obvious that the fact of the collective working group being composed of individuals of both sexes and all ages, must necessarily, *under suitable conditions*, become a source of human development; although in its spontaneously developed, brutal, capitalistic form, where the labourer exists for the process of production, and not the process of production for the labourer, that fact is a pestiferous source of corruption and slavery.'[19] Industrial labour and automated technology both promise the preconditions for woman's liberation alongside man's – but no more than the preconditions. It is only too obvious that the advent of industrialisation has not so far freed women in this sense, either in the west or in the east. In the west it is true that there was a great influx of women into jobs in the expanding industrial economy, but this soon levelled out, and there has been relatively little increase in recent decades. De Beauvoir hoped that automation would make a decisive, qualitative difference by abolishing altogether the physical differential between the sexes. But any reliance on this in itself accords an independent role to technique which history does not justify. Under capitalism, automation could possibly lead to an ever-growing structural unemployment which would expel women – the latest and least integrated recruits to the labour force and ideologically the most expendable for a bourgeois society – from production after only a brief interlude in it. Technology is mediated by the total social structure and it is this which will determine woman's future in work relations.

Physical deficiency is not now, any more than in the past, a sufficient explanation of woman's relegation to inferior status. Coercion has been ameliorated to an ideology shared by both sexes. Commenting on the results of her questionnaire of working women, Viola Klein notes: 'There is no trace of feminist egalitarianism – militant or otherwise – in any of the women's answers to our questionnaire; nor is it even implicitly assumed that women have a "Right to Work".'[20] Denied, or refusing, a role in *production*, woman does not even create the *pre*conditions of her liberation.

Reproduction

Women's absence from the critical sector of production historically, of course, has been caused not just by their physical weakness in a context of coercion – but also by their role in reproduction. Maternity necessitates periodic withdrawals from work, but this is not a decisive phenomenon. It is rather women's role in reproduction which has become, in capitalist society at least, the spiritual 'complement' of men's role in production.[21] Bearing children, bringing them up, and maintaining the home –

these form the core of woman's natural vocation, in this ideology. This belief has attained great force because of the seeming universality of the family as a human institution. There is little doubt that Marxist analyses have underplayed the fundamental problems posed here. The complete failure to give any operative content to the slogan of 'abolition' of the family is striking evidence of this (as well as of the vacuity of the notion). The void thus created has been quickly occupied by traditional beliefs such as Townsend's quoted above.

The biological function of maternity is a universal, atemporal fact, and as such has seemed to escape the categories of Marxist historical analysis. From it follows – apparently – the stability and omnipresence of the family, if in very different forms.[22] Once this is accepted, women's social subordination – however emphasised as an honourable, but different role (cf. the 'equal but separate' ideologies of Southern racists) – can be seen to follow inevitably as an *insurmountable* bio-historical fact. The causal chain then goes: Maternity, Family, Absence from Production and Public Life, Sexual Inequality.

The lynch-pin in this line of argument is the idea of the family. The notion that 'family' and 'society' are virtually co-extensive terms, or that an advanced society not founded on the nuclear family is now inconceivable, is widespread. It can only be seriously discussed by asking just what the family is – or, rather, what women's role in the family is. Once this is done, the problem appears in quite a new light. For it is obvious that woman's role in the family – primitive, feudal or bourgeois – partakes of three quite different structures: reproduction, sexuality, and the socialisation of children. These are historically, not intrinsically, related to each other in the present modern family. Biological parentage is not necessarily identical with social parentage (adoption). It is thus essential to discuss: not the family as an unanalysed entity, but the separate *structures* which today compose it, but which may tomorrow be decomposed into a new pattern.

Reproduction, it has been stressed, is a seemingly constant

atemporal phenomenon – part of biology rather than history. In fact, this is an illusion. What is true is that the 'mode of reproduction' does not vary with the 'mode of production'; it can remain effectively the same through a number of different modes or production. For it has been defined till now, by its uncontrollable, natural character. To this extent, it has been an unmodified biological fact. As long as reproduction remained a natural phenomenon, of course, women were effectively doomed to social exploitation. In any sense, they were not masters of a large part of their lives. They had no choice as to whether or how often they gave birth to children (apart from repeated abortion), their existence was essentially subject to biological processes outside their control.

Contraception
Contraception, which was invented as a rational technique only in the nineteenth century was thus an innovation of world-historic importance. It is only now just beginning to show what immense consequences it could have, in the form of the pill. For what it means is that at last the mode of reproduction could potentially be transformed. Once child-bearing becomes totally voluntary (how much so is it in the west, even today?) its significance is fundamentally different. It need no longer be the sole or ultimate vocation of woman; it becomes one option among others.

Marx sees history as the development of man's trans-formation of nature, and thereby of himself – of human nature – in different modes of production. Today there are the technical possibilities for the humanisation of the most natural part of human culture. This is what a change in the mode of reproduction could mean.

We are far from this state of affairs as yet. In France and Italy the sale of any form of contraception remains illegal. The oral contraceptive is the privilege of a moneyed minority in a few western countries. Even here the progress has been realised in a typically conservative and exploitative form. It is made only for women, who are thus 'guinea-pigs' in a venture which involves both sexes.

The fact of overwhelming importance is that easily available contraception threatens to dissociate sexual from reproductive experience – which all contemporary bourgeois ideology tries to make inseparable, as the *raison d'être* of the family.

Reproduction and Production

At present, reproduction in our society is often a kind of sad mimicry of production. Work in a capitalist society is an alienation of labour in the making of a social product which is confiscated by capital. But it can still sometimes be a real act of creation, purposive and responsible, even in conditions of the worst exploitation. Maternity is often a caricature of this. The biological product – the child – is treated as if it were a solid product. Parenthood becomes a kind of substitute for work, an activity in which the child is seen as an object created by the mother, in the same way as a commodity is created by a worker. Naturally, the child does not literally escape, but the mother's alienation can be much worse than that of the worker whose product is appropriated by the boss. No human being can create another human being. A person's biological origin is an abstraction. The child as an autonomous person inevitably threatens the activity which claims to create it continually merely as a *possession* of the parent. Possessions are felt as extensions of the self. The child as a possession is supremely this. Anything the child does is therefore a threat to the mother herself who has renounced her autonomy through this misconception of her reproductive role. There are few more precarious ventures on which to base a life.

Furthermore, even if the woman has emotional control over her child, legally and economically both she and it are subject to the father. The social cult of maternity is matched by the real socio-economic powerlessness of the mother. The psychological and practical benefits men receive from this are obvious. The converse of women's quest for creation in the child is man's retreat from his work into the family: 'When we come home, we lay aside our mask and drop our tools, and are no longer lawyers, sailors, soldiers, statesmen, clergymen, but only men. We fall again into our most human relations, which, after all, are the whole of what belongs to us as we are in ourselves.'[23]

Unlike her non-productive status, her capacity for maternity *is* a definition of woman. But it is only a physiological definition. So long as it is allowed to remain a substitute for action and creativity, and the home an area of relaxation for men, woman will remain confined to the species, to her universal and natural condition.

Sexuality

Sexuality has traditionally been the most tabooed dimension of women's situation. The meaning of sexual freedom and its connexion with women's freedom is a particularly difficult subject which few socialist writers have cared to broach. Fourier alone identified the two totally, in lyrical strophes describing a sexual paradise of permutations – the famous phalansteries. 'Socialist morality' in the Soviet Union for a long time debarred serious discussion of the subject within the world communist movement. Marx himself – in this respect somewhat less liberal than Engels – early in his life expressed traditional views on the matter: ' . . . the sanctification of the sexual instinct through exclusivity, the checking of instinct by laws, the moral beauty which makes nature's commandment ideal in the form of an emotional bond – [this is] the spiritual essence of marriage.'[24]

Yet it is obvious that throughout history women have been appropriated as sexual objects, as much as progenitors or producers. Indeed, the sexual relation can be assimilated to the statute of possession much more easily and completely than the productive or reproductive relationship. Contemporary sexual vocabulary bears eloquent witness to this –

it is a comprehensive lexicon of reification. Later, Marx was well aware of this, 'Marriage . . . is incontestably a form of exclusive private property.'[25] But neither he nor his successors ever tried seriously to envisage the implications of this for socialism, or even for a structural analysis of women's condition. Communism, Marx stressed in the same passage, would not mean mere 'communalisation' of women as common property. Beyond this, he never ventured.

Some historical considerations are in order here. For if socialists have said nothing, the gap has been filled by liberal ideologues. Wayland Young, in a recent book, *Eros Denied*, argues that western civilisation has been uniquely repressive sexually and, in a plea for greater sexual freedom today, he compares it at some length with oriental and ancient societies. It is striking, however, that his book makes no reference whatever to women's status in these different societies, or to the different forms of marriage-contract prevalent in them. This makes the whole argument a purely formal exercise – an obverse of socialist discussions of women's position which ignore the problem of sexual freedom and its meanings. For while it is true that certain oriental or ancient (and indeed primitive) cultures were much less puritan than western societies, it is absurd to regard this as a kind of 'transposable value' which can be abstracted from its social structure. In effect, in many of these societies sexual openness was accompanied by a form of polygamous exploitation which made it in practice an expression simply of masculine domination. Since art was the province of man, too, this freedom finds a natural and often powerful expression in art – which is often quoted as if it were evidence of the total quality of human relationships in the society. Nothing could be more misleading. What is necessary, rather than this naïve, hortatory core of historical example, is some account of the co-variation between the degrees of sexual liberty and openness and the position and dignity of women in different societies.

Some points are immediately obvious. The actual history is

much more dialectical than any liberal account presents it.
Unlimited juridical polygamy – whatever the sexualisation of
the culture which accompanies it – is clearly a total derogation
of woman's autonomy, and constitutes an extreme form of
oppression. Ancient China is a perfect illustration of this.
Wittfogel describes the extraordinary despotism of the
Chinese *paterfamilias* – 'a liturgical (semi-official) policeman
of his kin group.'[26] In the west, however, the advent of
monogamy was in no sense an *absolute* improvement. It
certainly did not create a one-to-one equality – far from it.
Engels commented accurately: 'Monogamy does not by any
means make its appearance in history as the reconciliation of
man and woman, still less as the highest form of such a
reconciliation. On the contrary, it appears as the subjugation
of one sex by the other, as the proclamation of a conflict
between the sexes entirely unknown hitherto in prehistoric
times'.[27] But in the Christian era, monogamy took on a very
specific form in the west. It was allied with an unprecedented
régime of general sexual repression. In its Pauline version,
this had a markedly anti-feminine bias, inherited from
Judaism. With time, this became diluted – feudal society,
despite its subsequent reputation for asceticism, practiced
formal monogamy with considerable actual acceptance of
polygamous behaviour, at least within the ruling class. But
here again the extent of sexual freedom was only an index of
masculine domination. In England, the truly major change
occurred in the sixteenth century with the rise of militant
puritanism and the increase of market relations in the
economy. Lawrence Stone observes: 'In practice, if not in
theory, the early sixteenth-century nobility was a polygamous
society, and some contrived to live with a succession of
women despite the official prohibition on divorce . . . But
impressed by Calvinist criticisms of the double standard, in
the late sixteenth century public opinion began to object to
the open maintenance of a mistress.'[28] Capitalism and the
attendant demands of the newly emergent bourgeoisie
accorded women a new status as wife and mother. Her legal

rights improved; there was vigorous controversy over her social position; wife-beating was condemned. 'In a woman the bourgeois man is looking for a counterpart, not an equal.'[29] At the social periphery woman did occasionally achieve an equality which was more than her feminine function in a market society. In the extreme sects women often had completely equal rights: Fox argued that the Redemption restored Prelapsarian equality and Quaker women thereby gained a real autonomy. But once most of the sects were institutionalised, the need for family discipline was re-emphasised and women's obedience with it. As Keith Thomas says, the Puritans 'had done something to raise women's status, but not really very much'.[30] The patriarchal system was retained and maintained by the economic mode of production. The transition to complete effective monogamy accompanied the transition to modern bourgeois society as we know it today. Like the market system itself, it represented a historic advance, at great historic cost. The formal, juridical equality of capitalist society and capitalist rationality now applied as much to the marital as to the labour contract. In both cases, nominal parity masks real exploitation and inequality. But in both cases, the formal equality is itself a certain progress, which can help to make possible a further advance.

For the situation today is defined by a new contradiction. Once formal conjugal equality (monogamy) is established, sexual freedom as such – which under polygamous conditions was usually a form of exploitation – becomes, conversely, a possible force for liberation. It then means, simply, the freedom for both sexes to transcend the limits of present sexual institutions.

Historically, then, there has been a dialectical movement, in which sexual expression was 'sacrificed' in an epoch of more-or-less puritan repression, which nevertheless produced a greater parity of sexual roles, which in turn creates the pre-condition for a genuine sexual liberation, in the dual sense of equality *and* freedom – whose unity defines socialism.

This movement can be verified within the history of the 'sentiments'. The cult of *love* only emerges in the twelfth century in opposition to legal marital forms and with a heightened valorisation of women (courtly love). Gradually thereafter it became diffused, and assimilated to marriage as such, which in its bourgeois form (romantic love) became a *free* choice for *life*. What is striking here is that monogamy, as an institution in the west, anticipated the idea of love by many centuries. The two have subsequently been officially harmonised, but the tension between them has never been abolished. There is a formal contradiction between the voluntary contractual character of 'marriage' and the spontaneous uncontrollable character of 'love' – the passion that is celebrated precisely for its involuntary force. The notion that it occurs only once in every life and can therefore be integrated into a voluntary contract becomes decreasingly plausible in the light of everyday experience – once sexual repression as a psycho-ideological system becomes at all relaxed.

Obviously, the main breach in the traditional value-pattern has so far been the increase in premarital sexual experience. This is now virtually legitimised in contemporary bourgeois society. But its implications are explosive for the ideological conception of marriage that dominates this society: that of an exclusive and permanent bond. A recent American anthology, *The Family and the Sexual Revolution*, reveals this very clearly: 'As far as extramarital relations are concerned, the anti-sexualists are still fighting a strong, if losing, battle. The very heart of the Judeo-Christian sex ethic is that men and women shall remain virginal until marriage and that they shall be completely faithful after marriage. In regard to premarital chastity, this ethic seems clearly on the way out, and in many segments of the populace is more and more becoming a dead letter.'[31]

The current wave of sexual liberalisation, in the present context, could become conducive to the greater general freedom of women. Equally it could presage new forms of oppression. The puritan-bourgeois creation of woman as 'counterpart' has produced the *pre-condition* for emancipation. But it gave statutory legal equality to the sexes at the cost of greatly intensified repression. Subsequently – like private property itself – it has become a brake on the further development of a free sexuality. Capitalist market relations have historically been a precondition of socialism; bourgeois marital relations (contrary to the denunciation of the *Communist Manifesto*) may equally be a precondition of women's liberation.

Socialisation

Woman's biological destiny as mother becomes a cultural vocation in her role as socialiser of children. In bringing up children, woman achieves her main social definition. Her suitability for socialisation springs from her physiological condition; her ability to lactate and occasionally relative inability to undertake strenuous work-loads. It should be said at the outset that suitability is not inevitability. Lévi-Strauss writes: 'In every human group, women give birth to children and take care of them, and men rather have as their speciality hunting and warlike activities. Even there, though, we have ambiguous cases: of course, men never give birth to babies, but in many societies . . . they are made to act as if they did.'[32] Evans-Pritchard's description of the Nuer tribe depicts just such a situation. And another anthropologist, Margaret Mead, comments on the element of wish-fulfilment in the assumption of a *natural* correlation of femininity and nurturance: 'We have assumed that because it is convenient for a mother to wish to care for her child, this is a trait with which women have been more generously endowed by a careful teleological process of evolution. We have assumed that because men have hunted, an activity requiring enterprise, bravery, and initiative, they have been endowed with these useful aptitudes as part of their sex-temperament.'[33] However, the cultural allocation of roles in bringing up children – and the limits of its variability – is not the essential problem for consideration. What is much more important is to analyse the nature of the socialisation process itself and its requirements.

Parsons in his detailed analysis claims that it is essential for the child to have two 'parents', one who plays an 'expressive' role, and one who plays an 'instrumental' role. [34] The nuclear family revolves around the two axes of generational hierarchy and of these two roles. In typically Parsonian idiom, he claims that 'At least one fundamental feature of the external situation of social systems – here a feature of the physiological organism – is a crucial reference point for differentiation in the family. This lies in the division of organisms into lactating and non-lactating classes.' In all groups, he and his colleagues assert, even in those primitive tribes discussed by Pritchard and Mead, the male plays the instrumental role *in relation* to the wife-mother. At one stage the mother plays an instrumental and expressive role *vis-à-vis* her infant: this is pre-oedipally when she is the source of approval and disapproval as well as of love and care. However, after this, the father, or male substitute (in matrilineal societies the mother's brother) takes over. In a modern industrial society two types of role are clearly important: the adult familial roles in the family of procreation, and the adult occupational role. The function of the family as such reflects the function of the women within it; it is primarily expressive. The person playing the integrative-adaptive-expressive role cannot be off all the time on instrumental-occupational errands – hence there is a built-in inhibition of the woman's work outside the home. Parson's analysis makes clear the exact role of the maternal socialiser in contemporary American society. [35] It fails to go on to state that other aspects and modes of socialisation are conceivable. What is valuable in Parsons' work is simply his insistence on the central importance of socialisation as a process which is constitutive of any society (no Marxist has so far provided a comparable analysis). His general conclusion is that: 'It seems to be without serious qualification the opinion of competent personality psychologists that, though personalities differ greatly in their degrees of rigidity, certain broad fundamental patterns of 'character' are laid down in childhood (so far as they are not genetically inherited) and are not radically changed by adult experience. The exact degree to which this is the case or the exact age levels at which plasticity becomes greatly diminished, are not at issue here. The important thing is the fact of childhood character formation and its relative stability after that.'[36]

Infancy

This seems indisputable. One of the great revolutions of modern psychology has been the discovery of the decisive specific weight of infancy in the course of an individual life – a psychic time disproportionately greater than the chronological time. Freud began the revolution with his work on infantile sexuality; Klein radicalised it with her work on the first year of the infant's life. The result is that today we know far more than ever before how delicate and precarious a process the passage from birth to childhood is for everyone. The fate of the adult personality can be largely decided in the initial months of life. The preconditions for the later stability and integration demand an extraordinary degree of care and intelligence on the part of the adult who is socialising the child, as well as a persistence through time of the same person.

These undoubted advances in the scientific understanding of childhood have been widely used as an argument to reassert women's quintessential maternal function, at a time when the traditional family has seemed increasingly eroded. Bowlby, studying evacuee children in the Second World War, declared: 'Essential for mental health is that the infant and young child should experience a warm, intimate and continuous relationship with his mother,'[37] setting a trend which has become cumulative since. The emphasis of familial ideology has shifted away from a cult of the biological ordeal of maternity (the pain which makes the child precious, etc.) to a celebration of mother-care as a social act. This can reach ludicrous extremes: 'For the mother, breast-feeding becomes a complement to the act of creation. It gives her a heightened sense of fulfilment and allows her to participate in a relationship as close to perfection as any that a woman can hope to achieve . . . The simple fact of giving birth, however, does not of itself fulfil this need and longing. . . . Motherliness is a way of life. It enables a woman to express her total self with the tender feelings, the protective attitudes, the encompassing love of the motherly woman.'[38] The tautologies, the mystifications (an *act* of creation, a *process* surely?) the sheer absurdities . . . 'as close to perfection as any woman can hope to achieve' . . . point to the gap between reality and ideology.

Familial Patterns
This ideology corresponds in dislocated form to a real change in the pattern of the family. As the family has become smaller, each child has become more important; the actual *act* of reproduction occupies less and less time and the socialising and nurturance process increase commensurately in significance. Bourgeois society is obsessed by the physical, moral and sexual problems of childhood and adolescence.[39] Ultimate responsibility for these is placed on the mother. Thus the mother's 'maternal' role has retreated as her socialising role has increased. In the 1890s in England, a mother spent fifteen years in a state of pregnancy and lactation; in the 1960s she spends an average of four years. Compulsory schooling from the age of five, of course, reduces the maternal function very greatly after the initial vulnerable years.

The present situation is then one in which the qualitative importance of socialisation during the early years of the child's life has acquired a much greater significance than in the past – while the quantitative amount of a mother's life spent either in gestation or child-rearing has greatly diminished. It follows that socialisation cannot simply be elevated to the woman's new maternal vocation. Used as a mystique, it becomes an instrument of oppression. Moreover, there is no inherent reason why the biological and social mother should coincide. The process of socialisation is, in the Kleinian sense, invariable – but the person of the socialiser can vary.

Bruno Bettelheim, observing Kibbutz methods, notes that the child who is reared by a trained nurse (though normally maternally breast-fed) does not suffer the back-wash of typical parental anxieties and thus may positively gain by the system.[40] This possibility should not be fetishised in its turn (Jean Baby, speaking of the post-four-year-old child, goes so far as to say that 'complete separation appears indispensable to guarantee the liberty of the child as well as of the mother).'[41] But what it does reveal is the viability of plural forms of socialisation – not necessarily tied to the nuclear family, nor to the biological parent.

Conclusion

The lesson of these reflections is that the liberation of women can only be achieved if *all four* structures in which they are integrated are transformed. A modification of any one of them can be offset by a reinforcement of another, so that mere permutation of the form of exploitation is achieved. The history of the last sixty years provides ample evidence of this. In the early twentieth century, militant feminism in England or the USA surpassed the labour movement in the violence of its assault on bourgeois society, in pursuit of suffrage. This political right was eventually won. Nonetheless, though a simple completion of the formal legal equality of bourgeois society, it left the socio-economic situation of women virtually unchanged. The wider legacy of the suffrage was nil: the suffragettes proved quite unable to move beyond their own initial demands, and many of their leading figures later became extreme reactionaries. The Russian Revolution produced a quite different experience. In the Soviet Union in the 1920s, advanced social legislation aimed at liberating women, above all, in the field of sexuality: divorce was made free and automatic for either partner, thus effectively liquidating marriage; illegitimacy was abolished, abortion was free, etc. The social and demographic effects of these laws in a backward, semi-literate society bent on rapid industrialisation (needing, therefore, a high birth-rate) were – predictably – catastrophic. Stalinism soon produced a restoration of iron traditional norms. Inheritance was reinstated, divorce inaccessible, abortion illegal, etc. 'The State cannot exist without the family. Marriage is a positive value for the Socialist Soviet State only if the partners see in it a lifelong union. So-called free love is a bourgeois invention and has nothing in common with the principles of conduct of a Soviet citizen. Moreover, marriage receives its full value for the State only if there is progeny, and the consorts experience the highest happiness of parenthood,' wrote the official journal of the Commissariat of Justice in 1939.[42] Women still retained the right and obligation to work, but because these gains had not been integrated into the earlier attempts to abolish the family and free sexuality, no general liberation has occurred. In China, still another experience is being played out today. At a comparable stage of the revolution, all the emphasis is being placed on liberating women in *production*. This has produced an impressive social promotion of women. But it has been accompanied by a tremendous repression of sexuality and a rigorous puritanism (currently rampant in civic life). This corresponds not only to the need to mobilise women massively in economic life, but to a deep cultural reaction against the corruption and prostitution prevalent in Imperial and Kuo Ming Tang China (a phenomenon unlike anything in Czarist Russia). Because the exploitation of women was so great in the *ancien régime*, women's participation at village level in the Chinese Revolution, was uniquely high. As for reproduction, the Russian cult of maternity in the 1930s and 1940s has not been repeated for demographic reasons: indeed, China may be one of the first countries in the world to provide free State-authorised contraception on a universal scale to the population. Again, however, given the low level of industrialisation and fear produced by imperialist encirclement, no all-round advance could be expected.

It is only in the highly developed societies of the west that an authentic liberation of women can be envisaged today. But for this to occur, there must be a transformation of all the structures into which they are integrated, and an *'unité de rupture'*.[43] A revolutionary movement must base its analysis on the uneven development of each, and attack the weakest link in the combination. This may then become the point of departure for a general transformation. What is the situation of the different structures today?

1. **Production:** The long-term development of the forces of production must command any socialist perspective. The hopes which the advent of machine technology raised as early as the nineteenth century have already been discussed. They proved illusory. Today, automation promises the *technical* possibility of abolishing completely the physical differential between man and woman in production, but under capitalist relations of production, the *social* possibility of this abolition is permanently threatened, and can easily be turned into its opposite: the actual diminution of woman's role in production as the labour force contracts.

This concerns the future. For the present, the main fact to register is that woman's role in production is virtually stationary, and has been so for a long time now. In England in 1911, 30 per cent of the work-force were women; in the 1960s 34 per cent. The composition of these jobs has not changed decisively either. The jobs are very rarely 'careers'. When they are not in the lowest positions on the factory floor they are normally white-collar auxiliary positions (such as secretaries) – supportive to masculine roles. They are often jobs with a high 'expressive' content, such as 'service' tasks. Parsons says bluntly: 'Within the occupational organisation they are analogous to the wife-mother role in the family.'[44]

The educational system underpins this role-structure. 75 per cent of eighteen-year-old girls in England are receiving neither training nor education today. The pattern of 'instrumental' father and 'expressive' mother is not substantially changed when the woman is gainfully employed, as her job tends to be inferior to that of the man's, to which the family then adapts.

Thus, in all essentials, work as such – of the amount and type effectively available today – has not proved a salvation for women.

2. Reproduction: Scientific advance in contraception could, as we have seen, make involuntary reproduction – which accounts for the vast majority of births in the world today, and for a major proportion even in the west – a phenomenon of the past. But oral contraception – which has so far been developed in a form which exactly repeats the sexual inequality of western society – is only at its beginnings. It is inadequately distributed across classes and countries and awaits further technical improvements. Its main initial impact is, in the advanced countries, likely to be psychological – it will certainly free women's sexual experience from many of the anxieties and inhibitions which have always afflicted it.[45] It will definitely divorce sexuality from procreation, as necessary complements.

The demographic pattern of reproduction in the west may or may not be widely affected by oral contraception. One of the most striking phenomena of very recent years in the United States has been the sudden increase in the birth rate. In the last decade it has been higher than that of underdeveloped countries such as India, Pakistan and Burma. In fact, this reflects simply the lesser economic burden of a large family in conditions of economic boom in the richest country in the world. But it also reflects the magnification of familial ideology as a social force. This leads to the next structure.

3. Socialisation: The changes in the composition of the work-force, the size of the family, the structure of education, etc. – however limited from an ideal standpoint – have undoubtedly diminished the societal function and importance of the family. As an organisation it is not a significant unit in the political power system, it plays little part in economic production and it is rarely the sole agency of integration into the larger society; thus at the macroscopic level it serves very little purpose.

The result has been a major displacement of emphasis on to the family's psycho-social function, for the infant and for the couple.[46] Parsons writes: 'The trend of the evidence points to the beginning of the relative stabilisation of a *new* type of family structure in a new relation to a general social structure, one in which the family is more specialised than before, but not in any general sense less important, because the society is dependent *more* exclusively on it for the performance of *certain* of its vital functions.'[47] The vital nucleus of truth in the emphasis on socialisation of the child has been discussed. It is essential that socialists should acknowledge it and integrate it entirely into any programme for the liberation of women. It is noticeable that recent 'vanguard' work by French Marxists – Baby, Sullerot, Texier – accords the problem its real importance. However, there is no doubt that the need for permanent, intelligent care of children in the initial three or four years of their lives can (and has been) exploited ideologically to perpetuate the family as a total unit, when its other functions have been visibly declining. Indeed, the attempt to focus women's existence exclusively on bringing up children, is manifestly harmful to children. Socialisation as an exceptionally delicate process requires a serene and mature socialiser – a type which the frustrations of a *purely* familial role are not liable to produce. Exclusive maternity is often in this sense 'counter-productive'. The mother discharges her own frustrations and anxieties in a fixation on the child. An increased awareness of the critical importance of socialisation, far from leading to a restitution of classical maternal roles, should lead to a reconsideration of them – of what makes a good socialising agent, who can genuinely provide security and stability for the child.

The same arguments apply, *a fortiori*, to the psycho-social role of the family for the couple. The belief that the family provides an impregnable enclave of intimacy and security in an atomised and chaotic cosmos assumes the absurd – that the family can be isolated from the community, and that its internal relationships will not reproduce in their own terms the external relationships which dominate the society. The family as refuge in a bourgeois society inevitably becomes a reflection of it.

4. Sexuality: It is difficult not to conclude that the major structure which at present is in rapid evolution is sexuality. Production, reproduction, and socialisation are all more-or-less stationary in the west today, in the sense that they have not changed for three or more decades. There is, moreover, no widespread *demand* for changes in them on the part of women themselves – the governing ideology has effectively prevented critical consciousness. By contrast, the dominant sexual ideology is proving less and less successful in regulating spontaneous behaviour. Marriage in its classical form is increasingly threatened by the liberalisation of relationships before and after it which affects all classes today. In this sense, it is evidently the weak link in the chain – the particular structure that is the site of the most contradictions. The progressive potential of these contradictions has already been emphasised. In a context of juridical equality, the liberation of sexual experience from relations which are extraneous to it – whether procreation or property – could lead to true inter-sexual freedom. But it could also lead simply to new forms of neocapitalist ideology and practice. For one of the forces behind the current acceleration of sexual freedom has undoubtedly been the conversion of contemporary capitalism from a production-and-work ethos to a consumption-and-fun ethos. Riesman commented on this development early in the 1950s: ' . . . there is not only a growth of leisure, but work itself becomes both less interesting and less demanding for many . . . more than before, as job-mindedness declines, sex permeates the daytime as well as the playtime consciousness. It is viewed as a consumption good not only by the old leisure classes, but by the modern leisure masses.'[48] The gist of Riesman's argument is that in a society bored by work, sex is the only activity, the only reminder of one's energies, the only competitive act; the last defence against *vis inertiae*. This same insight can be found, with greater theoretical depth, in Marcuse's notion of 'repressive de-sublimation' – the freeing of sexuality for its own frustration in the service of a totally coordinated and drugged social machine.[49] Bourgeois society at present can well afford a play area of premarital *non*-procreative sexuality. Even marriage can save itself by increasing divorce and remarriage rates, signifying the importance of the institution itself. These considerations make it clear that sexuality, while it presently may contain the greatest potential for liberation, can equally well be organised against any increase of its human possibilities. New forms of reification are emerging which may void sexual freedom of any meaning. This is a reminder that while one structure may be the *weak link* in a unity like that of woman's condition, there can never be a solution through it alone. The utopianism of Fourier or Reich was precisely to think that sexuality could inaugurate such a general solution. Lenin's remark to Clara Zetkin is a salutary if overstated corrective: 'However wild and revolutionary [sexual freedom] may be, it is still really quite bourgeois. It is, mainly, a hobby of the intellectuals and of the sections nearest them. There is no place for it in the Party, in the class-conscious, fighting, proletariat.'[50] For a general solution can only be found in a strategy which affects *all* the structures of women's exploitation. This means a rejection of two beliefs prevalent on the left:

Reformism: This now takes the form of limited ameliorative demands: equal pay for women, more nursery-schools, better retraining facilities, etc. In its contemporary version it is wholly divorced from any fundamental critique of women's condition or any vision of their real liberation (it was not always so). Insofar as it represents a tepid embellishment of the *status quo*, it has very little progressive content.

Voluntarism: This takes the form of maximalist demands – the abolition of the family, abrogation of all sexual restrictions, forceful separation of parents from children – which have no chance of winning any wide support at present, and which merely serve as a substitute for the job of theoretical analysis or practical persuasion. By pitching the whole subject in totally intransigent terms, voluntarism objectively helps to maintain it outside the framework of normal political discussion.

What, then, is the responsible revolutionary attitude? It must include both immediate and fundamental demands, in a single critique of the *whole* of women's situation, that does not fetishise any dimension of it. Modern industrial development, as has been seen, tends towards the separating out of the originally unified function of the family – procreation, socialisation, sexuality, economic subsistence, etc. – even if this 'structural differentiation' (to use a term of Parsons') has been checked and disguised by the maintenance of a powerful family ideology. This differentiation provides the real historical basis for the ideal demands which should be posed: structural differentiation is precisely what distinguishes an advanced from a primitive society (in which all social functions are fused *en bloc*).[51]

In practical terms this means a coherent system of demands. The four elements of women's condition cannot merely be considered each in isolation; they form a structure of specific interrelations. The contemporary bourgeois family can be seen as a triptych of sexual, reproductive and socialisatory functions (the woman's world) embraced by production (the man's world) – precisely a structure which in the final instance is determined by the economy. The exclusion of women from production – social human activity – and their confinement to a monolithic condensation of functions in a unity – the family – which is precisely unified in the *natural part* of each function, is the root cause of the contemporary *social* definition of women as *natural* beings. Hence the main thrust of any emancipation movement must still concentrate on the economic element – the entry of women fully into public industry. The error of the old socialists was to see the other elements as reducible to the economic; hence the call for the entry of women into production was accompanied by the purely abstract slogan of the abolition of the family. Economic demands are still primary, but must be accompanied by coherent policies for the other three elements, policies which at particular junctures may take over the primary role in immediate action.

Economically, the most elementary demand is not the right to work or receive equal pay for work – the two traditional reformist demands – but *the right to equal work itself.* At present, women perform unskilled, uncreative service jobs that can be regarded as 'extensions' of their expressive familial role. They are overwhelmingly waitresses, office-cleaners, hairdressers, clerks, typists. In the working class, occupational mobility is thus sometimes easier for girls than boys – they can enter the white-collar sector at a lower level. But only two in a hundred women are in administrative or managerial jobs, and less than five in a thousand are in the professions. Women are poorly unionised (25 per cent) and receive less money than men for the manual work they do perform: in 1961 the average industrial wage for women was less than half that for men, which, even setting off part-time work, represents a massive increment of exploitation for the employer.

Education
The whole pyramid of discrimination rests on a solid extra-economic foundation – education. The demand for equal

work, in Britain, should above all take the form of a demand for an *equal educational system*, since this is at present the main single filter selecting women for inferior work-roles. At present, there is something like equal education for both sexes up to fifteen. Thereafter three times more boys than girls continue their education. Only one in three 'A'-level entrants, one in four university students is a girl. There is no evidence whatever of progress. The proportion of girl university students is the same as it was in the 1920s. Until these injustices are ended, there is no chance of equal work for women. It goes without saying that the content of the educational system, which actually instils limitation of aspiration in girls, needs to be changed as much as methods of selection. Education is probably the key area for immediate economic advance at present.

Only if it is founded on equality can production be truly differentiated from reproduction and the family. But this in turn requires a whole set of non-economic demands as a complement. Reproduction, sexuality, and socialisation also need to be free from coercive forms of unification. Traditionally, the socialist movement has called for the 'abolition of the bourgeois family'. This slogan must be rejected as incorrect today. It is maximalist in the bad sense, posing a demand which is merely a negation without any coherent construction subsequent to it. Its weakness can be seen by comparing it to the call for the abolition of the private ownership of the means of production, whose solution – social ownership - is contained in the negation itself. Marx himself allied the two, and pointed out the equal futility of the two demands: ' . . . this tendency to oppose general private property to private property is expressed in animal form; *marriage* . . . is contrasted with the community of women, in which women become communal and common property.'[52] The reasons for the historic weakness of the notion is that the family was never analysed structurally – in terms of its different functions. It was a hypostasised entity; the abstraction of its abolition corresponds to the abstraction of its conception. The strategic concern for socialists should be for the equality of the sexes, not the abolition of the family. The consequences of this demand are no less radical, but they are concrete and positive, and can be integrated into the real course of history. The family as it exists at present is, in fact, incompatible with the equality of the sexes. But this equality will not come from its administrative abolition, but from the historical differentiation of its functions. The revolutionary demand should be for the liberation of these functions from a monolithic fusion which oppresses each. Thus dissociation of reproduction from sexuality frees sexuality from alienation in unwanted reproduction (and fear of it), and reproduction from subjugation to chance and uncontrollable causality. It is thus an elementary demand to press for free State provision of oral contraception. The legalisation of homosexuality – which is one of the forms of non-reproductive sexuality – should be supported for just the same reason, and regressive campaigns against it in Cuba or elsewhere should be unhesitatingly criticised. The straightforward abolition of illegitimacy as a legal notion as in Sweden and Russia has a similar implication; it would separate marriage civically from parenthood.

From Nature to Culture
The problem of socialisation poses more difficult questions, as has been seen. But the need for intensive maternal care in the early years of a child's life does not mean that the present single sanctioned form of socialisation – marriage and family – is inevitable. Far from it. The fundamental characteristic of the present system of marriage and family is in our society its *monolithism*: there is only one institutionalised form of intersexual or intergenerational relationship possible. It is that or nothing. This is why it is essentially a denial of life. For all human experience shows that intersexual and intergenerational relationships are infinitely various – indeed, much of our creative literature is a celebration of the fact – while the institutionalised expression of them in our

capitalist society is utterly simple and rigid. It is the poverty and simplicity of the institutions in this area of life which are such an oppression. Any society will require some institutionalised and social recognition of personal relationships. But there is absolutely no reason why there should be only one legitimised form – and a multitude of unlegitimised experience. Socialism should properly mean not the abolition of the family, but the diversification of the socially acknowledged relationships which are today forcibly and rigidly compressed into it. This would mean a plural range of institutions – where the family is only one, and its abolition implies none. Couples living together or not living together, long-term unions with children, single parents bringing up children, children socialised by conventional rather than biological parents, extended kin groups, etc. – all these could be encompassed in a range of institutions which matched the free invention and variety of men and women.

It would be illusory to try and specify these institutions. Circumstantial accounts of the future are idealist and, worse, static. Socialism will be a process of change, of becoming. A fixed image of the future is in the worst sense ahistorical; the form that socialism takes will depend on the prior type of capitalism and the nature of its collapse. As Marx wrote: 'What [is progress] if not the absolute elaboration of [man's] creative dispositions, without any preconditions other than antecedent historical evolution which makes the totality of this evolution – i.e. the evolution of all human powers as such, unmeasured by any *previously established* yardstick – an end in itself? What is this, if not a situation where man does not reproduce himself in any determined form, but produces his totality? Where he does not seek to remain something formed by the past, but is the absolute movement of becoming?'[53] The liberation of women under socialism will not be 'rational' but a human achievement, in the long passage from Nature to Culture which is the definition of history and society.

Women and Equality

¶I wrote 'Women and Equality' as the
T. B. Davie Memorial Lecture and delivered it at the University
of Cape Town in March 1975. Prior to the lecture, it was
published as a pamphlet in Cape Town. Subsequently, a
version of it appeared in an anthology I edited with Anne
Oakley: *The Rights and Wrongs of Women* (Harmondsworth,
1978).

The students of the University of Cape Town established this
annual lecture to commemorate a vice-chancellor who
consistently had fought the introduction of apartheid into the
university. He – and they – lost the battle, and the lecture –
always on some theme relating to academic freedom – is
preceded by a large procession across the campus with
extinguished torches.

For the lecture, perhaps arrogantly, I tried to deploy a
method used by Herbert Marcuse in *Eros and Civilization.* I
had always been somewhat disappointed in Marcuse's book
until I learned that, at the height of McCarthy's America, he
had written of something forbidden in terms of what was
allowed: psychoanalytic arguments masked political. In
speaking of women in seventeenth-century England, I hoped
to say something – very obvious – about how contemporary
racist South Africa appears even to liberals outside. Thereby
I hoped to salve my conscience.

Let us put first things first. There may be some in my country and yours who will want to argue that one group of people are not the equals of another group, they will contend that differences are not individual but general to a group and are a mark of inferiority or superiority. There are certainly, I think, limitations to the concept of equality. These are both problematic questions that I shall take up in the course of this talk, but I want to start by establishing a fact: democratic countries have as one of their highest aspirations, the attaining of equality by their citizens, but in no democratic country in the world do women have equal rights with men. Feminists, members of the by now practically world-wide Women's Liberation Movement, face a fair amount of abuse of one sort or another, but one of the most frequent sallies they receive is the confident assertion that they have nothing left to fight for bar the crumbs. This is not the case. No one is arguing that there are not other deprived groups in any given society; but feminists are stating and demonstrating that women *as women* are deprived and oppressed.

England has been a so-called democratic country for over three hundred years, equality has been a guiding principle yet this is how the authors of a very recent survey of women's rights in Britain introduce their researches:

> . . . At no level of society do [women] have equal rights with men. At the beginning of the nineteenth century, women had virtually no rights at all. They were the chattels of their fathers and husbands. They were bought and sold in marriage. They could not vote. They could not sign contracts. When married, they could not own property. They had no rights over their children and no control over their own bodies. Their husbands could rape and beat them without fear of legal reprisals. When they were not confined to the home, they were forced by growing industrialisation to join the lowest levels of the labour force. *Since then, progress towards equal rights for women has been very slow indeed.*[1] (My italics.)

The authors go on to document how in work, education, social facilities and under the law women are treated as men's inferiors and, despite appearances such as equal pay acts, equality is never attained: 'We have an Equal Pay Act but we don't have equal pay.'[2]

Equal Rights are an important tip of an iceberg that goes far deeper; that they are only a tip is both a reflection of the limitation of the concept of equality and an indication of how profound and fundamental is the problem of the oppression of women. The position of women in any given society can be taken as a mark of the progress of civilisation or *humanisation* within that society. There may be slave societies, such as that of the Ptolemies, in which there is an elite of privileged women, but it is not such an elite that we are talking about when we consider the position of women in general as the index of human advance: men and women actually become human in relation to each other and if one sex is denigrated then humanity itself is the loser. I don't mean this in the simple sense that any exploitation or oppression diminishes the dignity of the whole society – though that is, of course, the case – but in the rather special sense that it is precisely in his transformation of the functions of sexuality and reproduction into human communication (language and emotional relationship) that at a basic level man as an animal becomes man as human being.

That is the depth of the nature of the problem of the oppression of women. The position of women as a social group in relation to men as another social group goes far deeper, then, than the question of equal rights, but equal rights are an important part of it and, furthermore, the struggle for these rights has an intimate connection with the whole history of feminism as a conscious social and political movement.

But first, what are the strengths and limitations of the concept of equality? I want to give a parallel account: first, the meaning of the concept of equality followed by an attempt to relate it to the history of feminism, and then some suggestions on how we must, while never undervaluing it, go beyond equality. In attempting to establish such a general history, I am going to use the example I know best – that of England.

Fortunately England does provide something of a model – an exemplary case – of the historical connections I want to make. But, with obviously important variations, all capitalist and later industrial capitalist countries have crucial similarities and it should be possible to slot another particular example into the general framework provided by English history.

The economic development of capitalism is always uneven and the ideological world-view that goes with that economic development will likewise be uneven and not necessarily in a parallel manner. This consideration has two unrelated consequences for what I want to say here. Firstly, it means that you may find that what I say about the concept of equality or arguments about the position of women in England in the seventeenth century, in the country you know best, (a) fit better a different epoch and (b), are not precisely matched to the same economic events. As I don't intend to consider, except cursorily, the material economic and social base either of the development of capitalism or of the position of women, but only some particular ideologies and politics that go with it, this sort of comparison is one you will have to make independently. The society you are familiar with may be 'before' or 'behind' – it will certainly be different – though I trust you will recognise the similarities. The second consequence of the uneven development of any ideological world view has an effect that is intrinsic to this talk: as I am tracing a continuity in ideas, the discontinuities will get short shrift. The material position of women has zigzagged like a fairground cake-walk or the proverbial snail up the side of a wall – two slithers up and one slither down, sometimes one up and two down as the authors I quoted earlier record: '. . . progress towards equal rights for women has been very slow indeed. There have even been times when the tide seemed to turn against them. The first law against abortion was passed in 1803. It imposed a sentence of life imprisonment for termination within the first fourteen weeks of pregnancy. In 1832 the first law was passed which forbade women to vote in elections. In 1877 the first Trades Union

Congress upheld the tradition that women's place was in the home whilst man's duty was to protect and provide for her.'³ Certainly both the history of feminism and the ideology of equality in general and for women in particular offer a monument to the law of uneven development. It is a monument I shall largely pass by in selecting the continuous track.

Equality as a principle – never as a practice – has been an essential part of the political ideology of all democratic capitalist societies since their inception. In being this it has expressed both the highest aspiration and the grossest limitation of that type of society. The mind of liberal and social democratic man soars into the skies with his belief in equality only to find that it must return, like the falcon, chained to the wrist whence it came. For it is not only that capitalist society (which produces its own version of both liberal and social democratic thought) cannot produce the goods or practise what it preaches, but that the premise on which it bases its faith in equality is a very specific and a very narrow one. The capitalist system under which, in different ways, we live, establishes as the premise of its ideological concept of equality the economic fact of an exchange of commodities: a commodity is exchanged for another of roughly equal value. In overthrowing the noble landlords of a preceding period, the newly arising and revolutionary bourgeoisie made free and equal access to the production and exchange of commodities the basis of man's estate: individual achievement replaced aristocratic birth.

In England in the late fifteenth century, the absolutist monarchy first overcame the multiplicity of feudal lords and the multifariousness of competing jurisdictions of secular and temporal powers. As happened later in France, for example, the central power of the still largely feudal monarch created and integrated large economic areas and established an equality of duties. The notion of equality of duties stands midway between a system of privilege asserted by feudal landlords and the concept of equality of rights propounded by the capitalist middle classes in the seventeenth century in England and the late eighteenth century in France. The legal edifice which enshrined the new equality of rights replaced the harmony between a law of privilege and economic privilege with a complete disjuncture between legal equality and economic disparity – if disparity is not too mild a word to fit the bill.

In bourgeois ideology everyone has access to the dominant entrepreneurial class; in the capitalist economy that it expresses, of course, the majority of the people do not. For the accumulation of capital – which is the rationale of capitalism – profits must be made; for profits to be made there is one particular commodity that cannot be equally exchanged and it is the only commodity that the majority of the population possess – the commodity of labour power. In a capitalist system the person who only has one commodity to sell (his labour-power) is thought to be doing this in a free and equal way – no one enforces his labour and he is paid a 'fair' wage for the job. But, in fact, if profits are to be made and capital to accumulate, there is no way in which a wage could be *equal* to the proferred labour-power – the labour-power must produce *more* than the wage answers for, else where is the profit to come from? (The worker's labour-power, which is in a sense himself, produces a surplus.) The freedom to work is little more than the freedom not to go hungry: the equal bargaining power of employer and employee is the right of the employer to hire or dismiss the employee and the right of the employee to be dismissed or go on strike – without a wage.

Under capitalism 'equality' can only refer to equality under the law. Because it cannot take into account the fundamental inequities of the class society on which it is based, the law itself must treat men as a generalisable and abstract category, it must ignore not only their individual differences, their different needs and abilities, but the absolute differences in their social and economic positions. Since the seventeenth century the law has expressed this, its precondition.

Bourgeois, capitalist law is a general law that ensures that everybody is equal before it: it is abstract and applies to all cases and all persons. As the political theorist Franz Neumann writes: 'A minimum of equality is guaranteed, for if the law-maker must deal with persons and situations in the abstract he thereby treats persons and situations as equals and is precluded from discriminating against any specific person.'[4] In writing further of the concept of political freedom with which the bourgeois concept of equality is very closely linked, Neumann continues to analyse this particular capitalist notion of law in these terms:

> The generality of the law is thus the precondition of judicial independence, which, in turn, makes possible the realisation of the minimum liberty and equality that inheres in the formal structure of the law.
>
> The formal structure of the law is, moreover, equally decisive in the operation of the social system of a competitive-contractual society. The need for calculability and reliability of the legal and administrative system was one of the reasons for the limitation of the power of the patrimonial monarchy and of feudalism. This limitation culminated in the establishment of the legislative power of parliaments by means of which the middle classes controlled the administrative and fiscal apparatus and exercised a condominium with the crown in changes of the legal system. A competitive society requires general laws as the highest form of purposive rationality, for such a society is composed of a large number of entrepreneurs of about equal power. Freedom of the commodity market, freedom of the labour market, free entrance into the entrepreneurial class, freedom of contract, and rationality of the judicial responses in disputed issues – these are the essential characteristics of an economic system which requires and desires the production for profit, and ever-renewed profit in a continuous, rational capitalistic enterprise.[5]

The law, then, enshrines the principles of freedom and equality – so long as you do not look at the particular unequal conditions of the people who are subjected to it. The concept 'equal under the law' does not apply to the economic inequities it is there to mask. The law is general, therefore, as *men*, employer and employee are equal, the law does not consider the inequality of their position. Equality always denies the inequality inherent in its own birth as a concept. The notions of equality, freedom or liberty do not drop from the skies; their meaning will be defined by the particular historical circumstances that give rise to them in any given epoch. Rising as the slogan of a bourgeois revolution, equality most emphatically denies the new class inequalities that such a revolution sets up – the equality exists only as an abstract standard of measurement between people reduced to their abstract humanity under the law.

Those seem to me to be some of the limitations of the concept of equality – what of its strengths? When a rising bourgeoisie is struggling against an old feudal order, that is, before it has firmly constituted itself as the dominant class, in its aspirations it does in some sense represent all the social classes that were subordinate previously: its revolution initially is a revolution on behalf of all the oppressed against the then dominant class – the nobility. The ideological concepts that the bourgeoisie will forge in this struggle are universalistic ones – they are about *most* people and the society most people want. New formulations about 'human nature' will jostle with old ones and eventually set themselves up as permanent truths. New values, such as a belief in the supremacy of reason, will be treated as though they have always been the pinnacle to which men try to ascend. These ideas will seem to be not only timeless but classless. Equality is one of them. Equality is the aspiration of the bourgeoisie at the moment when as the revolutionary class it represents all classes.

The liberal universalistic concept of equality, encapsulating the highest and best aspirations of the society, is represented by these words of Jeremy Taylor's: 'If a man be exalted by reason of any excellence in his soul, he may please to remember that all souls are equal, and their differing operations are because their instrument is in better tune, their body is more healthful or better-tempered; which is no more praise to him than it is that he were born in Italy'.[6] Taylor recognises that there are differences but these should not count. It is this universalistic aspect of the concept that has continued in the most ennobled liberal and social-democratic thought within capitalism; because it is instituted as a demand of the revolutionary moment, it soars above the conditions that create it, but because this revolution is based on these conditions – the conditions of creating two new antagonistic 'unequal' classes – to these conditions it must eventually return trapped by the hand that controls even its flight.

A history of the concept of equality would run in tracks very similar to a history of feminism. First introduced as one of the pinnacles of the new society's ideology in revolutionary England of the seventeenth century, the notion of equality next reached a further high in the era of enlightenment in the eighteenth century and then with the French Revolution. Feminism likewise has both the continuity and the fits and starts of this trajectory. Feminism as a conscious, that is self-conscious, protest movement, arose as part of a revolutionary bourgeois tradition that had equality of mankind as its highest goal. The first expressions of feminism were endowed with the strengths of the concept of equality and circumscribed by its limitations.

Feminism arose in England in the seventeenth century as a conglomeration of precepts and a series of demands by women who saw themselves as a distinct sociological group and one that was completely excluded from the tenets and principles of the new society. The seventeenth-century feminists were middle-class women who argued their case in explicit relation to the massive change in society that came about with the end of feudalism and the beginning of capitalism. As the new bourgeois man held the torch up against absolutist tyranny and argued for freedom and equality, the new bourgeois woman wondered why she was being left out.

Writing on marriage in 1700 Mary Astell asked:

> . . . If Absolute Sovereignty be not necessary in a State how comes it to be so in a Family? or if in a Family why not in a State; since no reason can be alleg'd for the one that will not hold more strongly for the other . . .

And:

> If *all Men are born free*, how is it that all Women are born slaves? As
> they must be if the being subjected to the *inconstant, uncertain,
> unknown, arbitrary Will* of Men, be the perfect Condition of
> Slavery?[7]

How could men proclaim social change and a new equality
in the eyes of the Lord and consistently ignore one half of the
population? It is to the values of the revolutionary society
and against those of the old that the feminists appealed. The
old society was represented by arbitrary rule, superstition,
irrational custom and pointless pedantry of argument – more
problematic were the continued use of two otherwise rightly
respected sources, Aristotle and the Bible.

Aristotle's contribution to the debate on the status of
women can be summarised by his comment: '. . . and woman
is, as it were, an impotent male, for it is through a certain
incapacity that the female is female', and the arguments the
women made against this were organised around a thorough
refutation of any *natural* inferiority: there was no physical,
'bodily' difference in men and women's minds (it was left to
the nineteenth century to try and prove there was a
physiological racial and sexual defect here). The power of
reason was the mark of mankind's superiority over the beasts,
if women were deficient in this it could only be as a result of
their lack of educational and social opportunities for
improving their minds.

Considerable ingenuity was spent reinterpreting the
assumed misogyny of the Bible. Mary Astell demonstrated
that in crucial passages St Paul was arguing not literally but
allegorically, yet beneath the sophistication of her own
argument there is a simple appeal to the new commonsensical
aspect of reason: 'For the Earthly *Adam's* being *Form'd* before
Eve, seems as little to prove her Natural Subjection to him, as
the Living Creatures, Fishes, Birds and Beasts being Form'd
before them both, proves that Mankind must be subject to
these Animals.'[8]

The feminists ask for the equal status that they insist any reasonable person must grant they should have by right of all the professed values of the society. As the anonymous author of 'An Essay in Defence of the Female Sex' writes in her dedication to Princess Ann of Denmark: 'I have only endeavour'd to reduce the Sexes to a Level, and by Arguments to raise Ours to an Equality at the most with Men.'[9] The arguments for equality are still valid in all democratic societies and few of these feminist demands for equal rights (mainly to education and professional employment) have been adequately met. But the demands for equality are permeated with something more radical still.

I will select three aspects of the seventeenth-century feminists' arguments that make it clear this was the beginning of political feminism: first, in rejecting women as naturally different from men they are forced to define women as a distinct *social* group with its own socially defined characteristics. Second, as a result of this they see that men *as a social group* oppress women as a social group – they are not against men as such but against the social power of men; women's oppression, as they put it, is due to 'The Usurpation of Men, and the Tyranny of Custom'. Finally, while they want to be let into men's privileged sphere they also want men to learn something from women; though they wouldn't have used exactly these terms, the feminisation of men is as important as the masculinisation of women – they do not undervalue female powers, only their abuse. In the quotation from the anonymous author that I have just cited, we should note that there are two clauses: she wants to be equal to men *and* her arguments have endeavoured 'to reduce the Sexes to a Level'. There is a current Chinese slogan that says 'anything a man can do a woman can do, too'; feminism in the seventeenth century, as today, would add: 'anything a woman can do a man can do too' – though the seventeenth-century terms for this sexual 'levelling' are slightly different.

The mental agility of women is valuable. 'I know' (writes our anonymous author) 'our Opposers usually mis-call our

Quickness of Thought, Fancy and Flash, and christen their
own Heaviness by the specious Names of Judgement and
Solidity: but it is easy to retort upon 'em the reproachful ones
of Dulness and Stupidity with more Justice,'[10] and she goes on
to claim that potentially the women's world of care-for-others
could be as much a repository of the highest values of
civilisation as the men's world of pursuing material gain –
there is nothing in itself wrong with domesticity, it is only
women's enforced exclusive confinement thereto and men's
self-imposed exclusion therefrom that creates the evil; but
given this exclusiveness then indeed it is evil. As the Duchess
of Newcastle wrote in 1662:

> . . . men are so unconscionable and cruel against us, as they
> endeavour to Barr us all Sorts or kinds of Liberty, as not to suffer
> us Freely to associate amongst our own sex, but, would fain Bury
> us in their houses or Beds, as in a Grave; the truth is, we live like
> Bats or owls, Labour like Beasts, and Dye like worms.[11]

The early feminists do not consciously congregate as a
political movement but they do propose to establish female
groups usually for educational and self-educational purposes
– they want to develop 'friendship' among women. (The
concept of female friendship is very close to that of
'sisterhood' as it is advocated in the Women's Movement
today.) Clearly a larger rebellion crossed their minds:

> . . . women are not so well united [writes Mary Astell] as to form
> an Insurrection. They are for the most part Wise enough to Love
> their Chains, and to discern how very becomingly they sit. They
> think as humbly of themselves as their Masters can wish, with
> respect to the other Sex, but in regard to their own, they have a
> Spice of Masculine Ambition, every one woul'd Lead, and none
> will Follow . . . therefore as to those Women who find
> themselves born for Slavery, and are so sensible of their own
> Meanness to conclude it impossible to attain to anything
> excellent, since they are, or ought to be, the best acquainted with
> their own Strength and Genius, She's a Fool who would attempt
> their Deliverance and Improvement. No, let them enjoy the
> great Honor and Felicity of their Tame, Submissive and
> Depending Temper! Let the Men applaud, and let them glory in,
> this wonderful Humility![12]

It was left to later generations of women to try and devise a way of solving the problem of the masculine ambition to lead and of overcoming the apathy of feminine contentment – both are struggles that still continue. But less ironic and more strident than Mary Astell, the Duchess of Newcastle could wish she 'were so fortunate, as to persuade you to make a frequentation, association, and combination amongst our sex, that we may unite in Prudent consuls, to make ourselves as Free, Happy and famous as Men . . .'[13] In fact, a number of groups were formed and though they lacked the larger political unity and range of reference, such 'frequentations' do bear some resemblance to the small groups which are the distinctive unit of organisation within feminism today.

The seventeenth-century feminists are today frequently criticised for only wanting the liberation of the women of their own social class. Certainly whenever they explicitly thought of the labouring classes, it did not occur to them to consider that their own demands for access to education, the world of business and the professions were strikingly inappropriate for women (or men) of a lower class. When they talked of freeing 'half the world' they were oblivious of class differences. Yet I think to criticise them for being blinkered by their bourgeois vision is ahistorical and inaccurate. Insofar as they came from the revolutionary class of that epoch and that they pointed out the oppressions that still existed, they did speak for all women. I said earlier that at the point where it is challenging an old order, a revolutionary class speaks a universalistic language initially on behalf of all oppressed groups. If this is true in general, it must be true for women – the seventeenth-century feminists appealed in a universalistic language on behalf of women to the highest concepts of freedom and humanity of which their society was capable. Even the very precepts of revolutionary change, in any era, cannot transcend the social conditions that give rise to them. In demanding entry into a male world, the end of men's social oppression of women and equality *between* the sexes, the women were truly revolutionary. They had explanations but they did not have a theory of how women came to be an oppressed social group, but still today we lack any such full theoretical analysis. They understood clearly enough that in their own time they were being made to live like bats and they saw the contradictions between this oppression and the ideology of liberty and equality; at that historical point to go beyond such insight and such forceful protest could only be millenarianism – as they well knew. In a final dedication of her book on marriage to the Queen, Mary Astell addresses the future: 'In a word, to those Halcyon, or if you will *Millennium Days*, in which the Wolf and the Lamb shall feed together, and a Tyrannous Domination which Nature never meant, shall no longer render useless if not hurtful, the Industry and Understanding of half Mankind!'[14]

When feminism next really reached a new crescendo, with Condorcet and Mary Wollstonecraft and the French Revolution, it was the hurtfulness not the uselessness of the oppression of women that was uppermost in the writers' minds. The principles were clear; Condorcet was emphatic in stating them: 'Either no member of the human race has real rights, or else all have the same; he who votes against the rights of another, whatever his religion, colour or sex, thereby adjures his own.'[15] It is as bad to be tyrants as to be slaves, men and women are degraded by the oppression of women. But what is new to the argument, and best expressed in Mary Wollstonecraft's A *Vindication of the Rights of Woman* (1792) is the constant analysis of the damage done to women and therefore to society by conditioning them into inferior social beings. The theme is present in the seventeenth century, but a hundred years of confirmation has made its mark: 'femininity' has been more clearly defined as fragility, passivity and dependence – economic and emotional. Wollstonecraft inveighs against such false refinement:

> In short, women, in general . . . have acquired all the follies and vices of civilization, and missed the useful fruit . . . Their senses are inflamed, and their understandings neglected, consequently they become the prey of their senses, delicately termed

sensibility, and are blown about by every momentary gust of feeling. Civilized women are therefore so weakened by false refinement, that, respecting morals, their condition much below what it would be were they left in a state near to nature.[16]

Between the end of the seventeenth and the eighteenth century, it would seem that among middle classes the social definition of sexual differences had been more forcefully asserted; the behavioural characteristics of 'masculinity' and 'femininity' had drawn further apart. Behind Wollstonecraft's energetic analysis is a struggle with which we are still familiar: if a woman strives not to fall for the lure of feminine subservience she is labelled 'masculine', in which case what happens to her legitimate femininity or 'femaleness'? How can one be a woman, indeed womanly, and avoid the social stereotypes? The answer is a concept of humanity which more urgently unifies the social characteristics of men and women:

> A wild wish has just flown from my heart to my head, and I will not stifle it, though it may excite a horse-laugh. I do earnestly wish to see the distinction of sex confounded in society, unless where love animates the behaviour.[17]

In fact, Wollstonecraft, while asserting equality as a human right, has to some degree moved away from what I have characterised as an essentially liberal position into one that we might describe as radical humanism. Though like the seventeenth-century writers, her highest good is reason and she demonstrates that women are inferior because they have been subjugated – not, as is usually argued, that they are subjugated because they are inferior – yet there is a new political dimension to her feminism. Where her English predecessors were demanding the practice consistent with the revolutionary values of their society, Wollstonecraft, living in the double context of by then reactionary Britain yet having the inspiration of the French Revolution, wanted not a change *within* society but a change *of* society:

> I do not believe that a private education can work the wonders

which some sanguine writers have attributed to it. Men and women must be educated, in a great degree, by the opinions and manners of the society they live in . . . It may . . . fairly be inferred, that, till society be differently constituted, much cannot be expected from education.[18]

and,

Rousseau exerts himself to prove that all *was* right originally: a crowd of authors that all *is* now right: and I, that all *will be* right.[19]

In Wollstonecraft the millennium has come down firmly from heaven to earth.

The writer to whom I wish to refer finally in this sketch of the relationship between feminism and the concept of equality is John Stuart Mill. To offer a somewhat sweeping generalisation, after Mill, in England the feminist struggle moves from being predominantly the utterances of individuals about a philosophical notion of equality to being an organised political movement for the attainment, among other things, of equal rights. Of course, the one does not exclude the other, it is a question of emphasis.

In a lucid and powerful manner, Mill's essay, 'The Subjection of Women' (1869), written at the height of the Victorian repression of women, resumes with a new coherence the arguments with which we have become familiar. Thus he has a clear perspective on the argument that maddened the earlier writers, that women's characteristics and social status were 'natural': 'What is now called the nature of women is an eminently artificial thing – the result of forced repression in some directions, unnatural stimulation in others'[20] and, 'So true is it that unnatural generally means only uncustomary, and that everything which is usual appears natural. The subjection of women to men being a universal custom, any departure from it quite naturally appears unnatural.'[21] Mill also looks back with clarity on the history of democracy and of women's rights – or rather lack of them.

Where the seventeenth-century women looked to their own new society for change and Wollstonecraft, with the example of the first radical years of the French Revolution at hand, looked to change her society, Mill, writing from within an industrial capitalism that had hardened into fairly extreme conservatism, had to stand aside and argue from the best of the past and the hope of the future. Most importantly, the justice and morality he wanted have not yet been found in the world: 'Though the truth may not yet be felt or generally acknowledged for generations to come, the only school of genuine moral sentiment is society between equals.'[22] And – 'We have had the morality of submission, and the morality of chivalry and generosity; the time is now come for the morality of justice.'[23]

But Mill's lucidity, unlike Wollstonecraft's exuberance, forces him to constrict his own vision. Although at one moment he speculates that the reason why women are denied equal rights in society at large is that men must confine them to the home and the family, he does not pursue the implications of this insight and instead programmatically demands these rights. When it comes down to it, his equality is, quite realistically, equality under the law:

> . . . on women this sentence is imposed by actual law, and by customs equivalent to law. What, in unenlightened societies, colour, race, religion or, in the case of a conquered country, nationality, are to some men, sex is to all women; a peremptory exclusion from almost all honourable occupations, but either such as cannot be fulfilled by others, or such as those others do not think worthy of their acceptance.[24]

and:

> . . . the principle which regulates the existing social relations between the two sexes – the legal subordination of one sex to the other – is wrong in itself, and now one of the chief hindrances to human improvement.[25]

I am not arguing against Mill's position but trying to indicate a lack that is implicit in this perspective. Mill's concept of human beings that are freed from the artificial constraints of a false masculinity or femininity is somehow more abstract than that of the earlier feminists. The seventeenth-century women thought if men and women were equal they could gain some quality from each other; Mary Wollstonecraft's vision combined in one being the best of a female world with the best of a male world. Mill correctly argues that we cannot know what men and women will be like when released from present stereotypes but out of this correctness comes an elusive feeling that Mill, seeing so accurately women's horrendous subordination, failed to see their contribution. This turns on the question of the importance of the reproduction and care of human life – Mill does not see, as Wollstonecraft does, that there might be a gain in men really becoming fathers (instead of remote, authoritarian figureheads) as well as in women being freed to pursue the so-called 'masculine' virtues. That Mill's concept of humanity is abstract, that he did not seem to consider the contribution of 'femaleness' once freed of its crippling exclusiveness to women, may have been because he was a man; it may just as easily have been because of the different social circumstances from which he wrote. Because he was not living at the moment when the bourgeoisie was the revolutionary class, the universalistic aspect of such thought of which I spoke earlier must turn to abstraction, there is no other way in which it can refer to all people.

John Stuart Mill in a sense expresses the best and the last in the high liberal tradition. His ideals represent the best his society is capable of but they can no longer be felt to represent that society – as a consequence, there is a sort of heroic isolation to his philosophy. Because of his isolation, because of his abstraction, in this field Mill's thought pinpoints and 'fixes' the essence of liberalism:

> The old theory was, that the least possible should be left to the individual agent; that all he had to do should, as far as practicable, be laid down for him by superior powers. Left to himself he was sure to go wrong. The modern conviction, the fruit of a thousand years of experience, is that things in which the individual is the person directly interested, never go right but as they are left to his

own discretion; and that any regulation of them by authority except to protect the rights of others, is sure to be mischievous. This conclusion, slowly arrived at, and not adopted until almost every possible application of the contrary theory has been made with disastrous result, now (in the industrial department) prevails universally in the most advanced countries, almost universally in all that have pretensions to any sort of advancement. It is not that all processes are supposed to be equally good, or all persons to be equally qualified for everything; but that freedom of individual choice is now known to be the only thing which procures the adoption of the best processes, and throws each operation into the hands of those who are best qualified for it.[26]

Mill's philosophy is an overriding belief in the individual and in the right of the individual to fulfil his or her maximum potential. Mill's concept of equality is therefore an equality of opportunity. As a politician he fought for equal rights for women under the law.

Since Mill wrote, there has, I think, been, in an uneven way, a decline in the tradition of liberal thought. Today, exactly three-quarters of the way through the twentieth century, 'equality' would seem to have become a somewhat unfashionable concept. Equal rights are still strenuously fought for but equality as the principle of a just and free society rarely elicits the eloquent support it once received. I am neither a philosopher nor a political scientist and I am ill-equipped to analyse why this should be the case. I can, however, point to some observations we all might make.

The concept of equality as a high ideal flourishes as a revolutionary aspiration when it is confronted with two types of conservatism – as Mill's was in Victorian England. One type of conservatism is a direct reflection of the economic conditions of a society once the society has settled down after its revolutionary open-endedness. When class distinctions have rigidified, then the conservative ideology of capitalism can bear a striking resemblance to the old order the revolutionary bourgeoisie once overthrew. In its naked crudity this conservatism is found in Arthur Young's statement: ' . . . everyone but an idiot knows that the lower classes must be kept poor, or they will never be industrious'[27] or in a verse of a hymn popular in England in the years before the First World War:

> The rich man in his castle,
> The poor man at his gate,
> God made them high or lowly
> And ordered their estate.[28]

The best liberal traditions of liberty, equality and individualism, such as those represented by Mill, rarely engaged directly with conservatism of this sort, but their presence as an alternative *within* the same society hopefully acts to circumscribe the possible power of such reactionary stances.

There is another conservative tradition that is more testing for the liberal conception of individualism and equality and that is Tory radicalism. Where conservative conservatism argues that there are generic differences which must be the basis of differences between groups of people, Tory radicalism, like liberalism and, for that matter socialism and communism, argues that there are differences between individuals. The litmus test here for establishing a distinction between the political philosophies is to see what happens to these individual differences. Tory radicalism always offers a place in the past, a romantic golden age when society was small enough for all these differences to flourish – merely as differences, be they handicaps or advantages. The liberal concept that I have presented here, argues that we are all different but these differences can only be realised in their infinite variety if we are given equal opportinities to make what we individually and differently can of them. The socialist and communist perspective suggests that 'equality' in capitalist society is based on class inequality; in a classless society there will still be differences or inequalities, inequalities between individuals, strengths or handicaps of various kinds. There will be differences between men and women, differences among women and among men; a truly just society based on collective ownership and equal distribution would take these inequalities into account and give more to those who needed more and ask for more from those who could give more. This would be a true recognition of the individual in the qualities that are essential to his humanity.

When the liberal concept of equality – the ideal of a revolutionary bourgeoisie – has to oppose not conservatism, as it did in Mill's case, but a system of thinking such as that of socialism which looks to a new future, then its own radicalism is weakened and that is what has been happening in a somewhat sporadic fashion since the last part of the last century.

A crisis in the history of the concept of equality can, I think, be marked by one book that epitomises the problem: the publication of the Halley Stewart lectures that the socialist historian, R. H. Tawney gave in 1929. The book, entitled *Equality*, is a most moving document – a humanitarian plea for equality as, quite simply, a correct, indeed *the* correct principle of civilisation. The framework within which Tawney argues for equality is that of moral and ethical philosophy, the terms in which he assesses the progress of equality are those of poverty and disparity of opportunity particularly in education. There is no underlying analysis of a class-antagonistic society and even in the lengthy epilogue written in 1950 the racial minorities in Britain are not mentioned, the position of women is not hinted at. Yet Tawney's own recommendations transcend the limitations of his belief in equality: he must argue for redistribution of wealth and for more collective provision of social services. His argument follows the liberal tradition but starts to look beyond it and sees that the freedom of privilege must be controlled; freedom in a class society is freedom for one class to exploit another.

It was not malicious oversight that made Tawney fail to see women as a deprived group – when he was writing women were simply not seen as a group at all. Ten years before he wrote and roughly fifteen years after his epilogue they were seen as a group once more. Feminism had in both cases pointed to the fact. In 1974, using the very criterion by which Tawney estimated the march of equality – poverty – a survey carried out in Britain found that women were the single most impoverished social group. The survey was not carried out by feminists, but feminism had made the investigators conscious of this category: women were found both to be a distinct group and an underprivileged one.

The fight for equal rights for women today takes place against this weakening of the liberal conception of equality. This talk is a plea both to remember that ideal and to realise its limitations. Too many revolutionary groups would skip the present and think that given both a falseness in the conception and its ultimate unrealiseability, 'equality' is not something to be fought for: too many not-so-revolutionary groups think that equal rights are attainable under class-antagonistic systems and are adequate. Equal rights will always only be rights before the law but these have by no means been won yet nor their possible extent envisaged. A new society that is built on an old society that, within its limits, has reached a certain level of equality clearly is at a better starting point than one that must build on a society predicated on privilege and unchallenged oppression. At a more general level, there seems to me no doubt that civilisation and human dignity are better served by as many people having as many rights as possible.

Aspects of Feminism

¶ 'Aspects of Feminism' are four lectures originally presented as 'The Chancellor's Lectures' at the University of Victoria, Wellington, New Zealand in August 1974. They were taped and transcribed and then bought by Liz Fell for the Australian Broadcasting Commission and broadcast as a Radio Special project in Australia early in 1975. Parts of the third lecture were printed later in the Australian periodical, *Nation Review* (Vol. 5, No. 21, March 7—13, 1975).

If I remember rightly, the first two were prepared in England in the summer weeks before I went to New Zealand. They certainly owed a great deal to work I had done with women colleagues and students while I had been teaching the previous Easter in the American Studies programme of the State University of New York at Buffalo. The first essay uses the anthropological writings I was then reading. In America there was a flowering of feminist anthropology. My interest in psychoanalysis at that period involved a possibility I subsequently felt to be mistaken: a link – clearly proposed by such works as *Totem and Taboo* – between psychoanalysis and anthropology. Certainly women found one crucial definition of themselves within the family, and psychoanalysis seemed to offer a way of understanding how kinship structures were internalised. Lévi-Strauss's work helped the potential analysis.

It was also a period when English women, but more extensively American women, were visiting China. I did not myself go to China (then) but I heard and read many reports of those who did. Mao Tse-Tung's essay 'On Contradiction' I had always found useful for teaching students about dialectical materialism. Both lectures are heavily indebted to these experiences.

The third and fourth lecture seem to me rather different. They use the contemporary arguments and preoccupations of feminists as a spring-board, but both lectures reach back into something earlier in myself. Both were written in New Zealand, a country I had left as a three-year-old child, thirty years before. It was a most important visit. For me New Zealand always was, and is, the world I have lost. Its extraordinary beauty and the kindness of the people I had known as a baby, somehow confirmed this sense of *temps perdus*. There is a nostalgia in the lectures. Romanticism is about a similar nostalgia. So is hysteria.

As a child and teenager I had been deeply caught up in the poetry of the Romantics and as a student and teacher I had thought about romances and romantic novels. Prompted by feminist speculations, the third lecture moves into literature for illustration and psychoanalysis for explanation.

The fourth lecture had originally been planned as 'Nora and Dora' – the heroine of *A Doll's House* and Freud's hysterical patient. It grew out of hand and had to be cut in half. It is still growing. This was the beginning of an interest that is with me now: the connection between femininity and hysteria – the subject in part of the last essay in this collection. Yet though this one looks forward, Freud also claimed that 'hysterics suffer from reminiscences'. I wasn't particularly hysterical in New Zealand – but certainly as I drafted this with the Southern Alps behind me and the untrod beaches before, only minutes from the spot where I was born, I suffered from reminiscences. Once more by way of Ibsen – a long-standing love – it brought together the politics of Marxism, the questions of feminism, the example of literature and the explanations of psychoanalysis.

1: *What is Feminism?*

In an essay entitled 'On the Sexual Theories of Children', Freud wrote:

> If we could divest ourselves of our corporeal existence and could view the things of this earth with a fresh eye as purely thinking beings, from another planet for instance, nothing perhaps would strike our attention more forcibly than the fact of the existence of two sexes among human beings, who, though so much alike in other respects, yet mark the difference between them with such obvious external signs.[1]

Feminists are also struck by the numerous human insignia that divide the sexes and they are, I hope, looking at the matter with a fresh eye. Men and women are like each other and are distinct from other animate or inanimate forms, yet whatever constitutes the difference between men and women is socially insisted upon in human societies and always elaborated. It is this social stress on the difference between men and women that is the subject of feminism.

I would suggest that what is important is that feminism in initiating a system of thought, transforms the ideological notion that there is a biological opposition between the sexes which determines social life, and asserts instead that there is a contradiction in the social relations between men and women. This contradiction – which is never static, as a biological opposition would be – shifts, moves and is moved and is therefore one force among others that effects social change and the movement of human history itself.

If we proceed to look at a social relationship between the sexes we can see that this has certain implications for the way we consider the question of the oppression of women, which is, after all, what feminism is about. Even the most progressive thought (both without and within feminism) tends to view women either in isolation from the men of their society or only in relation to the women of other societies. At its crudest, this argument will take the form of a European pointing out that though it is true that women in, say, Italy have a raw deal, women in America enjoy all the wealth-earning power glories of the so-called matriarchy. Somewhat more sophisticated research will engage in the type of cross-cultural argument that shows that Arapesh men are gentler and more feminine than the stereotype of women within advanced capitalist societies. In other words, this type of research tries to show that as there are no absolutes and all values are relative, there is no universal oppression of women.

But as feminists, what we should be talking about is not relativism but a social relationship. What we are therefore concerned with has two aspects: first we are concerned with the particular relationship between men and women within a particular society; and second, we have to draw from that particular relationship any universal features of it that we can. The cross-cultural work that has to be done is to discover the relationship between Arapesh men and women, American men and women, and then to discover what is common not to the men on their own or to the women on their own, or to a man and a woman of different societies, but what is common to the relationship between men and women itself.

Every society makes some distinction between the sexes. This does not mean that every society makes the biological male into a social man, or a biological female into a social woman. Among the Mohave, an American Indian group, for instance, a male in his own behaviour and in the regard of others, can be a social female or vice versa. Nor does it mean that all societies have only two social sexes; among the Navaho there are three gender groups, masculine, feminine and the nadle, an intersex person who may or may not have intersex physiological morphology. Thus, all societies make a distinction between at least two social sexes and a distinction, which, with all the many variations, can be described as a distinction between social men and social women. Some societies mark the difference in extreme ways, others only marginally, but the distinction has always been there.

Across the world, throughout history and, indeed, within prehistory, woman's situation has varied enormously, but relative to the man of her society, woman has always held a very particular place. Since the distinction between the sexes among human beings is a social one (whatever its coincidence with biology), and human beings distinguish themselves from other primates and animals in general by their organisation of society, we can expect the social distinction between the sexes to find expression in ways that are relevant to this organisation.

Reducing the background of my argument about the contradiction in the social relationship between men and women which forms the basic premise of feminism, to its simple essentials, we should argue that mankind transforms nature both by its labour and by its social organisation. It is not that other primates do not have skills or know the use of primitive tools, that animal groups have no systems of communication – clearly they do – but the learned accumulation of both the techniques of labour and the complexities of language is a characteristic peculiar to humans. Humans – male and female – form not groups, but societies.

If then, both labour and social organisation and with it, language, are human characteristics, we would expect to find that the universal social distinction between the sexes takes up its place within these terms. This, indeed, would seem to be the case.

The division of labour by sex is a universal feature of human society. Whatever the degree of overlap, whatever the weight of labour carried by either men or women, a distinction is made between the work predominantly done by men and that predominantly done by women. In this case, it is not a question of which group's labour provides the chief source of a society's subsistence – in some, woman's labour contributes virtually nothing, in others practically the whole – the question is rather what we can find to be a constant characteristic of women's work as it relates to men's. Here it would seem that in all societies, relative to their men, women undertake more childcare. The Nuer man of East Africa may nurture the young more than a man or even an upper-class woman in England, he may cuddle and care for, but a Nuer woman still does that bit more than he does. Even if we exclude her physiological ability to breastfeed, the Nuer woman's social role as nurse is more extensive than that of the man of her tribe.

In a short note written for *The American Anthropologist*, Judith Brown speculated that the contribution women make to the subsistence of their society was determined by the compatibility of the main subsistence activity with child care. She wrote:

> I would like to suggest that the degree to which women contribute to the subsistence of a particular society, can be predicted with considerable accuracy from a knowledge of the major subsistence activity. It is determined by the compatibility of this pursuit with the demands of childcare . . . Nowhere in the world is the rearing of children primarily the responsibility of men, and only in a few societies are women exempted from participation in the subsistence activities. If the economic role of women is to be maximised, their responsibilities in child care must be reduced or the economic activity must be such that it can be carried out concurrently with childcare.[2]

Since we are interested in human society, and the social relationship between the sexes, what has to concern us here in the physiological and biological arguments that are bound to be made, is that the females of all species of animals, including humans, give birth, and females of all primates can give primary nourishment to their young. However, what should interest us, in fact, are not the similarities between humans and animals, but the differences. And, in this case, the relevant physiological fact is that the human infant is born prematurely; it is less well-developed at birth, and hence more dependent. This in turn means a reduced capacity for instinctual behaviour and an increased capacity for learning.

It is not that women do have a 'natural animal instinct' for mother love that matters in this context – they may or may not do so – but that the social organisation of mankind requires women to be the group that provides for the human animal becoming a social being at this primary level. Mother love is a social requisite even where it coincides with a natural urge.

The sexual division of labour with its characteristic of more child care for women would seem to be a significant element in the organisation of human society, It can be either oppressive or non-oppressive. The second universal feature that I want to isolate in the structures of social organisation is the taboo on incest. Just as the universal division of labour according to sex is a universal form with a very various content – in some societies men farm and in others, women – so the taboo on incest is a universal proscription with a very diverse expression – some societies forbid marriage between brothers and sisters, others desire precisely that union for their ruling groups. Again, we have to remember that we're talking about a general social system. The taboo on incest seems to us so natural precisely because it is a key point at which mankind organises its own animal nature into a social nature.

A human kinship system, which is a system within which the taboo on incest is contained, organises human behaviour in a symbolic manner: 'Human kinship is above all a symbolic organisation of behaviour, a cultural construct upon the biological individuals involved.' Kinship involves the socialisation of sexuality into prescribed patterns and the naming of the kinsfolk with whom one may or may not have sexual relations. In other words, it involves both social interchange and language. Whom you call 'mother' may not be your biological mother, but your naming her such tells you your place in a social relationship to her.

The kinship system, like the sexual division of labour, utilises and institutes a social distinction between social men and women. Going back to Freud's quotation, we note that the visitor from outer space was struck (if we looked around us at the literature on the subject we may think that he was indeed struck dumb) by the elaborate effort that the human species has made to distinguish between two sexes which otherwise are so alike. Indeed, we might be right in thinking that this very inordinate desire to thus socially distinguish is one of the marks of human society. Primates such as chimpanzees and baboons, are characterised by a natural biological division between the sexes. As mankind starts to master nature (and we must remember that it is always man's own nature as well as external nature that is bound up in this question of the control of nature, that it is a process that has not only gone on throughout prehistory and all recorded history but is still very much going on and will always go on), it would seem that a natural division between the sexes, such as the primates know, would gradually be overcome. Instead, we find that far from being overcome, it is forcefully redefined in social terms – no primates distinguish between the sexes as assiduously as humans do. In the gap between our hypothetical expectation of mankind's control of its own nature, and hence what we would expect to be a gradual social elimination of natural differences and what, in fact, we do, which is to reinforce sexual differences – lies the question to which we have to address ourselves.

The social behaviour of primates is one of reciprocity: feed and be fed, protect and be protected, produce survival and survive by reproduction. It would also seem that in their most residual elements, the two features of human life that distinguish it from the lives of other primates and, in addition to this, are also universal features of human society – the social divisions of labour by sex and the kinship system – are also reciprocal relationships. In fact, they could be defined as systems set up to ensure reciprocity. The anthropologist Claude Lévi-Strauss suggests that the sexual division of labour is an artificial device whereby the two sexes, who in their human ability to labour could be so alike, are yet kept distinct and hence, mutually dependent. In proposing this, Lévi-Strauss is extending the work of Marcel Mauss on the significance of the gift. Mauss defines the gift as the first form of social contract – if you give a gift it is expected that you will at some point be given something in return. According to Lévi-Strauss, what else is the kinship system but a complex giving of people to each other in the understanding that one day you will be given someone in return? At first sight, then, it would seem that human kinship and the sexual division of labour reinterpret at a social level the natural reciprocity of primate groups. But do they?

Reciprocal relations are dual relationships – give and take/ take and give; but social relations cannot be dual relations because a dual relation is a closed system – a happy or vicious circle. Any social relationship must have as a minimum a third element and a fourth which gives meaning to the third: the gift and the significance of a gift. It is this meaning that transforms a piece of meat exchanged between primates to a shell necklace exchanged between humans – the one is reciprocal survival, the other symbolic of social relations. For two sounds to move from animal communication to become language, a third and fourth term must intervene: the space between the words and the meaning it thus gives to their relationship.

Because of this, it seems that, contrary to most anthropology that has been concerned with explaining the position of women, the key event that marks the human-isation of the primate is kinship and its attendant event language, and that the sexual division of labour is not causal but consequent upon this. In other words, where, for instance, Engels in *The Origin of the Family, Private Property and the State* argues that a natural division of labour becomes a social division of labour which becomes oppressive only with the accumulation of wealth and, hence, property, I think we should see that kinship and language already structure human beings into socially different places before you have any massive accumulation of wealth. Or, to put it schematically, instead of a theory that goes as follows: the natural division of labour among the primates becomes the social-sexual division among humans which becomes organised oppressively by kinship and then by class society, my suggestion goes as follows: the natural division of labour among primates is first transformed by human kinship and language which for its functioning sets up its social human division of labour by sexes. This may seem a pointless quibble – and after all, how can anyone tell whether the egg or chicken came first – but, in fact, it is not an argument about a chronological priority of events, but about the structural place of women's oppression.

Kinship organises sexuality in such a way that it prescribes social relations. To do this it exchanges people from one group to another and sometimes within a group. As a system it doesn't matter who is exchanged, and, doubtless, a complex anthropology of any given society would find within it that various categories of people are being exchanged. However, what we are looking for within kinship systems, just as it is what we are looking for in class society, is both what is the main social relationship and what is the principal system of organisation? It would seem that whatever other exchanges go on, women are always exchanged between men, thus though it may well be that there are some societies in which some women exchange some men, there are none in which women are not exchanged predominantly by men. Clearly the particular conditions of any kinship group's material base for survival will affect the form of kinship or the form of family organisation, that is to say whether it is agricultural, pastoral, or so on. Later, of course, the form of family will also be determined by class structures. But the other aspect of a material base will also be determinate; that base is the reproduction of human life. Mankind transforms external nature for the production of the needs of life and transforms its own nature, not for the reproduction of the species, but for the reproduction of society. In exchanging women, humans transform the primate ability to continue the species and give a social form to the reproduction of human society. In exchanging women in a way that ensures the reproduction of

the society, the sexual division of labour that ties women to
child care in a particular social manner is instituted.

Exactly at which point these conditions become oppressive
of women is hard to determine. Engels' thesis would suggest
that, while labour (as he sees it, the male-dominated
sphere) was primitive, it had no more importance than the
reproduction of people (the female-dominated sphere), and
that hence the sexes occupied equilateral positions. But
behind this analysis (and despite its intentions) there seems to
me to be a biological determinism – that is to say, that because
women give birth they got left behind when labour and
production, which determine social change, leaped ahead.
At the very least, the exchange of women (itself possibly a
determinate system within the various exchanges of kinship)
was a precondition for women's oppression. I think it may be
more than a precondition. It made their productive labour
dependent on their ascribed social functions as mothers,
nurses and educators and those functions were already
constituted in their 'future': they were subordinate functions.

The question of matrilineal or patrilineal societies –
inheritance down the mother's line or down the father's line –
is likewise a vexed one. Because of the role of the mother's
brother, even where the line of descent is traced through
women (matrilineality), women as reproducers are exchanged between men. But in that the exchange is only one
exchange among many and in that the role of the mother's
brother is only one aspect even of this situation – the husband
will probably come to live in the wife's place of residence for
instance, he may even be given some gift as recognition of his
move of social and geographical location (the male equivalent
of bride-price) – then the woman's situation is potentially less
oppressive. No more than are class societies uniformly
exploitative are kinship systems uniformly oppressive.

What I'm suggesting, however, is that we have a situation
which is doubly determined. The internal movement of
kinship systems is determined by the nature of the exchange
of women. But the relationship *between* the kinship

88

organisation and the economic mode of production of the
larger society and the eventual subordination of kinship to
class means that class determines the particular form of
kinship. There is a contradiction *within* kinship between men
and women whose determining moment is the exchange of
women, and there is a contradiction *between* kinship systems
and the mode of production.

I'm suggesting that the exchange of women always
determines the nature of the kinship group from within, but
this is not the same as saying that this particular exchange is
always dominant. In matrilineal, matrilocal tribes it would
not seem to be dominant and this would make the position of
women very different from that within patrilineal societies.

The woman who is exchanged is the promise of the next
generation – no one wants to receive or, therefore, give, an
infertile woman. In the kinship system heterosexuality is
assured as the dominant mode and in the exchange of
women, women become confined not to the species, as is
often argued, but to the social task of reproduction – to
mankind's transformation and humanisation of its own
nature.

At first sight, there is nothing in itself oppressive about this
situation, nor, of course, is it an exclusive one – women do
other things than get exchanged. But it is in the interlocking
of this determinate aspect of kinship (which in most societies
which are, after all, patrilineal ones, is also the dominant one)
and the sexual division of labour that I think we have to start
asking questions about women's oppression. If in her note in
The American Anthropologist Judith Brown is correct and we
can gauge the degree of women's contribution to the
subsistence economy by the extent to which women's work is
compatible with child care, then we can see that women's
contribution to production is determined by their place in the
system of the reproduction of human beings. As the level of
production dominates over that of reproduction in society as
a whole, we can see that women's ability to produce being
dominated by their having to reproduce has very serious

consequences. In other words, it is not only, as Engels claims, that as production gets more advanced, class societies come to dominate over kinship groups and women, who are bound to the kinship family, become oppressed. It would seem that in the pre-class intersection of the kinship exchange system and the sexual division of labour (the system which still continues), as the people whose ability to produce is determined by the demand to reproduce social human beings, women must hold a subordinate position to men whose ability to reproduce not themselves but the other material conditions of their society (such as the reproduction of capital), depends on the social demand for them to produce those material goods in the first place.

Thus it is not just a question of class society – the dominance of production over reproduction – coming to dominate over the organisation of the society by kinship (and thus men coming to dominate over women) but rather that within the very system of kinship and its implications for the division of labour the conditions of men's domination over women are instituted.

What implications does this have for feminism? I want to end not by answering this question – because it's too big a question – but by giving two illustrations that might help direct the way in which we should look for answers. The first illustration I've borrowed from an observation I heard an American anthropologist, Norma Diamond, make recently about the Chinese communes. On her visit to the Chinese communes, she noticed that despite egalitarian job pos-sibilities, communal, domestic and child-care facilities and a political policy of sexual equality, women in the communes rarely held positions with as high a status attached to them as did the men. Being a feminist, and a good scholar, she asked two questions: 'Why not?' and 'What particular charac-teristics did the few women who had managed to get important positions have in common?' To cut a long story short, she found that as a result of the Chinese policy of not only eradicating faults in social practices but also of building on social strengths, many communes were based on old pre-liberation kinship groups. The evil practices, whereby the father of the family was absolute head often with rights of life and death over the rest of the family, whereby the older generation oppress the younger, whereby women were literally chattels without any rights at all, problems of inheritance, and so on, were all absolutely removed, and most of the social reforms that feminists in the west craved for were instituted. But the seemingly harmless residual organisation of kinship was retained. Communes often had old kin names, and the old kin groups had been patrilocal, that is to say, a woman moved to her husband's place of residence on marriage. This practice continued in the communes. Now the women who had high status positions were married women who had, for some reason, stayed in their original commune – their commune of origin. For example, they had married youths who had come out from the cities during the Cultural Revolution. Other women were either unmarried and therefore likely to leave their commune of origin or had come to the commune on marriage. In both cases, they had not the same positions of power – in one case because they were going to leave and in the other case because they had just arrived and had not the well-established influential ties. In other words, an apparently harmless means of social organisation, invisible unless one looked for it, had quite serious consequences for women.

The more frivolous illustration comes from our own type of society. It exemplifies how kinship still operates even if concealed beneath other complex ideologies and other forms of organisation. The daughter of the Queen of England married a commoner. Her father, who himself was not the king, gave her away to her husband, to whose place of residence she then removed. Princess Anne, as she herself said, is an 'old-fashioned' girl and she embellished the proceedings by promising to honour and obey her husband.

But even without the 'extras' of a patriarchal religious ceremony, the exchange of women and all its consequences still goes on in our society. It has, I think, important implications not only for women's subordination to men in the family but for the unequal sexual division at the place of work. Feminism needs to bring the unseen structures of kinship into the light of day.

2: Feminism as a Political Movement

In 'What is Feminism?', I described how in the exchange of women within the kinship system and in the sexual division of labour there resides a contradiction in the social relationship between men and women. What are the implications of this? Contradiction or contradictoriness describes the movement by which anything changes and develops. Everything that develops contains at least two elements which are in contradiction with each other, these can move place and become identified, in which case they will, as a unity, enter into a new contradictory relationship with another new element. There is a contradiction within anything that can change and one between it and its relationships to other things. This concept of contradiction and the unity of opposites is the concept of dialectical materialism. Mao Tse-Tung gives an illustration of one aspect of this process which feels pertinent to feminism as a relatively new field of knowledge. I suggest that we can transfer what Mao Tse-Tung says to our field of study. Mao writes:

> When we engage in study . . . [we have] . . . the contradiction in the passage from ignorance to knowledge. At the very beginning of our study of Marxism, our ignorance of or scanty acquaintance with Marxism stands in contradiction to knowledge of Marxism. But by assiduous study, ignorance can be transformed into knowledge, and blindness in the application of Marxism, into mastery of its application.[1]

The contradiction between ignorance and knowledge becomes resolved when ignorance is transformed into knowledge, the contradiction between the two forms a new unity – in this case, a new level of knowledge. But this knowledge then, of course, enters into a contradictory relationship with another new aspect of knowledge, in which case our first unity of ignorance and knowledge, which was knowledge, becomes ignorance in relation to the new knowledge, and so on . . .

How does this apply to a contradiction in the social relations between men and women? It is here that we must recollect the supremacy for feminism of this argument of a social contradiction between the sexes, over and above that which posits a static, biological opposition between the sexes. What we are talking about in proposing a resolution of a contradiction in the social relationship between men and women, is not men becoming women, or vice versa, as physiological androgynes, but the present social meanings of masculinity and femininity becoming resolved in a unity of their previous contradictions. To give a simple illustration – if the nurturant definition of women as social beings (as we discussed in relation to child care in 'What Is Feminism?') and the protective definition of men were to become resolved into a unity, this unity would enter into a new contradictory relationship with an, as yet, unforeseen possibility of human behaviour. In other words, nurturance and protection would become unified – would be a new form of social relationship and something else would enter in as a human possibility in contradiction to this new definition of persons. But this particular contradiction in the social relations between men and women as it has so far been known in history, would in this instance have then been resolved.

There is nothing in itself oppressive in a contradiction, but the history of the contradiction between men and women within kinship groups has, in an uneven way, been a history of an oppressive relationship. To go back to Mao Tse-Tung:

Why is there identity between war and peace and none between war and a stone? Why can human beings give birth only to human beings and not to anything else? The sole reason is that the identity of opposites exists only in necessary conditions. Without these necessary given conditions there can be no identity whatsoever.[2]

Clearly the analogy between war and peace is what we have to bear in mind when we think about the contradiction in the social relations of men and women; we're not looking at women and stones which could never form either a contradictory relationship or a unity. The meaning of identity is first that each element is the condition of the other's existence – and we have seen how kinship and the sexual division of labour make both men and women as social beings preeminently this (the one could not exist without the other) and second, that in certain conditions the one can be transformed into the other. What are the conditions that might make such a unity possible?

Given our ignorance of the history of this social relationship between men and women at this point, one cannot answer this definitively. A history of women that looks at their social meaning in relation to men from both a dialectical materialist and a feminist perspective (or, indeed from either) is only beginning to be attempted. So, using just two sources, I want to sketch two moments in the history of women which might prove significant for examining this question. This historical reconstruction is purely speculative – it is only a possible way of looking at things. I want to choose the rise of the middle-class city state in late sixth-century BC Athens and the rise of bourgeois capitalism in seventeenth-century England.

In the ninth and still in the eighth century BC, the heroic codes of Greece describe a society which is essentially male. The behaviour of women is literally prescribed by men; if they offend the laws which demand chastity, the problem is one to be handled by the men whose honour has been abused – they must fight it out between them. Heirs can be adopted and bred from concubines and the kinship groups can scarcely be said to resemble families as we think of them.

In the seventh century, clan ties are beginning to give way to emerging social classes, and the later Greek polis is visible in a form of society that has an agricultural base but an urban centre with the state controlled by an hereditary aristocracy, but one subject both to internal conflict and increasing opposition from the lower classes. Between the conflict of the upper and lower classes, a middle class of successful farmers arises, and for this middle class the position of women takes on a new significance. To quote from an article on the subject:

> In the rising 'middle classes' . . . there was far greater fragmentation and far deeper divisions between class members. For these people a policy of aggressive individualism and fierce competition was dictated; the nuclear family was a necessity of life for this group, and the wife was part of a corporate effort which made possible her husband's ascent up this economic social scale. In particular, the most important function of women, that of providing an heir, was crucial to the survival and the continuance of the family in an era when availability of land was increasingly restricted and the continuance of rights over family land dependent upon the existence of an heir. From the point of view of this class, women's sexuality emerges as a threat and as a potentiality which requires regulation and supervision.[3]

In the traditional clan society with its heroic code, women are insignificant objects of exchange – perhaps enjoying by virtue of their insignificance a certain freedom of behaviour and certainly a freedom from abuse. With the increased importance of women for the rising middle classes in Athens, comes a new element of misogyny: women matter and therefore must be minded. There is no question that both systems oppress women, but they do so very differently. Another principle of the contradiction within anything is that the contradictory elements are in an uneven relationship – that unevenness most clearly manifests itself here: as women gain, they lose.

In the sixth century it was clearly recognised that women

had both an integral place in the city state and yet had to be excluded from public life and by the sixth century the control of the state had virtually been wrested from the aristocracy by the middle classes. The rapid growth of colonisation and of commercial activity brought the city states of Greece, controlled by the middle classes, into being: new laws of succession cleared the way for the advent of private property by allowing a man to make a will bequeathing his property to his family instead of it having, as hitherto, to be returned to the clan. Landed property and its income, not birth, was the new principle of the agrarian economy. The new definition of the state was a union of households. The laws governed the household and successsion and prescribed the procreative function of women; this situation gave women both duties and rights.

The earlier heroic age seems to have conceived of men's and women's spheres as separate, coexisting but unrelated. The home, where man and woman form a unity, was utterly unimportant. The middle classes of the Greek democracies made a man's headship of his household – of his home – the principle for his incorporation in the city state. The private and the public are thus separated and the private – the home – is subordinated to the public:

> Women had before been conceived as an aspect of life in general; now they are seen as an aspect of men's existence . . . [this] means that the inferiority of women, their subservience to men, has to be explicitly recognised. Formerly women's inferiority was merely implied by the fact that the cultural ideal (the hero), was male . . . [and so] where the early aristocracy had ensured a free and leisured life for itself by concentrating in its hands all economic and social privilege, the democracies of Ancient Greece secured liberty for all its citizens by inventing a system of private property which required women to legitimate it and slaves to work it.[4]

The contradiction in the social relations of men and women certainly existed in the heroic age. But it would seem that the antagonism in the contradiction becomes intense

and able to be protested against from a political point of view
when, within class society, women and men get closer
together, more alike – a new unity – but then the women's
sphere is made an essential sub-category of men's – when the
public and the private are separated and the latter, enclosing
women, is subordinated to the former. At these points,
feminism arises as an articulate expression of the intensification and formation of a new contradiction. In one
sense, Plato would seem to have been a proto-feminist,
dreaming up a polis in which upper-class women would be
given equal opportunity with upper-class men, dreaming too
– in a jokey, self-critical way – about the resolution of the
contradiction.

Before going into the characteristics of feminism in its first
expressions, I want to jump to the English seventeenth
century. In this instance I don't want to go into even the
skimpy detail with which I glanced at the changing place of
women in classical Greece.

Comparisons are frequently made between the rise of the
Greek middle classes and the rise of the capitalist bourgeoisie.
Obviously the differences between them are as great as the
span of the twenty-three hundred years of human history can
make them. But for the moment, whilst recognising that that
span of history marks the difference for women too, let us look
at the similarities.

From the patrilineal systems of the upper class under
feudalism, capitalism was inaugurated, as was the Greek city
state, by colonisation and, at a super-structural level, by an
intellectual renaissance that stressed human reason and the
necessarily artificial character of human society. The small
family was instituted, and family, rather than lineal,
inheritance. Women in the new middle class cease to occupy
their own separate, if unequal, sphere (as upper-class women
under feudalism would seem to have done). The public and
private are separated. The private is made important but at
the expense of being harshly relegated as subordinate to the
public.

Feminism in the dominant class arises again from the conditions set up by a bourgeois state and the particular nature of the exchange of commodities that becomes more complex under capitalism but was there in a less developed form in the early Greek city state. An apparently free exchange of commodities takes place among citizens. Money represents the value of the commodities and the labour power that went into creating them is totally obscured. Here in the market places of Athens and the very different ones of seventeenth-century England, the nature of the economic exchange gives rise to an ideology of free and equal citizens. No wonder the societies felt the need to explain and justify the exclusion of their own class of women from the rights of this apparently free and equal society; no wonder a feminist vision of equality was forthcoming.

Interestingly, the first expressions of feminism are aristocratic. Plato and the women writers of the last third of the seventeenth century realise – if unconsciously – that within the terms of their society, the condition of equality between men and women is freedom from labour, including female labour. The ideal is an aristocratic one. Plato wants his women of the guardian class in his ideal polis, to be free from domestic work, child-rearing and marriage. The family and its property, the household and domestic work are all to go. There is to be equality of opportunity in this, the guardian class, and a spirit of 'brotherhood'. The work will be done by another class.

The seventeenth-century feminists came from the lesser gentry, they were sisters of curates, and perhaps schoolteachers or governesses. They explicitly compared the general situation of women with that of slaves and other deprived groups. Like Plato, they appealed to reason and the values of civilisation: 'Custom and the reliance on authority were their two great enemies.'[5] They, too, expressed the unity and then the intensification of the contradiction as it came into being anew, in the social relations between men and women, in a class that brought men and women into proximity, had an ideology of equality, yet had to subordinate women's work as reproducer of people to men's task of the reproduction and production of capital.

The lineage of the Greek heroic age and English feudalism was patrilineal. There is no doubt that in such systems there is not only a contradiction but probably an antagonistic one, between men and women, but the struggle here would seem to be from two separate spheres for domination of the one over the other; or, at least, as the authority and power is held by men, women try to subvert it – whether they try to subvert it by subcultural protest, such as that of the witches, or whether they try to subvert it by what is known as 'an open battle' between the sexes. The struggle between men and women under feudalism, is for power.

Chaucer's Wife of Bath, a lusty, resourceful woman who has buried several husbands, tells a tale of a knight who raped a maiden and was condemned to death by King Arthur. The Queen gets the knight a reprieve on condition that after a year and a day he should return with the answer to the question: 'What thyng is it that wommen moost desiren?' (What is it that women want?). To cut a long story short, after failing miserably in his quest, just as his time is up, the knight meets a hideous old hag who promises to tell him the answer to the question provided in return he grants her whatever she asks. The knight agrees and the hag gives him the answer, that what women most want is 'maistrie' (mastery), in particular over their husbands. The hag asks the knight to marry her. Feeling utterly wretched he, of course, has to do so. To console him she asks him which he would prefer – that she were old, ugly and faithful, or young, beautiful and false? Worn down and at a loss from tossing sleeplessly all night, the knight gives up and leaves it to his wife's judgement:

> 'My lady and my love, and wife so deere,
> I put me in your wise governance.
> I do no fors the wheither of the two;
> For as you liketh, it suffiseth me.'
> 'Thanne have I gete of yow maistre,' quod she,

'Syn I may chese and governe as me lest?'
'Ye, certes, wyf,' quod he, 'I holde it best.'[6]

She has, in other words, got mastery over him to choose and govern as she wishes. Having thus won 'maistre' over her husband, the old crone announces that she will be both young and faithful and, above all, obey and serve him in whatever way gives him pleasure.

In all its details, the medieval battle is a battle for power, a male and a female way of dominating over the other sex. Of course one sex gives up, even if in a subtle, complicated way. In a patrilineal clan or lineage system the contradiction between men and women, then, takes the form of a power struggle. When the clan (as in the Greek heroic age) or the 'line' (as in feudal England) changes – through a trans-formation in the economic mode of production – into a kinship system dominated by the small, individual family which gains in importance at the cost of being made harshly subordinate, women's status rises in relation to men's; instead of struggling for power from a different sphere, women become a part of men's life, they are inferiorised within men's sphere – which is the dominant sphere; they gain and they lose.

Within the middle classes of sixth- to fifth-century Greece and seventeenth-century England, there is not so much a situation of two separate spheres for men and women from which they struggle; there is a situation of greater propinquity. As women in this social sense become more like men, the struggle is not for power between two different areas but for equality within the same one. Feminism, after its initial individual visions of an aristocratic utopia, starts as a middle-class movement for equal rights – but it does not end there.

So far we have been looking only at the dominant class – dominant in the sense both of ideological and economic control. But, in fact, slaves outnumbered citizens at times in the Greek city state by as many as four to one and in England by the time mercantile capitalism had developed into industrial capitalism in the nineteenth century, the wage slaves of that system constituted roughly 65 per cent of the population. It would seem that in neither the slave nor the working-class population would the conditions be such as to bring about a shift and an intensification in the contradictions in the social relations of men and women such as was seen in the middle classes.

It is clearly the case that in a number of capitalist countries, throughout a large part of the nineteenth century and, of course, in the twentieth century, there is an important working-class feminist movement. As a very broad generalisation it would seem true to say that this, at first, was centred on issues of work – the earliest demands for female participation in the first male friendly societies and then trade unions, alternative women's trade unions and latterly, perhaps the demand that housework should be regarded and remunerated as a job. As an organised movement, feminism undoubtedly has both middle- and working-class dimensions, but I'm tentatively suggesting that the conditions that are crucial to its first expression are found within the situation of the middle classes. It is not, in other words, as is sometimes argued, privilege that makes middle-class women rebel, but a real change that takes place, initially in their particular social conditions.

Despite the fact that working-class women make demands for equality with working-class men, for the right to equal participation in the working-class organisations as well as demands against another class for such things as equal pay, yet as a class – because of their participation at the same place in production – men and women in the working classes are unified. However, this is only as a class and in relation to another class, not to each other as men and women. In other words, one element of a contradiction may be resolved in relation to another element, but the contradiction still remains in other respects. To give a familiar illustration – in a struggle against imperialism, a colonised national bourgeoisie will unite with the peasantry that it usually exploits, but the contradiction between the bourgeoisie and the peasantry as classes still remains. It is only in their nationalism, struggling against an imperial power, that the contradiction between the two classes is resolved. So the working class as workers against the bourgeois middle class resolves the contradiction between men and women workers, but in their social relationship as men and women *within* their class, the contradiction remains. It is this factor which unifies women across class lines.

In the middle class, men and women do not occupy the same place in production and though they are, of course, members of the same class they're not unified, as such, through their place in production – through, in this case, their ownership or management of the means of production. The new contradiction is a heightened one because their class unity rests on their social differences – in the middle class, the woman's place in the home is the condition of the man's place in society, and vice versa. Among the earliest working-class men and women in cottage industry, the work is in the home, men and women are unified in their work and the place where they work. With industrialism, the proletarian home is eroded, as all members – men, women and children – are out at work. Set against this, the separation of home and work and the wife's relegation to the home, and the husband's relegation to work (or rather 'business') is a condition of the middle class.

If the key event within kinship for the oppression of women is the exchange of women and the way it establishes the nature of the division of labour between the sexes, the initiating moment for feminism might well be when, instead of the separation of kinship from production within the dominant class (as it was in the Greek heroic age or under English feudalism), the former is subordinate as a condition of control or ownership of the latter. In the middle class, women are exchanged only for their subordinate roles as social reproducers – not, as among peasants or the working class, as additional workers in production. In this situation, the two aspects of the contradiction become intensified – the contradiction within kinship and the contradiction between it and the mode of production.

It would seem, then, quite predictable that as a democratic bourgeois system initially intensifies the contradiction between men and women within that class, feminism would first be expressed by middle-class women at the outset as a retrospective aristocratic ideal, then as a demand for equal rights and opportunities with middle-class men. But the difference between the Greek slave community and the capitalist working class is that the working class is in a position to struggle against the conditions of its existence – the exploitation of its labour power and the appropriation of its products in a new way. In England, the presence of working-class struggle – male and female – and in nineteenth-century America of slave struggle – male and female – gives a new context to feminism, a new possibility for the resolution of the social contradiction of men and women. Confronted, as Plato and seventeenth-century women were not, with the struggles of a class other than their own, feminists in the nineteenth and twentieth centuries have been given conditions in which they have not simply had to react to the shift and the intensification of the contradictions between the social position of themselves and their own middle-class men, but to consider the wider meaning of the contradiction itself. And as capitalism has developed, the implications both of the sexual/social division of labour within industry and of the need for all women to be social reproducers of the labour force as well as workers have intensified the contradictions for working-class women as a sex.

I think this is posing the question of the relationship of social class, race and feminism in a somewhat different way from the usual presentations of the issue. I am suggesting that there always has been a contradiction in the social relations between men and women, differently expressed in different societies and social classes. The contradiction intensifies for the middle classes and makes them the first to focus on the issue, but as the contradiction is universally present, feminists from all classes become aware of it. The struggle in the social relations between the working classes and the bourgeoisie is a class struggle, the struggle in the social relations between men and women is a woman's struggle.

In *The Symposium*, Plato has Aristophanes imagine the unity of men and women as a hermaphrodite – each half has found the other half that it longed for and was incomplete without. This is an imaginary transformation of opposites into a unity and is a characteristic process in much mythology. Such ideas are conjured up in fantasy by the many real and concrete transformations that take place but cannot be grasped as yet. The resolution of today's contradiction will be a new unified social being in contradiction with a new social possibility. It will not be an androgyne. Feminism has found that the contradiction in the particular social relations of men and women today can, as with all contradictions, all forms of learning, only become a unity through struggle.

3: Romantic Love

In her book, *The Dialectic of Sex,* Shulamith Firestone writes:

> A book on radical feminism that did not deal with love would be a political failure. For love, perhaps even more than childbearing, is the pivot of women's oppression today.[1]

These are strong words, but they are indicative of an attitude to love, and to romantic love, in particular, that is prevalent within the women's movement today. In this talk I want to ask three questions. First of all, what has the women's movement got to say about love? Secondly, I'm going to try and find some definition of what I think are the psychological characteristics of romantic love. How does it come about? What is it? How do we fall romantically in love? And then, finally, I want to discuss whether there is, in fact, a difference for men and women in the state of being in love. These three topics are clearly related.

For Shulamith Firestone, it is men who, on account of their insatiable power lusts, cannot know the meaning of true love and women who, deprived of power, can give such love but are inevitably exploited when they do so. Men want, as all humans want, to be loved, but men do not want to waste time giving love. So a man romantically falls for some falsely idealised woman in order to get her to give to him the love that he craves for the rest of his life. Firestone argues that there is nothing wrong with love itself, what is wrong are the forms it can take in a sexually inegalitarian society and, as all societies so far have been sexually unequal, love has always been distorted away from its potential. Men have short, sharp phases of romantic idealisation wherein they elevate in a false, dishonest way the one woman that through their love they want to honour and remove from her gender inferiority as a woman. Firestone argues that social and economic oppression of women is no longer sufficiently powerful on its own to keep women in their inferior status; to bolster it, the disastrous ideology of romantic love has been called in. She argues:

> Romanticism develops in proportion to the liberation of women from their biology. As civilisation advances and the biological bases of sex class crumble, male supremacy must shore itself up with artificial institutions . . . where formerly women had been held openly in contempt, now they are elevated to states of mock worship. Romanticism is a cultural tool of male power to keep women from knowing their condition . . . Today, with technology enabling women to break out of their roles for good . . . romanticism is at an all-time high.[2]

To summarise her position: true erotic love is impossible in our society. Romanticism conceals a distorted, false eroticism and romanticism is, today, the name of the game of women's oppression. In the language of the Women's Movement, it is 'pedestal treatment'.

In *The Female Eunuch*, Germaine Greer offers a different approach. Through an analysis of literature she traces the changing ideology of love – it is a sensitive and fascinating account. I think it is one of the best parts of her book. It is because her picture is historically richer that I think that it is legitimate for me ultimately to use it to draw a different conclusion from that which she offers in her analysis. In other words, I'm going to use some of her material to advance a different argument.

Like Shulamith Firestone, Germaine Greer feels that romantic love is a perversion of real love and she, too, sees it as false, stifled eroticism. This does not, of course, prevent it from having produced great literature. But Germaine Greer accounts for its falsity, not as Firestone does, in sexual class terms, but in social class terms. To Germaine Greer, medieval epics of romantic love were the province of the nobility who had the time and means to luxuriate in idle adulterous fantasies. Unlike these aristocrats, medieval peasant men and women must have genuinely worked and genuinely loved on the level of realism, the realism of their shared need and mutual dependence. In Greer's account, during the sixteenth century, the move from the Catholic to the Protestant Church was reflected in the new ideology of marriage. For the rising Protestant middle classes of the sixteenth and early seventeenth century, marriage could no longer be an arranged business deal between powerful lineages as it had been among the nobility; it had to be seemingly free and equal. Because of this, from having been this sort of fantasy province of a small nobility, romantic love came to replace parental coercion as that which forced one into marriage. From being excitingly adulterous and oppositional to the social *status quo* in the Middle Ages, romantic love became a prelude to Establishment marriage of modern times. Firestone and Greer, then, give us two feminist accounts of romantic love.

Let us now consider what constitutes the most obvious characteristics of romantic love from a psychological perspective. Love is a huge and elusive topic – being in love, by its very definition, is about the Great Unknown; to be in love is not to understand it; if you understood it, you would not be in it. Yet despite this, I think we can use a working definition of romantic love that describes it even if it does not yet explain it. Romantic love seems to me to seek an ideal; if it attains its idealised object, then it ceases to be romantic love. If it realises what it has been seeking, if it gains its ideal, then the love may turn either to disillusionment, quite often to hate, alternatively – and this is the hope within marriage – the romantic lover can recognise the non-ideal status of his love object, and thus transform what was once romantic love into affectionate love, something much more muted. Whatever happens, the romance dies out with the attainment. Romantic love dreams of consummation, but never achieves it without in the process setting in motion its own dissolution.

If romantic love cannot be consummated, then there is an essential contradiction between romantic love and Christian marriage. It is this contradiction between romantic love and marriage that inspired what I think is still the classical book on the subject of love: Denis de Rougement's *Love in the Western World*. De Rougement's central thesis is that love and marriage do not go together like a horse-and-carriage. Quite the contrary. What seems to go together is not love and marriage, but love and death. De Rougement was pre-occupied with love and death, partly, I think, because he wrote his book in 1940 at the beginning of the Second World War and preoccupations with love and death are always at their height in wartime. Nevertheless, despite the particular date of his book, I think he is correct – love and death are the twin components of romantic love.

De Rougement was interested in the topical and typical wartime anxiety about the survival of marriage in the western world. This is the question he asks at the beginning of his book:

Once the existence of the ill has been recognised must the institution of marriage bear the blame for it, or is there something fatal to marriage at the very heart of human longing? Has the so-called 'Christian' notion of marriage, as many people suppose, really brought about this turmoil; or is there a notion of love abroad in the world which, although we do not yet realise it, renders the marriage bond intolerable in its very essence?[3]

The answer that de Rougement comes up with is that there is indeed a type of love abroad in the world, which by its very nature is opposed to marriage, and this love is romantic love. He traces it back in the west to the twelfth-century heresy of Catharism – or the faith of the Albigensian people, which brought into being the epics and lyrics of romantic love. The notion of romantic love that de Rougement finds deriving from this twelfth-century heresy and its literary forms is a notion of love that is, in itself, and by its very nature, anti-marriage. It is also, by definition, anti-life. It is strongly connected with death, indeed, it finds its apotheosis in death. Even in its very conception, it opposes the main forces of life – that is to say, it opposes sexuality, and, in particular, the reproduction and propagation of the species. To de Rougement, romantic love is adulterous, not because of the thrills of illicit sex (as Germaine Greer proposes) but because it is simply not interested in procreation or any form of legitimate union or marriage. Indeed, de Rougement argues that romantic love is not about sexuality at all. The twelfth- and thirteenth-century romances are only about an ideal longing that is expressed in what sounds to our modern, over-sexualised ear, to be sexual terms. The real terms of this medieval love are, he argues, not sexual but mystical terms. It is our anachronistic error that we hear it in the wrong way.

I want now to reconsider what we have learned from these three accounts – the feminist analyses of Firestone and Greer and the general hypotheses offered by de Rougement, in order to try and understand something further about the nature of romantic love and within this, the relative positions of men and women as romantic lovers. To do this I am going to reformulate the whole conception of the shift in romantic love from medieval to modern times as, in particular, Greer and de Rougement describe it.

I think it is true that in the twelfth and thirteenth century adulterous romantic love is a search for some unattainable ideal and that at the end of the sixteenth century this becomes harnessed as one of the main means to marriage. But while I think that that shift is true and truly described by Greer and de Rougement, I am not sure that that is the most important thing to say about it. What I want to point out is that love in the twelfth-and thirteenth-century romantic epic and lyric had the male as the romantic lover; the subject of the passion is the man. What happens at the end of the sixteenth and the beginning of the seventeenth century – and is much more forcefully with us today – is that we no longer have a dominant strain of romantic literature in which the man is the subject of the passion. Instead, we have romantic fiction in which the woman is the object of the romantic tale itself. It is this object, not the male subject, with whom the reader or listener is asked to identify.

That may sound an over-subtle distinction but it seems to me to be a highly significant one. In other words, romance has moved from being about a male subject to becoming a commodity about women, for women. The woman who reads the popular romantic novels of say Barbara Cartland or Denise Robbins or stories in women's magazines, has to identify with the sexual object of the romance. It is not that the woman has become the sexual subject of the romance, but that the actual romance has shifted from being about a sexual subject – who is male – to being about a woman – who is the object of romance. The woman in the romance today may indeed aspire to some dark romantic hero, but he is not the subject of the romance and nor is she – the romance itself is the subject. The woman has to make herself into a suitable sexual object in order to win this man. The romance has shifted from being the poetic utterance of a free, aspiring subject to being an opiate of a trapped sexual object. To me this is the key to the shift from romantic love as a description of oppositional, adulterous love in the Middle Ages to its becoming part of conformist, marital love in modern times.

If there has been this shift in the literary presentation of romantic love, it will be likely that it reflects not only an historically changing relationship between men and women but some more fundamental, less historically specific distinction that is set up between men and women, both as romantic lovers and as objects of romantic love. To look at this question, it is first necessary to consider in greater detail the general psychological characteristics of romantic love. De Rougement, as we have seen, fights strongly against the idea that there is a common factor of sexuality that underlies all forms of romantic love. Instead, the qualities he ascribes to romantic love are the psychological characteristics of narcissism and bisexuality. In other words, romantic love is self-love and offers the neglected possibilities of the other sex that are always contained within every human being. At least as regards the male lover (whom de Rougement is describing), what the lover would seem to be seeking is the lost feminine part of himself – the eternal feminine who inspires the very art that is being written, but the eternal feminine that can, of course, only be re-met in death. It is the other half of himself that the romantic lover searches for. He cannot find it except in his own annihilation which, of course, is very much what happened to Narcissus himself. When he looked in the pool, all Narcissus wanted was himself and, as all he wanted was himself, he could only have himself in death – the other half of himself, his own shadow.

In repudiating an explanation of passionate, romantic love in terms of sexuality, de Rougement has reiterated, I think, a common misunderstanding about the concept of Eros. But I do not think that either Firestone or Greer solve the problem by simply reinvesting romantic love with stifled sexuality or eroticism. I think there is certainly some form of sexuality underlying romantic love but we have to be very careful to specify what type of sexuality it is. If we use the psychoanalytic notion of Eros, we may be able to understand the general human ability to feel romantic love. What we're discussing is something that happens before the child has his love and sexuality directed to another object. A person's self is initially very much a body-self – a body-ego. We come into the world as bodies and the world we come into is a world of words and perceptions. Our very 'creation' of ourselves involves a perception and a relationship to our own body – the way the baby relates to its body and the way it perceives its relationships can, in a complex sense of the term, be labelled sexual.

Sexuality is not limited, as in conventional morality, to genital intercourse with its procreative powers. It includes all that as adults we still possess but that we have come to regard as perverse. There are certain areas of the infant's body, for instance, the mouth and the anus, that have a heightened sensitivity, and these erotogenic zones coincide with dominant aspects of the baby's sensual or sexual relationship to itself. Genital sexuality is initially no different from other forms of sexuality but the way it is controlled and socialised gives it a different significance. Unlike other forms of sexuality, genital sexuality comes up against the universal taboo of incest. Instead of sucking the mother's breast or pleasing the toilet trainer, the child has its genital desires for one or other of its parents, forbidden. All that matters in this context is that the first body-self, the pregenital self, is perceived as important in itself.

The autonomous, or auto-erotic pleasure of the erogenous zones has its perceptual equivalent in self-love, the concept of narcissism. It is only with genital love and the implications of the tabooed, incestuous love for the parents that love and sexuality take on their meaning of interpersonal relationships – that is, love between people. Before this particular juncture, sexual feelings are from a body point of view, auto-erotic and imaginatively narcissistic. Furthermore, this pre-Oedipal infant does not have a body-ego or self that in psychological terms, it meaningfully, or symbolically distinguishes as masculine or feminine. This pre-Oedipal child is psychologically bisexual.

It seems to me that it is exactly this area of pre-interpersonal sexuality that we are talking about in the case of romantic love. Its characteristics – narcissism and bisexuality – agree with those that de Rougement has isolated; but its sexual, or rather its erotic nature, accord with what the feminist writers depicted and what de Rougement denies. I suggest that de Rougement is wrong to think that the origin of romantic love is non-sexual and only mystical. Narcissism and bisexuality are certainly erotic states although they are not dominated by genitality, nor do they express themselves in a relationship between two people. They're about the self but it is a sexual self.

To the general conglomeration of sexuality, both in its narcissistic and its interpersonal or Oedipal phase, Freud, in his later work gave the name of Eros. Where in his earlier thinking he had seen an opposition between the sexual and the self-preservative instincts, he later saw a conflict or a contradiction between Eros and what he called the death drive. He proposed that the sexual drives strove to stabilise the species and hence force the individual to live and propagate on behalf of the species. But against this, the death drive pushes the individual towards stasis, towards his own annihilation and hence the annihilation of the future of the race. Human drives are versatile and can both amalgamate and separate. The death drive can only be seen in its concrete manifestations, either simply as destructiveness or, in conjunction with the sexual drive, as sadism. I think that we can see that Eros and the death drive are very intertwined in all the greatest portrayals of romantic love. One might almost say that where interpersonal procreative love, that is, some form of legitimate or married love, is the triumph of sexuality over death, the species over the individual, romantic love, being only about the individual, is the triumph of death over life.

Romantic love is about the self, it is erotic, but does not have a sexual object that it is ultimately different from itself. The lady of the courtly epic, Goethe's eternal feminine, Cleo the poet's muse, the feminine principle of *fin de siècle* artists, are all, in the last resort, metaphors for the lost female part of the original, psychologically bisexual self. That is the general distinguishing quality of romantic love as such. But there is an important assumption here – an assumption that gets us back to one of our original questions. Just as we are getting to a definition that separates romantic love from marital love and sees romantic love as achieving annihilation only in death because it is a search for the other side of the lost shadow of the bisexual, narcissistic self, we must note that there is an important assumption behind this definition of romantic love. And that assumption is that the romantic lover is male. We do not hear of an ideal gentleman or a masculine principle or some eternal masculinity that a woman strives for as a completion of the lost half of her bisexuality. The dark handsome stranger of romantic fiction will not complete the woman on the imagined plane but on a realistic one of marriage. By then the romance will be over. She has, as it were, 'realistically' found her other half. Her romantic love will be resolved in marriage and the wife's task, if she is not to lose her husband to his need for romance with other women, is to re-create the romance *ad infinitum* – this is the message of most women's journalism today. For a woman, romantic love then does not end in the death-like contemplation of self-annihilation – of loss of self in the larger cosmos – as it does for a man, because she finds her other half, without which, in any case in social life, she would not be a whole person. The male romantic lover, on the other hand, has only the sense of fantasised, internal incompleteness; reunion with his lost feminine half would not complete his actual life, but only perfect his being in death.

Why should there, in psychological terms, be this difference? Boys and girls, though alike as human animals, are born into a world that expects very different things of them. Girls must want to grow up, marry and have babies. Boys must want to do these things, too, if the species is to survive, but their strongest desire must be different. For boys, in a patriarchal society, the desire must be to go beyond the

reproduction of the species and create new ways of living, production, technology and so on. When a girl emerges from her earliest narcissistic phase, as I have described it, into her first object love, it is the same as the boy's. She loves the mother who gave birth and succour to her, but she must abandon this incestuous desire in a manner different from the boy's. She must transfer to loving the father. To do this she must want to become lovable for him. So she retains her earliest narcissism to help her become a pretty little girl for her father. Though she must never actually win the father – that too would be incestuous – she does not wholly abandon this pattern of relationship and, in fact, tries to repeat it when she attracts a man as her father-substitute and starts a family of her own on the model of the one she has come from. The girl's secondary narcissism is a repeat of her first narcissism, a narcissism of becoming a sexual object – a woman who makes herself beautiful for men.

The first narcissism, the primary narcissism of the boy and the girl, is not essentially different – but it has a very different fate. Like the girl, the boy takes the mother as first love-object, but he does not give up his tabooed desire by substituting the father for the mother. He gives her up by identifying with the father and learning that if he puts his mind to other things, one day he'll go on and work like his father and have a woman of his own at the same time. The boy does not, therefore, need to re-deploy his early narcissism to make himself an attractive object, as the girl has to do to make herself attractive to the father. He re-uses his early narcissism as a secondary formation, simply to prove his own sense of subjecthood, or to search for that lost complete self of his early, narcissistic days.

The earliest narcissism, the primary narcissism of both sexes – to which the romantic lover returns – is certainly erotic, but it is different for each. Women have to go back and use their narcissism to become attractive sexual objects. Boys go back to use it to strengthen their own subjecthood. Romantic love – pre-social, pre-interpersonal, bisexual, narcissistic, a struggle between Eros and death – is, for a man, a return to his earliest self, a search for the self-completion that, on entering the world of being only a man, was taken from him. Male romantic love looks backwards, or if it looks forward, it looks only to death – which is itself a return to the inert from which we came. For the woman, the narcissism of her romantic love is the mark of her attractiveness, first to her father and later to her lover. Women's bisexuality is externalised in finding, quite literally, another half with which to complete themselves. The romantic love of women looks forward, forward to marriage.

In the late sixteenth and early seventeenth century, a new ideology of men and women as equals started to be established. Marriage was supposed to be a contract between equals, but the equality was notional. Romantic love shifted from being the male subject's search for his lost feminine self to being a consolation for a woman's future confinement in domesticity – she needs to have the luck and the appeal to win the handsome, dark stranger as her lawfully wedded husband.

In some of the best romantic novels, such as those of the Brontës, something mars the glory of the strong, attractive man. Hareton in *Wuthering Heights* is a bit of a buffoon, Rochester in *Jane Eyre* is partially blinded and maimed – there are many other examples. There was no pretended equality between men and women during the Middle Ages and the male romantic lover flourished, at least in literature. After the seventeenth century, the woman becomes the object of the tale. But we should look more closely and realise that, if women cannot be romantic lovers as subjects of their own search for self, then in any true sense, men cannot be so either. The end of these later romantic novels is the confinement and the submission of the woman and usually some form of emasculation of the man. A false sexual equality has introduced romantic fiction that ends in marriage. But romantic fiction that makes woman the sexual object, makes man the sexual object too – in the new popular romantic novels nobody is romantic subject. A false equality can only equalise downwards.

4: Feminism and Femininity at the Turn of the Century

According to Aristotle, 'woman is, as it were, an impotent male, for it is through a certain incapacity that the female is female.' Although it would be a generalisation, it would not be an unfair one to suggest that during the nineteenth century, this incapacity of the female, when it was liked, was called 'charm' or one of a dozen epithets that described that insubstantial notion of 'femininity', and when it was disliked was called 'hysteria'. As one American churchman put it in the 1890s:

> The excessive development of the emotional in her nervous system ingrafts on the female organisation a neurotic or hysterical condition which is the source of much of the female charm when it is kept within due restraint. In moments of excitement, it is liable to explode in violent paroxysms. Every woman carries this power of irregular, illogical and incongruous action and no-one can foretell when the explosion will come.

I want to speculate on some of the links between hysteria, femininity and feminism. The medical history of hysteria and its connection with femininity is a complex one and I shall only mention it here. It is often argued that hysteria as a diagnostic category is now redundant. The hysteric has vanished. On the other hand, if we move away from the medical usage to lay usage, I think we will find that the term hysteria is still quite prevalent. For example, although schizophrenia became a fashionable diagnosis in the 1960s, it is only in very special circles, I imagine, that a husband made late for work by some agitated protests of his wife shouts at her, 'Stop being so schizophrenic!' But there are few women who have not found themselves at some point or other described as 'hysterical' – from 'She's just an hysterical bitch' to a kindlier, 'Jenny, darling, we'll sort it all out, but don't get so worked up and hysterical' – a man's reasonableness against a woman's emotionality.

Although in some epochs, it has been quite clearly stated by both medical practitioners and lay people that hysteria was to be found in men, it has always been primarily associated with women. The Egyptians connected its symptoms with a wandering womb – the uterus had a life of its own end and it had to be moved back from its hysterical tracks by persuasion, by evil tastes or attractive smells. Often a male deity was employed to lure it back into place. The Greeks believed that of itself, the womb wanted to generate children and had to be appeased by passion and love; marriage was a prescribed remedy for hysterical spinsters and widows. Roman ideas of hysteria were closely indebted to Greek Hippocratic medicine, and generally throughout antiquity the con- nection between sexuality, particularly female sexuality and hysteria was explicit.

However, the connection becomes more pronounced, and in a totally different way, from the fifth century AD onwards. The change comes with Christianity and its notion that sex was tainted with sinful eroticism and hence that abstinence, hitherto the *cause* of the painful disease of hysteria, was now a virtue that had to be recommended. As Ilsa Veith writes:

> [This] . . . altered the social attitude towards the hysteric and changed him from a sick human being beset with emotional needs and physical distress into someone more or less wilfully possessed, bewitched, in league with the devil, even heretical.[1]

Only marital, procreative intercourse, could, at least in Augustinian doctrine, be unlustful – the rest, for women, was witchcraft. Thus hysteria was removed from the field of a medical problem to that of a social disgrace, and from the jurisdiction of doctors, to that of the Church and its executors.

Twentieth-century feminism, searching for its own history, has started to identify the witches as its first valiant spokeswomen. If we regard feminism as a conscious political movement with a need for a theory as well as a practice, then the claim seems to me to be a slim one. On the other hand, if we are looking for pre-political manifestations of feminism, for spontaneous protest, then the point would seem valid. One can see the witchcraft that was prevalent European practice from the ninth century to the early seventeenth century, either as mass hysteria or as unconscious feminism. The link between the two perspectives is, of course, the close association of *femininity* and hysteria. I shall come back to this later, but pre-political feminism (at whatever date it arises) is bound to be a protest by women in terms of their definitional and denigrated characteristic – emotionality. If femininity is by definition hysterical, feminism is the demand *for* the right to be hysterical.

If women are oppressed, then the psychological characteristics that describe femininity are bound to be debased and those that define masculinity are bound to be elevated. In a spontaneous protest, debased characteristics are going to be revalued. At this point, and at this point alone, feminism is a battle of female hysteria against male obsessionality, or women's emotions over man's rationality.

From this perspective, it is certainly plausible to see the witches of the Middle Ages as using – if unconsciously – their hysteria to flout the patriarchal powers. Certainly, those powers took it that way. At the end of the fifteenth century in Germany alone, an average of 600 witches manifesting hysterical symptoms were executed each year. As we shall see, the later nineteenth-century physicians, preachers and husbands or fathers who had to deal with hysterical women, found them manipulative, using their hysteria as a devious way of getting power. The medieval church authorities were not at all embarrassed by this way of looking at the matter. If it was the nineteenth and twentieth centuries that deployed the notion that woman, the incomplete male, wanted to castrate men in revenge, in the fourteenth and fifteenth centuries it was explicitly maintained that by casting enchantment over

it, the woman could take away the power of the male organ –
deprive the man of his sexual potency. The terminology may
just about shift but there is something very constant in the
features of this so-called battle between the sexes.

The mass sub-cultural protest of the witches and its hyper-
political repression by patriarchal authorities started to die
out in Europe in the early seventeenth century. Tracts
questioning the validity of witchcraft asserted reason over
superstition and offered a diagnosis of the event quite
explicitly in terms of hysteria. John Webster in his *The
Displaying of Supposed Witchcraft,* claimed that its symptoms
were occasioned by 'Melancholic Dreams or Hysterical
Imaginings', and hysteria itself started to be re-analysed.

There were various theories connecting hysteria with
mental or emotional sensitivity. By the nineteenth century
the battleground on which women and men fought in an
unconscious, pre-political manner, was not witchcraft with
its hysterical manifestations, but hysteria as a disease.
Women used hysteria simultaneously to exaggerate and
refute the 'stereotypes of their nature'. Against this assault,
patriarchal power offered the home. To put it somewhat
glibly, at a simple *social* level, hysteria, with its malingering
invalidism, tantrums and wilfulness was the nineteenth-
century woman's protest against confinement in the home-
sweet-home of bourgeois industrial capitalism.

Tracing the literature of magazines and journals from
1820–1860, Barbara Weller notes what she calls the growth
of 'The Cult of True Womanhood'. Piety, purity, sub-
missiveness and a love of domesticity characterise true
womanhood. The chores of cooking, cleaning, sewing, and
the like, are designated 'housecraft' and the art is that of
'home-making'. In a world governed by the ideologies of love
and religion, as is the home, one must be sure not to call work,
work. But as the reality was usually so far from this domestic
ideal, the magazines enticed women into domesticity, not
only by extolling virtue, but also by sneaking hints that only
through marriage could a woman better her position in the

uneven balance of power. As one article on 'Matrimony' put it:

> The man bears rule of his wife's person and conduct. She bears rule over his inclinations: he governs by law, she by persuasion . . . the empire of the woman is an empire of softness . . . her commands are caresses, her menaces are tears . . . to him the law, to her the subtlety.[2]

As one Reverend Samuel Miller preached:

> How interesting and important are the duties devolved on females as wives . . . the councillor and friend of the husband; who makes it her daily study to lighten his cares, to soothe his sorrows, and to augment his joys: who, like a guardian angel, watches over his interests, warns him against dangers, comforts him under trials; and by her pious, assiduous, and attractive deportment, constantly endeavours to render him more virtuous, more useful, more honourable and more happy.[3]

The novelist, George Meredith, let one of his heroines have a pretty shrewd picture of what was going on in this world of men and women. As Diana of the Crossways puts it: 'We women are the verbs passive of the alliance. We have to learn, and if we take to activity with the best intentions, we constitute a frightful disturbance. We are to run on lines like steam trains or we come to no station, dashed to fragments.' The women who did not keep to the lines of submission and domesticity – at least in the middle classes – dashed to fragments in hysteria or constituted a frightful disturbance with feminism.

But while women were unconsciously protesting against a patriarchal definition of their characters by becoming hysterical, and while doctors and philosophers were haggling over the definition of the disease, what were women *consciously* doing with their disease? In England, at any rate, the demise of witchcraft in the seventeenth century coincided with the rise of an explicitly political demand by women for equality. In other words, with the end of feudalism and Catholicism and the rise of Protestantism and capitalism, conscious feminism replaced witchcraft. In America, witch-

craft survived longer, and feminism as a conscious protest
started later and all the more forcefully.

It was, among other things, against their definition as
hysterics that nineteenth-century feminists protested – no
doubt, they often did so hysterically. For as many nineteenth-
century feminists pointed out, male hysteria was called
patriotic enthusiasm. Indeed feminism, then, as now,
inevitably oscillated between asserting that feminine emotion
(hysteria) was valid but undervalued, and claiming that the
demands for equality were not emotional but rational. The
arguments throughout nineteenth-century feminism and
today are both that women have the same capacities as men,
and should have the same rights, and that they are distinct
and have their own cultural contribution to make. Both
arguments are correct and only mutually exclusive when
neither is granted.

If unconsciously women protested against submission and
domesticity by withdrawing into hysteria in the nineteenth
century, consciously feminists challenged nineteenth-
century concepts of motherhood and wifehood. In the
United States, the enormous National Association for
Women held that marriage was responsible for women's
oppression and, until it was influenced at the end of the
century by the rise of imperialism and ideas that the nation
was but a larger family, this feminist association system-
atically attacked the mystifications that surrounded the
nineteenth-century family. As Charlotte Perkins Gilman,
one of the greater theorists of the nineteenth-century
women's movement, put it, on two different occasions:
'family unity is bound together with a tablecloth' and
'anybody can be a mother. An oyster can be a mother. The
difficult thing is to be a person.'

It is this dilemma of how to be person if one is a woman, that
Nora, in Ibsen's A Doll's House embodies. The play brings
together the dilemmas of femininity in a patriarchal society:
how to be a charming woman, a responsible mother and a
person in your own right. Nearly a hundred years later, the

play is still relevant for feminism. Nora is the gay child-wife of a minor official, Helmer. He treats her as a doll, as her father did before him, and – a point often missed – she in her turn tends to treat their children as dolls. But in the past Nora has not only secretly worked, but also secretly and, in a sense, innocently, committed forgery, in order to get enough money to save her husband's life. It is when Helmer finds out about his wife's act and responds to it with utter duplicity that Nora questions the meaning of their marriage and her own suitability as a mother. At the end of the play, Nora leaves both husband and children.

In his notes for the play written in Rome in September 1878, Ibsen defined its themes thus:

> There are two kinds of spiritual laws, two kinds of conscience, one in man and a wholly different one in woman. They do not understand each other, but woman is judged in practical life according to man's laws, as if she were not a woman, but a man.

> The wife in the play does not know the ins and outs of right and wrong, natural feeling on the one side, and belief in authority on the other, both confuse her.

> A woman cannot be herself in today's society, which is an exclusively male society, with laws written by men and with prosecutor and judge who judge women's conduct from a male point-of-view.

> She has committed forgery, and this is her pride, for she has done so from care of her husband, to save his life. But this man with his everyday honesty, stands firmly planted on the law's foundation, and regards the matter with a male eye. The mental struggle. Depressed and confused by her faith in authority, she loses her faith in her moral right and her ability to bring up her children. Bitterness . . .

> . . . everything must be borne along. The catastrophe approaches mercilessly, inevitably. Despair, struggle and defeat.[4]

Ibsen's statement is about one sort of feminism – the assertion of values that do not simply criticise the *status quo* but come from another system of morality altogether. It is a precarious assertion, easily leading into the elevation of women over men as better human beings. But I don't think Ibsen's conception need induce that sort of banal speculation in us. If we take Ibsen's words seriously, then it seems to me that what we have is the painful and serious struggle of a woman whose honesty compels her to abandon the tricks of femininity a patriarchal society imposes on her and assert feminist values, humanist values that attack the very root of patriarchy.

Until the crisis when Helmer discovers how she saved his life by fraudulent means, Nora's femininity quite clearly verges on the hysterical – the word is used, her acts imply such behaviour. Interestingly enough, contemporary critics of the play urged Nora to have a more mature sense of responsibility to her home. Without quite realising what they did, these critics advocated exactly what the play was attacking. In different European and Scandinavian countries, aspiring playwrights adapted A Doll's House into acceptable versions. Most leading actresses refused to play Nora's final desertion of her home. The first verson to be played in England was called The Breaking of a Butterfly. Helmer was an ideal husband who took his wife's crimes on his shoulders (thus showing the British authors and audiences to be more gullible to fantasy than the 'butterfly' Nora), the forged note is stolen back from the villain and the crisis of marriage is overcome in reconciliation and happiness. Other versions merely had Helmer leading Nora back to the children's bedroom, whereupon her resolution to leave is broken and we are left to assume that the young woman can gain maturity by recognising the importance of motherhood. Anti-Ibsenites wrote sequels: Walter Besant described the state of the family Nora had deserted – Helmer, her husband, takes to drink, her son engages in forgery, as his mother had done, and her daughter commits suicide. Pro-Ibsenites responded. But the first performance of the play as Ibsen wrote it was given in the Bloomsbury drawing-room of Karl Marx's daughter, Eleanor. Eleanor, Edward Aveling, Bernard Shaw and May

Morris played respectively, Nora, Helmer, Krogstadt and Mrs Linde. Aveling wrote, 'Ibsen sees a lop-sided modern society suffering from too much man, and he was born a woman's poet.'[5]

Obviously some social conditions have changed since the play was written in the 1870s, obviously important aspects of the marriage relationship have been, if not revolutionised, then at least reformed. But is A *Doll's House* dated, as many critics argue? Its most recent critic, Elizabeth Hardwick, thinks that nowadays Nora and Helmer would have separated long ago as they were so obviously unsuited as a couple. Certainly, if Sophocles had written *Oedipus Rex* today, it would not have been about the King of Thebes. I'm not, however, suggesting that A *Doll's House* has the culturally 'eternal' status of *Oedipus Rex*, but I do think it is about something that cannot be dated without a far more profound change in the relationship between the sexes taking place than has so far occurred. The immediate social context may have altered, although probably not as much as we would like to think – but Nora's dilemma, her choice between capricious femininity or feminism and Helmer's dilemma as at the end he offers to change but cannot see how; Nora's awareness of his fragile masculinity and his limited vision of her female possibilities; the problem of what a true marriage could be; are still with us and will be with us as long as a society that denigrates not individual women, but women as a group, remains with us.

If we want to answer those critics who tell us the play is dated on a less elusive level, I think we can simply ask one question. If the social conditions have changed, as these critics claim, why have not the responses of the critics likewise altered in certain key respects? Elizabeth Hardwick, to me Ibsen's most sensitive critic at the moment, writes of Nora leaving her children thus:

> . . . the severance is rather casual and it drops a stain on our admiration of Nora. Ibsen has put the leaving of her children on the same moral and emotional level as the leaving of her husband

and we cannot in our hearts, assent to that. It is not only the leaving but the way the play does not have time for suffering, for changes of heart. Ibsen has been too much of a man in the end. He has taken the man's practice, if not his stated belief, that where self-realisation is concerned, children shall not be an impediment.[6]

I do not want to suggest that self-realisation should come before children, nor that women or, for that matter, men, should leave their children; though I would not agree to a dogmatic opposite. That is not the point. Elizabeth Hardwick is voicing in today's idiom what yesterday's bowdlerisers did to the play: she is echoing what it is attacking. She, too, though less grossly, in her heart of hearts would stop Nora leaving. I would argue that it is *not* a question of Ibsen's masculine sensibility predominating at the end, it is a question of the meaning of motherhood in a world where women are unequal. Women do not have economic and hence social and personal independence; they are judged by a patriarchal law. Natural instinct – an oyster can be a mother, as Charlotte Perkins Gilman put it – is not enough. If you infantilise women by making them both statutorily dependent and psychologically passive, should you simultaneously ask them to be responsible mothers? Helmer is a poor father – he actually can stand neither the noise of his children nor the sight of sewing that furnishes the doll's house he cherishes. Nora is a bad mother, she loves, cuddles, plays with her children – but as dolls. I think it is relevant to the pieties that our societies utter about the joys of motherhood to end by pointing out that it is useless to say that we must make more of motherhood, and to give a higher status to the woman who cares for our nation's future, if the context of motherhood today is one that erodes self-realisation and the becoming of a social person. From the day before we learn to speak, we learn that women are mothers; it is time to remind ourselves that mothers are women and social motherhood will only have the high status it should have when the position of women, as such, has been changed.

Part II   The Novel: Women
                       and Children
_____

Wuthering Heights: Romanticism and Rationality

¶ 'Wuthering Heights: Romanticism and Rationality' is one among a number of essays and lectures I have written on Wuthering Heights. As with the majority of these, it was never published – indeed, it was not really written for publication. It was produced as a piece of background writing to what one day might have been a chapter of a Ph.D. I have selected it because it illustrates the preoccupations I have already described: growth, romanticism, the historical self, hysteria, femininity.

Virginia Woolf wrote that Emily Brontë was a greater poet than her sister, Charlotte: 'there is no "I" in Wuthering Heights . . . there is love, but not the love of men and women'. In a different essay on Wuthering Heights, I had written of Heathcliff as the 'poem' within the novel. I had forgotten this until I looked at the last essay in this collection, written twenty years later.

This was written at a time – 1963 or 64 – when there was a movement away from Leavisite criticism and the beginning of an interest in using psychodynamic analyses of novels: Hillis Miller, Steven Marcus . . . In an excellent department of English Literature at Reading University where I then worked, this was not, however, the practice. But the sensibility and cultured intelligence of the professor, Donald Gordon, facilitated any approach that justified itself.

In a wider context there was the humanism of Raymond Williams, and the concerns of Richard Hoggart and Stuart Hall. Generously interpreted, psychological understanding of fictional characters fitted in there too. Since then there has been a division within this sort of criticism: either away from the psychodynamics of the characters into a sociology of the genre or, alternatively, via linguistics, Lacan and Derrida into a psychoanalysis of the text and beyond.

(All references to *Wuthering Heights* are to the Heather edition, Allan Wingate, London, 1949. The classification of the poems follows C. W. Hatfield's edition, Oxford University Press, 1941.)

Emily Brontë's society was so small that she was able to grasp nearly everything about it. Within these narrow confines she explored the depths. If the family is to be a society, intensity must make up for extensiveness; depth for breadth. In one sense, it is this limiting context that is the cause of the cosmic quality so often commented on in *Wuthering Heights*. The universe has become the family, and a microcosm has become the cosmos.

There is a further way in which Emily Brontë's brief and uniform existence shaped the novel. Her subjects were infancy, adolescence, early childhood and death. No formal work, no marriage splintered her childhood from her maturity; the perpetuation of her poems, the Gondal saga from early childhood until her death shows that this unbroken growth was echoed in her imaginative life. Her childhood *directly* entered her adulthood; there was no break between them. It is this continuity of experience which enabled Emily Brontë to give such meaning to the theme of growth in her novel. Not only does every character who ever lives at Wuthering Heights, grow up, but there is a constant interpenetration of their past and present. With one interesting exception (Heathcliff) all the adult characters are at some time categorised as childish in their behaviour. As adults both generations can indeed behave as children. The first narrator of the story, Lockwood, says of the second Cathy: 'She flung the tea back, spoon and all and resumed her seat in a pet; her forehead corrugated and her red under-lip pushed out like a child's ready to cry' (p.27).

In turn, as children, all the characters can be extremely mature. Nelly Dean's role of realising this interpenetration of past and present, of childhood and adulthood is crucial. For this second narrator is the nurse and this allows for a continuity of insight which a description of the disruptions to their growth experienced by the main characters would forbid. For though the characters feel their crises as disruptive, they naturally also feel their own consistency in the face of these – to them – external events.

> 'Should I always be sitting with you?' [Catherine] demanded. 'What good do I get? What do you talk about? You might be dumb, or a baby, for anything you say to amuse me, or for anything you do either!' 'You never told me before that I talked too little, or that you disliked my company, Cathy!' exclaimed Heathcliff, in much agitation (p.82).

Heathcliff is astonished that he is something different for Catherine from what he was; Catherine herself cannot understand why people did not always know she was, in fact, 'a young lady'. This is the Romantic's sense of his own continuity in time which the critic Poulet comments on. The interpenetration of childhood and adulthood is confirmed and intensified by the interpretive role of Nelly. As a nurse she can make judgements:

> [Catherine] beat Hareton, or any child at a good passionate fit of crying (p.96).

And she can offer explanations:

> [Heathcliff] struggled long to keep up an equality with Catherine in his studies and yielded with poignant though silent regret: but he yielded completely. . . then personal appearance sympathised with mental deterioration: he acquired a slouching gait

and ignoble look; his naturally reserved disposition was exaggerated
in almost idiotic excess of unsociable moroseness (p. 80).

And looking back retrospectively, she endorses the
coherence that they feel in their lives despite their crises of
change: '[Edgar] had the sense to comprehend Heathcliff's
disposition: to know that, though his exterior was altered his
mind was unchangeable and unchanged'(p. 112).

In *The Mill on the Floss*, George Eliot fails to protract
Maggie's growth beyond adolescence – the conclusion of the
novel is a sentimental addendum. Until his last completed
novel, *Our Mutual Friend*, Dickens only manages to mature
his heroes by juxtaposing adult and infant states; his own
profoundly dislocated life was reflected in this ruptured
progress in his art. For him, change was so serious a trauma,
that fictionalised it was expressed as absence, a gap – the
critical illnesses of David Copperfield, Esther Summerson,
Pip. But Emily Brontë could apprehend the violence of any
alteration. (When Emily was sent away briefly to school at
Miss Wooler's, it seemed to Charlotte that this breakage in her
sister's life would literally be the death of her.) But Emily
could experience and resist change personally and thereby
write about it as a novelist. Dickens' art was clearly
therapeutic: an initial obsession with children, passing
through a medial stage of retrospective comprehension of
childhood *(David Copperfield* and *Great Expectations)*, to a final
interest in arriving at maturity *(Our Mutual Friend* and *Edwin
Drood)*. But Emily's interest in children is a concern with the
part of the life cycle she has most fully experienced. For her,
there was nothing to evade, only changes to explain:
childhood being the key in the process of exploration.

Nelly Dean is nurse or companion to all the main characters, of both generations. Her matter-of-fact comments not
merely check the mysticism of the protagonists, they also
offer an alternative explanation of the characters in terms of
their environment. At no point does Emily Brontë allow an
essentialist judgment to become incontestible:

The master's bad ways and bad companions formed a pretty example for Catherine and Heathcliff. His treatment of the latter was enough to make a fiend of a saint. And truly, it *appeared* as if the lad were possessed of something diabolical at that period (p.78, my italics).

The two attitudes are counterpointed. Heathcliff feels himself, quite plausibly, as an unexplained 'being'. But Nelly, at a moment in the novel when Heathcliff has indeed come nearest to an inexplicable, archetypical being, refuses such a simple answer:

Is he a ghoul or a vampire? I mused. I had read of such hideous incarnate demons. And then I set myself to reflect how I had tended him in infancy and watched him grow to youth, and followed him almost through his whole course; and what absurd nonsense it was to yield to that sense of horror. 'But where did he come from, the little dark thing, harboured by a good man to his bane?' *muttered Superstition*, as I dozed into unconsciousness (p.329, my italics).

The whole story is told because an idle southerner, Lockwood, wishes to understand the character of his adult neighbour, Heathcliff. He feels a completely spurious identification with him. Lockwood is a parody of romanticism. But the person Lockwood asks for an account – Nelly Dean – has the clue to the present because she knows the past. This makes of the novel more than a presentation – it is an explanation. This feature permeates all the analyses of character. Edgar Linton in his pain and fury can accost Heathcliff thus:

'I've been so far forbearing with you, sir . . . not that I was ignorant of your miserable, degraded character, but I felt you were only partly responsible for that' (p.125).

Nelly herself punctuates her account of Heathcliff's growth with explanatory remarks and, as character not narrator, comments on the dislikeable young Heathcliff:

I divined, from this account, that utter lack of sympathy had rendered young Heathcliff selfish and disagreeable, if he were not so originally (p.217).

and she protests against the second Cathy's mistreatment of Hareton:

> 'Had you been brought up in his circumstances, would you be less rude? He was as quick and intelligent a child as ever you were; and I'm hurt that he should be despised now, because that base Heathcliff has treated him so unjustly' (p.253).

Many of the characters offer the same kind of explanations for their own behaviour. Thus Linton Heathcliff to the young Cathy Linton:

> 'You are so much happier than I am, you ought to be better. Papa talks enough of my defects and shows enough scorn of me, to make it natural I should doubt myself. I doubt whether I am not altogether as worthless as he calls me' (p.257).

Growth is the key interaction in the novel: thematically and structurally the novel is explicative. The one depends upon the other, for only childhood explains the adult.

The structure and time-scheme of the novel hardly ever allow childhood to disappear from it. In the introductory section the heroine – Catherine Earnshaw – is first seen as the ghost of a twelve-year-old child; Nelly's story then opens with the childhoods of Catherine, Heathcliff and Hindley. Their childhood ends and their tormented adolescence begins with Catherine's enforced stay at the Grange. This is the means of introducing other children: Edgar and Isabella Linton. Even with the emergence of this generation (Catherine, Heathcliff, Edgar and Isabella) into youth and early adulthood, infancy does not disappear from the novel – Hareton – the son of Hindley and Frances – is born. This is followed by a stress on the early adolescence of Cathy Linton – daughter of Catherine Earnshaw and Edgar Linton – then on the late adolescence of Linton Heathcliff – son of Isabella Linton and Heathcliff. But the thematic focus of the novel is the first generation. Catherine Earnshaw begins and ends the book; Heathcliff is absent from the chronicle for over three years, but these occupy only seven pages of the novel.

Nearly all the critics read the story in two halves – the story of the first and then the second generation. It is, however, much more the story of Heathcliff and, above all, of the childhood, youth and death of the first Catherine. In the second half, the descendants are manipulated by Heathcliff to expiate Catherine's mistaken marriage choice, to satisfy his obsession with her. In one sense, the novel is as much about death as about life. Death is always counterposed here with youth, never age (except for the original parents). Catherine Earnshaw and Linton Heathcliff die before their majority. Hindley dies just as the triple relationship between Catherine, Linton and Hareton commences. Heathcliff's death is set against the pastoral youth of Catherine and Hareton. Of the central characters only three live into full adulthood and in each case it is an adulthood blighted by the crisis of youth or at most very early manhood (both Hindley and Edgar are twenty-one when their wives die).

The marriage of the second Cathy and Hareton is a temporary lull, a bit of Victorian prettiness, not a solution to the passions explored by Heathcliff and Catherine Earnshaw. These passions are the central concern of the novel. But they are not mysterious and abnormal, as many critics have maintained. On the contrary, their intensity is not only *felt*, but is also explained.

Catherine is nearly six, Hindley ten, when Heathcliff is offered to them as a token of their father's love. All Hindley's primogenitural claims are threatened by his father's present of a gypsy boy and a broken violin. In this crisis, his growth towards a habitual and stable position in the adult world is checked. His response is childish: 'when he drew out what had been a fiddle, crushed to morsels in the greatcoat, he blubbered aloud' (p. 51). His response creates the very situation that he fears. His father starts to favour the rejected orphan. Like the violin, harmony is shattered. Heathcliff becomes a usurper taking Hindley's possessions and being offered the love of his father and sister. His mother – who had latterly aided and abetted the dissolution of his expectations – dies after two years and, finally, his nurse, Nelly, flattered by her success with the sick Heathcliff, refuses to countenance his oppressions of the latter. 'Thus Hindley lost his last ally.' The break in Hindley's filial world is complete when he is declared a reprobate by his father and exiled to college. From an early point he had lost his fraternal role to Heathcliff. At first, with Catherine, he had kept Heathcliff out: 'They entirely refused to have it in bed with them, or even in their room' (p.52). Catherine and Heathcliff, however, become inseparable – Hindley later reverses and re-enacts this physical separation. He does his utmost to exclude Heathcliff, in particular, from Catherine's society. When Hindley comes back, an adult, to his father's deathbed, he has adapted himself. In maturity, he will both relive in reverse his adolescence and simultaneously be the person he should have been if Heathcliff had not come to interrupt his growth; he will be the master. Because this is no longer a natural transition, it is both painful and brutal. To be what as a child he had been brought up to understand he was going to be, has had to become premeditated revenge on others. Only a complete outsider is unimplicated in his crisis. Only with his wife, who comes from afar and has no experience of his story, can he be the sort of person his childhood was leading him towards. His clinging to her is the pathetic yearning of someone who does not want to be committed to his own chosen response to an early crisis, a choice that grew bigger than its moment of incarnation – the urge to exclude a child imposter.

Heathcliff's infant predicament is very different. Genuinely fond of Mr Earnshaw who rescued him from the streets of Liverpool, his attitude cannot be free from ambiguity. For the paternal favouritism exposes him to other cruelties. This ambivalence is reflected in the dual nature of his other relationships. Typically, he is indifferent to the brutality of people who have no other purchase on him – either formal (they are not his relatives) or authentic (they have never been kind to him for himself, but only to placate Mr Earnshaw). Mr Earnshaw dies and, through Hindley's agency, Heathcliff reverts to his six-year-old condition: his waifdom and deprivation:

> He had by that time lost the benefit of his early education; the continued hard work, begun soon and concluded late, had extinguished any curiosity he once possessed in the pursuit of knowledge, and any love for books or learning. His childhood's sense of superiority, instilled into him by the favours of old Mr Earnshaw, was faded away (p.80).

Thus, instead of being able gradually and naturally to assert his autonomy, and so establish some equality in his relationship with Catherine, Heathcliff becomes entirely dependent on her: 'she taught him all she knew'. His former need is intensified, the nature of his love confirmed. What should have happened gradually as infancy advanced has to wait until adulthood. He cannot break free until he is forced to leave and come back on his own terms. The rebellion that would initiate equality in their relationship is postponed until adulthood.

> Mrs. Linton sat down by the fire, flushed and gloomy. The spirit which served her was growing intractable: she could neither lay nor control it. He stood on the hearth with folded arms, brooding on his evil thoughts (p.124).

But in their childhood she is his only friend and benefactor. He loves her with the intensity of a first and only attachment. The passionate side of the relationship is at this stage expressed by him. Catherine has alternative affections; Heathcliff has none. His rejection by Catherine is the most serious crisis undergone by the three first-generation children. Hindley's is a desertion spaced over two years. But Heathcliff's is more dramatic. He is left an exploited farm-hand and the intervening attentions of Mr Earnshaw and Catherine might as well not have existed; as an adolescent he becomes once more the waif he was in infancy. Catherine's desertion of him is a re-enactment of previous traumas, the form it takes places her on the side of his enemies: 'If you wash your face and brush your hair, it will be all right: but you are so dirty' (p.67). Heathcliff, too, at the age of sixteen must go away in order to readapt to his shattered world. Catherine enters a state of delirium. Their childhood is over.

At a first reading Catherine Earnshaw may seem an exception of the general analysis offered here. For throughout she is shown as larger than the comprehension of her describers, and larger than the sum of her circumstances. Within the novel she is rarely explained or analysed by others beyond their assertions of her characteristics. She is a plausible child and adolescent, but her 'nature' seems to precede the events, she appears fascinating, enigmatic, pure essence where the others are created through their existence. But the appearance is deceptive. Catherine is internally 'explained' in the very structure of the novel, which creates her as an intelligible person.

When Heathcliff enters the family, Catherine is still a child not, like Hindley, on the verge of adolescence. Her first reaction is aggressive, not like his a collapse. She is barely six. An intrusion into her established circle can be for good or evil. She has lost a whip but gained a brother: 'They had christened him "Heathcliff": it was the name of a son who died in childhood' (p.52). But for Catherine, Heathcliff does not have to be only a brother. She is young enough to accept him as such, but she is also old enough to accept him as more. Offered as a brother, Heathcliff also comes to Catherine as a contemporary playmate. Others curb and contain her but with Heathcliff she is supremely free to display her identity.

> She liked exceedingly to act the little mistress; using her hands freely, and commanding her companions. She did so to me, but I would not bear slapping and ordering; and so I let her know . . . she was never so happy as when [she was] turning Joseph's curses into ridicule, baiting me, and doing just what her father hated most – showing how her pretended insolence, which he thought real, had more power over Heathcliff than his kindness; how the boy would do *her* bidding in anything and *his* only when it suited *his* own inclination (p.56).

At twelve, Catherine dramatically experiences the death of

her father – an event which confirms her intimate
dependence on Heathcliff.

> 'Oh he's dead, Heathcliff! He's dead! . . .'
> I ran to the children's room: their door was ajar, I saw they had
> never lain down, though it was past midnight; but they were
> calmer and did not need me to console them (p. 58).

This does not, therefore, prove to be a serious crisis in itself,
nor does Hindley's cruelty to Heathcliff threaten her: 'They
forgot everything the minute they were together again.'

The isolation which Hindley inflicts on Catherine and
Heathcliff in their early adolescence only in part affects
Catherine. He forces her into some dependence on
Heathcliff, but this is not as critical as his on her. She has had
in the past, and is to have in the future, alternatives. New
prospects open up to her; Edgar Linton takes over the role that
should have been Heathcliff's. Catherine is aware of a break
with her past; her divided state is confirmed by outside
attempts to create a rift between her childhood and
adulthood: 'Why, Cathy, you are quite a beauty! I should
scarcely have known you: you look like a lady now!' her
brother tells her. Henceforth her actions display the tension
of her position. Catherine's own self-revelations to Nelly
illustrate what has happened. Her use of the term 'love'
epitomises, in its ambiguity, the transference her affections
have undergone.

> 'It would degrade me to marry Heathcliff now; so he shall never
> know how I love him: and that, not because he's handsome,
> Nelly, but because he's more myself than I am . . . Heathcliff
> does not know what being in love is!' (p. 92).

The tragedy is that Catherine cannot grow consistently with
Heathcliff; they are separated and she must anchor her whole
growth on another, a stranger. In doing so she becomes as
alien to herself as she is to Heathcliff; she tries to feel that she
was always what she has become – a young lady – but she
cannot recognise herself in this role. She tries to find her past
in her present, but cannot. With Edgar she lives a death-in-

life, invalid existence, for in choosing him she forecasts what she is later, in fact, to become – a self-murderer. Heathcliff cries out to her:

> 'Why did you betray your own heart, Cathy? I have not one word of comfort. You deserve this. You have killed yourself . . . You loved me – then what *right* had you to leave me? What right . . . for the poor fancy you felt for Linton? . . . I have not broken your heart – *you* have broken it; and in breaking it, you have broken mine . . .' (p.170).

She is the agent of separation because her life and her choices confirm the disruptions which society provokes. She is offered the temptation of bourgeois glamour – first, when she breaks her foot and is nursed at the Grange, second, when Edgar Linton asks to marry her. She *chooses* this separation from Heathcliff and in her choice are contained all the other separations that were imposed on them, but which they had resisted. Thus the first real break with her childhood and her unity with Heathcliff apparently comes with her confinement at the Grange. But retrospectively Catherine does not see it as this alone. When married to Edgar, in her final illness, Cathy describes her delirious dream to Nelly:

> 'The whole last seven years of my life grew a blank. I did not recall that they had been at all. I was a child; my father was just buried, and my misery arose from the separation that Hindley had ordered between me and Heathcliff, I was laid alone, for the first time and, rising from a dismal dose after a night of weeping, I lifted my hand to push the panel aside, it struck the table-top . . . supposing that at twelve years old I had been wrenched from the Heights, and every early association and my all in all, as Heathcliff was at that time, and been converted at a stroke into Mrs. Linton . . . wife of a stranger, an exile, an outcast, thenceforth, from what had been my world' (p.136).

Here, interestingly, the three occurrences of one year, her father's death, Hindley's discriminating treatment of Heathcliff, and her first entrance into the Grange, have merged with her later marriage to Edgar Linton and are shown to have formed *a composite crisis* at the age of twelve.

The different moments and meanings of her separation from Heathcliff have fused into one. It is at this age – the age of her dream, the age of twelve, the year of the first separation from Heathcliff, that she haunts the book. Indeed, this same conflation of the different episodes is confirmed in Lockwood's dream:

> – my fingers closed on the fingers of a little, ice-cold hand! The intense horror of nightmare came over me: I tried to draw back my arm, but the hand clung to it, and a most melancholy voice sobbed, 'Let me in – let me in!' 'Who are you?' I asked, struggling, meanwhile, to disengage myself. 'Catherine Linton', it replied. shiveringly (why did I think of *Linton*? – I had read *Earnshaw* twenty times for Linton) (p. 40).

On the threshold of adolescence, Catherine's life has been disrupted. As elsewhere, after this initial trauma, all crises re-enact the first one. For Hindley, the death of his wife, Frances, echoes the death of his mother and all its attendant desertions. For Heathcliff, Catherine's estrangement epitomises the alien quality of his infant world. For Catherine her two removals to the Grange finalise the continual separations from Heathcliff with which her childhood was punished: 'She was much too fond of Heathcliff. The greatest punishment we could invent for her was to keep her separate from him' (p. 56). That her adult torment is the direct equivalent of her childhood fears is further made evident by the imagery of the novel. Separate, both Heathcliff and Catherine feel themselves in some sort of hell, the language of both clearly expresses this: Catherine: 'I had risen in angry rebellion against Providence. Oh I've endured very very bitter misery Nelly' (p. 111), and Heathcliff: 'Two words would comprehend my future – *death* and *hell*: existence after losing her, would be hell' (p. 158). The metaphors are picked up from their childhood. In her twelve-year-old diary, Catherine records: 'Joseph asseverated, 'owd Nick would fetch us as sure as we were living; and *so comforted we each sought a separate nook to await his advent*' (my italics, p. 37).

The relationship of Catherine and Heathcliff arises out of

different circumstances for each; their actions converge with this distinction. For Heathcliff, Catherine is the focal point of the universe, as Nelly says: she is his all: 'his friend, and love, and all!' (p.93). And as he says: 'I am surrounded with her image! The most ordinary faces of men and women – my own features mock me with a resemblance. The entire world is a dreadful collection of memoranda that she did exist!' (p.325). Dead, she becomes his 'heaven'.

By definition, the characteristic of an obsession is singularity of purpose, intensity of concentration. Heathcliff is obsessive. Catherine's love arises out of a totally different response and totally different needs. Where Heathcliff suffers from singularity, Catherine is plagued by the problems of division: 'She was full of ambition – and this led her to adopt a double character without exactly intending to deceive anyone' (p.79). She is the agent of separation, as Heathcliff is of unity. She breaks the relationship by her absence as Heathcliff perturbs all by his presence; as he tells her:

> '. . . misery and degradation, and death, and nothing that God or Satan could inflict would have parted us, *you*, of your own will, did it' (p. 170).

In her delirium, Catherine envisages two means of return to her own authenticity. Authenticity is unity with Heathcliff and – which is the same thing – unity with herself, her undivided self in childhood or death:

> 'Oh, I'm burning! . . . I wish I were a girl again, half savage and hardy, and free . . . Why am I so changed? . . . I'm sure I should be myself were I once among the heather on those hills . . . [Joseph's] waiting till I come home that he may lock the gate. Well, he'll wait a while yet. It's a rough journey, and a sad heart to travel it; and we must pass by Gimmerton Kirk to go that journey! . . . Heathcliff, if I dare you now, will you venture? If you do, I'll keep you. I'll not lie there by myself: they may bury me twelve feet deep, and throw the church down over me, but I won't rest till you are with me. I never will! . . . He's considering – he'd rather I'd come to him! Find a way, then! not through that kirkyard. You are slow! Be content, you always followed me!' (p. 137).

'She drew a sigh, and stretched herself, like a child reviving, and sinking again to sleep. . . She lies, a sweet smile on her face; and her latest ideas wandering back to pleasant early days' (p. 175).

The intervening strains of adolescence are cancelled, the adult dies a twelve-year-old child; as this child she haunts her brother-lover and the beginning of the novel.

Emily Brontë, uncluttered with diverse experience, could trace through an almost complete life cycle; not literally her own or her brother's or sisters'. Isolated, her mind turned for release and enrichment to fantasy or fiction. Strenuously sane, Emily, unlike her elder siblings, mostly projected herself into the latter. *Wuthering Heights* is in the tradition of her poems, the Gondal saga, started at the age of twelve. But Emily could not have created art out of mirror-to-life portrayal; her fiction had to be larger than her experience. It is here that the romantic heritage enters most obviously into her novel.

Immune from the disintegrating effects of urban industrialism, Emily Brontë's romanticism is not the straining after golden-age pastoral ideals that makes and mars some of Dickens' tortured work; nor is it the bizarre, reintegrating construct of a genius like Blake. Like all Romantics, Emily does try to render whole what is splintered. But the disruptive agent is not for her, as it was for her contemporaries and successors, the industrial revolution; nor, as it was for her sisters, the discrepancy between personal experience and conventional morality. The divisive world that Emily tried to unite was more fundamental than this.

Three Gods within this little frame
Are warring night and day.

Heaven could not hold them all, and yet
They are held in me
And must be mine till I forget
My present entity. (No. A27, p. 220.)

Division existed in the individual himself: in the novel it was a state of being complete in oneself yet, simultaneously, nothing without others. As a separate entity apprehending the world around – nature and animals, yet again partaking of their existence because without them (in this specific context) one would not be the same person. Although this idea bears resemblances to Wordsworth's philosophy, it is not pantheism. Wordsworth's philosophy is a faith – man is man, in unity with nature. Emily's seems a value judgement: people exist in towns, in the south of England, in decorative parklands, but they exist more authentically on the moors and with animals because here there is no place for sophistication.

Many of the ideas in *Wuthering Heights* are mystical; but the framework of the novel, the matter-of-fact and the satirised pseudo-romantic narrators (Nelly and Lockwood), ensure a permanent rational control over Emily Brontë's own powerful romantic imagination.

F. R. Leavis claimed that Emily Brontë: 'broke completely, and in the most challenging way, both with the Scott tradition that imposed on the novelist a romantic resolution of his themes, and with the tradition coming down from the eighteenth century that demanded a plane-mirror reflection of the surface of "real" life.' This statement does suggest part of the truth. At the centre of the novel, is the romantic notion of the affinity of separate forms. There is a strong ontological preoccupation – the language of soul, spirit and essence:

> Heathcliff's more myself than I am. Whatever our souls are made of, his and mine are the same . . . I cannot express it; but surely you and everybody have a notion that there is or should be an existence of yours beyond you. What were the use of my creation, if I were entirely contained here? My love for Heathcliff resembles the eternal rocks beneath: a source of little visible delight, but necessary . . . Nelly, I *am* Heathcliff! He's always, always in my mind: not as a pleasure . . . but as my own being (p.94).

But these statements are always made in dialogue: their vagueness – 'I cannot express it' – is not attributable to the author who has her position mediated by the narrators', from whom in turn she distances herself. The 'essentialist' attitude is conveyed only by the self-awareness of the chief protagonist; it is not an assertion such as D. H. Lawrence would have made, a point established through emphatic repetitive statement from the outside. Consequently it can coexist with an 'existential' viewpoint offered, as we have seen, explicitly by Nelly, and confirmed by the whole structure of the novel.

Emily Brontë's unusual existence: her isolation from industrialism and her immersion in a family from which she almost never departed, enabled her to have certain insights which were unavailable to many of her contemporaries who were more subject to the conventions of Victorian custom and the alienating experiences of an industrial society. Above all, she felt that there should be continuous growth from birth to adulthood, and when this was prevented the cleavage was seen by her as disastrous. The experiences of childhood were as profound as those of adulthood. Maturity and immaturity interact in childhood and adulthood.

The greatness of *Wuthering Heights* lies in the *rationality* of its romanticism: the dialectic between the two constitutes the whole form and force of the novel. The astringent rationalism of *Wuthering Heights* can be seen in its deliberately controlled use of typical romantic devices: orphanage, ghosts, dreams. Above all, it is inseparable from the form of the novel: the mode of double narration. Nelly Dean is a constant disintoxication of the characters. Lockwood is a disintoxication of the romantic material of the story itself. This rationalism is fundamentally linked to the whole use of childhood: the two are for the most part identical in the book. This is most clearly seen in the figure of Nelly Dean, the narrator who is precisely a nursemaid, whose relationship to the characters is by definition mediated through childhood. This device allows Emily Brontë to explain all her characters, while presenting them with romantic and ontological intensity. Thus, contrary to received critical notions, there are no mysteries in *Wuthering Heights*. The nature and actions of every character in the drama are fully intelligible because they are always related to the total biographical development of the person and, above all, to what we now know to be the most critical phase of life: childhood. This is true of Hindley, Edgar, Hareton, Heathcliff and even Catherine Earnshaw – who seems initially to have an 'ontological' privilege within the book. In *Wuthering Heights*, Emily Brontë translated the conceptual awareness we now have of the interrelation of childhood and adulthood into a most unusual novel. This achievement prochronistically was almost certainly made possible by her exceptional life-history: telescoped in time and place to a unity which allowed her to recreate the existential unity of human life, in art.

The Ordeal of Richard Feverel: A Sentimental Education

¶ 'The Ordeal of Richard Feverel: A Sentimental Education' appeared in *Meredith Now* (Routledge and Kegan Paul, London, 1971). The collection of essays was edited by a friend and colleague at Reading University, Ian Fletcher. I remember that when I read Meredith's works in preparation for this essay I was intrigued and bewildered. I was not at home in burlesque as a literary mode; I had always missed the point about 'take-off' as a way of dealing with painful subjects. And this novel was far from being just or even predominantly that, in any case.

I had long been interested in Rousseau's work and finding a connection between Meredith and Rousseau helped me to sort out something about this greatly underestimated novel.

(All references to *The Ordeal of Richard Feverel* are to the Modern Library edition, New York, 1950.)

I

. . . It is so crystalline and brilliant in its principal passages, there is such purity mingled with its laxness, such sound and firm truth in the midst of its fantastic subtleties, that we hesitate whether to approve or condemn; and we have a difficulty even in forming a judgement on such strange contrarieties.

The Times, 14.10.59.

The Times finally affirmed the purity of *Richard Feverel*; Mudie's Library banned it on account of its immorality. Bewilderment and misunderstanding were yet more rampant than prudery. The novel is a medley of romantic interludes, prosaic detail, burlesque, melodrama, pathos, fantasy, realism – everything except the naturalism which Meredith deplored. With hindsight, it has now been heralded as the first modern novel and earned for Meredith a reputation as the first highbrow novelist. Despite ingenious critical rationalisation, the novel in its original, unedited form[1] remains intrinsically perplexing.

Sir Austin Feverel, of Raynham Abbey in the Thames Valley, is author of a book of aphorisms, 'The Pilgrim's Scrip', and of a system for educating boys into unsullied manhood. Both book and system are directed mainly against the corrupting influence of women. A realistic appraisal of the rotten state of society and, in particular, of women within it, if applied and rejected scientifically in education, could produce an ideal man and therefore an ideal society. Basing his Utopianism on this misanthropic premise, Sir Austin brings up his son Richard accordingly. The novel is the story of Richard's life. But Sir Austin's apparently objective theory is the result of a traumatic experience. His wife ran off with his best friend and dependant, the poet Diaper Sandoe, leaving him nothing but the baby Richard.

Richard grows up at the Abbey surrounded by the Feverel family of dependants: his Uncle Hippias, dyspeptic glutton; his aunt, Mrs Doria Forey, and her daughter, Clare; his cousin and tutor, the epicurean Adrian Harley ('The Wise Youth'), a man as hard and cynical as Sir Austin claims to be (in an early draft he edited Sir Austin's 'Pilgrim's Scrip' – without this detail the relationship between the two is still retained in the novel). Also in residence is Richard's Great Aunt Grantly, nicknamed 'The Eighteenth Century',

wealthy and a gourmet. Frequent visitors are his Uncle
Algernon, who in the course of the story loses a leg and takes
to drink to help his balance; and his cousin, Austin
Wentworth, who was seduced by, married and is separated
from his mother's housemaid, a man of kindness and
integrity, a Republican, a philanthropist. For a period of his
boyhood (and later in adult life) Richard has a companion in
Ripton Thompson, son of his father's solicitor, and he finds a
competitor in the Etonian youth, Ralph Norton of the
neighbouring Poer Hall. He has an 'adoptive' mother in his
father's friend and admirer, their widow neighbour, Lady
Blandish. The custodian of the whole system is the butler,
'Heavy' Benson, a vengeful misogynist deserted by his wife.

The Feverel family are supposed to be pursued by a malign
fate ('Mrs Malediction'), the enduring of which constitutes
their 'Ordeal'. Sir Austin only came to believe this
superstition when his wife deserted him and he suffered an
'Ordeal'. On his seventh birthday, Richard, in a hypnagogic
state, sees a lady at his bedside. This 'Mrs Malediction' turns
out to be his mother, but that it is a bad omen is confirmed by
the fact that Uncle Algernon loses his leg in a game of cricket
that day.

After his wife's desertion, Sir Austin retreated from his
noble prodigality into austerity, the only festive occasions at
the Abbey being Richard's birthdays. On his fourteenth
birthday, when his healthy flesh is beginning to feel the chains
of the 'system', Richard, refusing to submit to medical
examination, goes pheasant-shooting with Ripton Thompson. They are whipped by Farmer Blaize for poaching on his
land; and in vengeance Richard bribes an unemployed
labourer, Tom Bakewell, to set fire, with his aid, to the
farmer's ricks. Bakewell is caught and imprisoned. After
much manoeuvring, bribery and confession, Bakewell is
released and employed as Richard's attendant. Richard has
confessed all, and father and son are reconciled; the system
triumphs.

In adolescence Richard takes to poetry, but his father

manages to make him burn his poems. This repressive act ends the true confidence between them. This is the 'Magnetic Age' and all notion of love must be kept from Richard. His cousin Clare, intended by her mother as Richard's wife, unbeknownst to all, is deeply in love with him. She is removed from Raynham. Benson controls the flirtatious activities of the housemaids. Sir Austin, however, is seen by Richard kissing Lady Blandish's hand. This opens his eyes. Perturbed, his father leaves Raynham in search of a young uncorrupted Eve, future bride for Richard. Meanwhile, Ralph Norton reveals to Richard that he is in love with Clare; immediately after this Richard sees Lucy Desborough, orphan niece of Farmer Blaize. It is love at first sight. Their love is spied on by Heavy Benson, who writes warning Sir Austin. Sir Austin summons Richard to him in London, retains him there while it is arranged that Lucy be sent back to the convent where she was educated. Sir Austin and Richard return to Raynham. Richard finds Lucy gone, and on the night of his birthday sets out to pursue her, but falls desperately ill.

On recovery Richard seems to have forgotten his love. Once more the system triumphs. But in spring, on arriving with his Uncle Hippias in London, Richard discovers Lucy is temporarily there. His love revived, he meets her, installs her in lodgings with a Mrs Berry and marries her. At the church he finds he has lost the wedding-ring and has to take that of Mrs Berry. Lucy and Richard leave to honeymoon in the Isle of Wight. The Feverel family discover the marriage and Mrs Berry turns out to be a housemaid whom Sir Austin dismissed for witnessing him in tears over his deserted infant son.

Sir Austin's reaction to the forbidden marriage is to blame the inadequacies of humanity rather than his system. He remains formally charitable, but, despite Lady Blandish's interventions, will not see Richard. Adrian Harley arrives in the Isle of Wight and persuades Lucy to persuade Richard to return to London without her and await his father alone.

In London, despite Richard's efforts to prevent it, Clare is married to an old man. Richard tries to reform the prostitutes

and courtesans of London, and he takes his mother away
from Diaper Sandoe and places her in lodgings with Mrs
Berry. Richard is seduced by one of the women he was
reforming, Mrs Mount, and comes to feel so ashamed that he
cannot return to Lucy, who, though pregnant, is herself
pursued by a Lord Mountfalcon – husband to Mrs Mount. Sir
Austin comes to London to be reconciled to Richard, but
Richard is out of town. Mrs Berry fearing that worst, goes to
fetch the ignorant Lucy and installs her in her house. Richard
will not see her, but asks his father to receive her alone at
Raynham Abbey. Sir Austin prevaricates.

At this point Clare commits suicide, leaving a diary
confessing her love for Richard. Richard, feeling himself a
virtual murderer, goes abroad 'to cleanse' himself. Lucy has a
son. Austin Wentworth returns from the tropics and, on
hearing the whole story from Adrian, goes to Lucy and takes
her and the child and Mrs Berry to Raynham, where Sir
Austin welcomes them. (Mrs Berry discovers that her
husband, who deserted her, has become Sir Austin's valet.)

In Germany with a philanthropic acquaintance of Isle of
Wight days, Lady Judith Velle, Richard dreams of liberating
Italy. He opens no letters from England and only at last hears
of his son's birth from Austin Wentworth, who joins him in
Germany. At the news, Richard rushes alone into the forest,
and there, in a thunderstorm, 'the Spirit of Life' illumines him
and he has a 'sense of purification'. He starts out immediately
for England. Stopping in London *en route* to Raynham, he
receives an old letter from Bella Mount explaining that she
was offered bribes to seduce him so that Lord Mountfalcon
might be able to seduce Lucy in his absence. Outraged
Richard rushes to insult Mountfalcon and thereby provoke a
duel. Mountfalcon tries to cool the whole affair, but his
message to this effect is never given, as Ripton Thompson (its
recipient) delays too long. At Raynham a wretched Richard is
sanctimoniously welcomed by his father and formally
reconciled. After a brief and passionate encounter with Lucy
in which he acknowledges and she forgives his infidelity, and

an intensely emotional glimpse of his son, Richard rushes out without explanation to fight his duel in Northern France.

The final scenes are described by Lady Blandish in a disillusioned letter to Austin Wentworth. Richard, seriously wounded, is visited by the whole family. Because they are fearful that her emotionality will disturb him, Lucy is not allowed to sit with Richard. He recovers, but she from her superhuman efforts at self-control has contracted brain-fever and dies. Mrs Forey is reminded of Clare's death and becomes distracted. The novel ends with Richard pictured as 'dead-in-life'.

The story starts in gladness to end in sadness; from gay childhood to disillusioned maturity. The style apparently reflects this shift: the novel opens with wit, even burlesque, passes through lyricism and ends with the brevity of tragedy. Contemporary reviewers deplored the gratuitous cruelty of Lucy's death,[2] and critics have continued to see the novel as a comedy in which the pathos of his story overtakes the author: Meredith, despite himself, goes deeper than the frivolity of his comic intentions and creates a tragedy.[3] It is inadequate to answer these charges of inconsistency with citations from Meredith's later developed theories of comedy, or offer the trite rejoinder of the seriousness of real comedy; though these statements would be true. The point is rather that the novel is not inconsistent, but heterogeneous; not chaotic, but strangely inclusive. Furthermore, it is this simultaneously and diversely in terms of the relationship of its content and its style. For example, Meredith is not only an 'intellectual' novelist in the sense that he overtly discusses 'ideas', but also in that, through echoes and allusions to other literature (most obviously Greek legends, the Bible, Shakespeare and Goethe), he verbally reiterates or questions others' concepts. At times it seems that Meredith is discussing the form of his novel while in the process of writing it; in this way following on from Sterne, preceding Joyce and being atypical of his own period. One of the most interesting features of the *Ordeal of Richard Feverel* is the relationship of 'The Pilgrim's Scrip' to the whole novel. The novel opens:

Some years ago was printed, and published anonymously, dedicated to the author's enemies, a small book of original Aphorisms, under the heading, THE PILGRIM'S SCRIP . . . Modern Aphorists are accustomed to make their phrases a play of wit, flashing antithetical brilliancies, rather than condensing profound truths. This one, if he did not always say things new, evidently spoke from reflection, feeling, and experience . . . His thoughts were sad enough; occasionally dark; here and there comical in the oddness; nevertheless there ran through the volume a fire of Hope; and they did him injustice who said he lacked Charity . . .

On the subject of Women, certainly, the Aphorist seemed to lose his main virtue. He was not splenetic: nay, he proved in the offending volume he could be civil, courteous, chivalrous towards them: yet, by reason of a twist in his mental perceptions, it was clear he looked on them as domesticated Wild Cats . . .

He gravely declared . . . 'I expect that Woman will be the last thing civilized by Man.'

Singular to say, the one dangerous and objectionable feature in this little volume, preserved it from limbo. Men read, and tossed it aside, amused, or weary. They set the author down as a Sentimentalist jilted . . . They, let us suppose, were Sentimentalists not yet jilted' (pp. 1–3).

Autobiographical critics, rightly connecting Meredith's and his baby son Arthur's desertion by his wife, Mary Peacock, with the theme of the novel, have seen Sir Austin and his system as Meredith's cautionary tale of himself. This is too simple. So is the notion that Meredith was completely condemning Sir Austin's system and 'The Pilgrim's Scrip', when what is striking in the novel is precisely that he sometimes approves and sometimes rejects it. He thereby offers an apparently realistic appraisal of it. The main and most fallacious claim that Sir Austin makes for his own aphorisms is their realism: 'He conceived that the Wild Cats [Women] would some day be actually tamed. *At present it was best to know what they were*, (p. 3, my italics). By ironising the realism of Sir Austin, Meredith wittily calls in question his own. Sir Austin then is not just 'a caution' to himself but a take-off of himself for setting up that caution. 'The Pilgrim's Scrip' is the work of 'a sentimentalist jilted', and so in a way is the novel, but of a sentimentalist who knows he is jilted and therefore is no longer a sentimentalist. Hence the Edenic passages of Lucy and Richard's first meeting and of Richard's resurrection in the German forest are not, as is often thought, the poet Meredith bursting through his cynic's shell, but the very contained romanticism of an author who can contextualise these lyric strophes in a fallen world. The author/narrator and Sir Austin are never one and the same, but their opinions coincide as well as diverge.

'The Pilgrim's Scrip' illustrates Meredith's preoccupation with form in another way. *The Times* reviewer regarded it as an obtrusive chorus in Greek fashion; rather it is a 'play-within-a-play' serving not only as a commentary, but as a directive. Yet it is more interesting than this. The characters within the novel created by Meredith are yet in search of an author who will describe their salient features in abstract. Meredith creates his flesh-and-blood characters, but the pre-novel blueprint of them is the work of 'The Pilgrim's Scrip', except that it is, of course, a post-novel abstract of them:

> 'Your Aunt Helen, I was going to say, my dear boy, is an extraordinary woman. It was from her originally that the Pilgrim first learned to call the female the practical animal. He studies us all, you know. THE PILGRIM'S SCRIP is the abstract portraiture of his surrounding relatives'. (Adrian Harley, p. 407.)

A further twist of the joke is that Meredith's flesh-and-blood characters are often just sketches, caricatures. Or a further twist, that 'the female' is conventionally called a 'practical animal' and Adrian is mocking Sir Austin for sensitive observation that only produces a commonplace. Meredith maintains a constant interrelationship between the scrip and the novel, so that the scrip is even used to comment on its own author: Sir Austin is with Lady Blandish after Richard has recovered from his first illness and with this his first love flush:

> Lady Blandish had been sentimentalizing for ten years. She would have preferred to pursue the game. The dark-eyed dame was pleased with her smooth life and the soft excitement that did not ruffle it. Not willingly did she let herself be won.

'Sentimentalists,' says THE PILGRIM'S SCRIP, 'are they who seek
to enjoy Reality, without incurring the Immense Debtorship for a
thing done' . . .

However, one who could set down, Dying for Love, as a
Sentimentalism, can hardly be accepted as a clear authority.
Assuredly he was not one to avoid the incurring of the immense
Debtorship in any way: . . .

[Sir Austin] expounded to her the distinctive character of the
divers ages of Love . . . And while they sat and talked, 'My wound
has healed,' he said. 'How?' she asked. 'At the fountain of your
eyes,' he replied and drew the joy of new life from her blushes,
without incurring further debtorship for a thing done (pp. 266–7).[4]

Meredith, then, is writing a novel about a man writing a book
of aphorisms conceived from the characters in his novel.

This game that Meredith plays with the art of novel-writing
is less intricately, but still interestingly, worked out also in his
treatment of the hero, Richard. At many junctures he stands
back and calls him 'Hero'. This denomination looks two ways
– it obviously describes the role Richard has in the novel, but it
also depicts Richard's own role-playing:

He [Richard] is foolish, God knows; but for my part I will not
laugh at the Hero, because he has not got his occasion. Meet him
when he is, as it were, anointed by his occasion, and he is no
laughing matter (p. 552).

Or:

Richard was too full of blame of himself to blame his father: too
British to expose his emotions. Ripton divined how deep and
changed they were by his manner. He had cast aside the Hero,
and however Ripton had obeyed him and looked up to him in the
heroic time, he loved him tenfold now (p. 562).

Meredith treats Lucy, less frequently, in the same way: 'The
Heroine, in common with the Hero, has her ambition to be of
use in the world – to do some good: and the task of reclaiming a
bad man is extremely seductive to good women' (p. 499). This
meeting of the language of the art of fiction with that of the

role of the character within it parallels at a linguistic level that between 'The Pilgrim's Scrip' and the novel structure at a formalist level. It also ensures a constant distancing of the author and reader from the characters, helped also, of course, by the wit and irony. It is maintained even at the end: the death of the heroine and spiritual annihilation of the hero are summarily described in a letter from Lady Blandish – hardly a device to encourage tragic participation. This 'distancing', an eighteenth-century or pre-Brechtian 'alienation', is highly atypical of the mid-Victorian novel: Meredith looked 'before and after' for his method.

II

> Ordeal: Judicial trial in use in the Middle Ages under the name of 'judgement of God': trial by water, trial by fire . . .
> *Larousse.*

> Anything . . . which . . . severely tests character or endurance, a trying experience.
> *N.E.D.*

The Feverels have always considered themselves subject to a divine trial, their response to which is misinterpreted by the world as severe eccentricity or mild insanity:

> [Sir Austin] had regarded his father, Sir Caradoc, as scarce better than a madman when he spoke of a special Ordeal for their race; and when, in his last hour . . . the old Baronet caught his elder son's hand, and desired him to be forewarned, Austin had, while bowing respectfully, wondered that Reason was not vouchsafed to his parent at that supreme instant. From the morning hills of existence he beheld a clear horizon. He was no sooner struck hard than Sir Caradoc's words smote him like a revelation. He believed that a curse was in his blood; a poison of Retribution, which no life of purity could expel; and grew, perhaps, more morbidly credulous on the point than his predecessor: speaking of the Ordeal of the Feverels, with sonorous solemnity as a thing incontrovertibly foredecreed to them . . . Sir Austin, strong in the peculiar sharpness of the sting darted into him, held that there was an entire distinction in their lot: that other men were tried by puny ailments; were not searched and shaken by one tremendous

shock, as of a stroke of Heaven's lightning. He indicated that the Fates and Furies were quite as partial as Fortune (pp. 16–17).

This Fate is nicknamed 'Mrs Malediction': 'Often had she all but cut them off from their old friend, Time, and they revived again. Whether it was the Apple-Disease, or any other, strong constitutions seemed struggling in them with some peculiar malady' (p. 14). Having undergone his Ordeal in his wife's desertion, Sir Austin is convinced that it is the 'Apple-Disease': 'What he exactly meant by the Apple-Disease, he did not explain: nor did the ladies ask for an explanation. Intuitively they felt hot when it was mentioned' (p. 12). Whether the 'Apple-Disease' is sexuality in general or, more specifically, venereal disease is unprovable and largely irrelevant to the larger themes, though interesting for an evaluation of the type of novel.[5] To Sir Austin it is as though God put woman in the garden to tempt Adam (as did, in a minor way, but in a major literary tradition, the Satan of *Paradise Regained* to tempt Christ). The Feverels as Adam's heirs in each generation undergo a repetition of this original 'Ordeal'. Meredith thus makes Sir Austin use the term 'Ordeal' in its limited ancient sense. One of the brilliances of the book is that Meredith takes up the term and redeploys it in its more generalised and psychological sense; the 'Ordeal' that primarily Richard, and secondarily Sir Austin, undergo is the trial of enduring their inherited notion of the family's divine Ordeal; the 'ordeal' of an Ordeal.

Sir Austin, believing in a perfected Paradise that can be regained, educates his only son Richard to be a new Adam: 'By advancing him to a certain moral fortitude ere the Apple-Disease was spontaneously developed, there would be something approaching to a perfect Man' (p. 12). He is not preparing Richard to avoid the fight, but bracing him for the struggle. The boy's childhood is marked by a number of crises which always fall on his birthdays. On the boy's seventh birthday, 'Mrs Malediction' (in fact, his exiled mother), has visited Richard's bedside; Sir Austin is relieved to find the Ordeal deflected on to his brother Algernon, who loses a leg that day. On his seventh birthday a protesting Ricky is declared morally and physically fit. On his fourteenth birthday Richard refuses to submit to medical examination: 'For in Richard's bosom *a fate was working*, and the shame of the insult, as he thought it, rankled' (p. 42, my italics). He escapes with Ripton from the festivities, offends Farmer Blaize, provokes the firing of the farmer's rick, and, when finally apologising for the episode, meets (though he does not acknowledge the farmer's niece) – Lucy Desborough. When Sir Austin overhears the boys discussing their crime, the same language is in operation: 'A sensation of infinite melancholy overcame the poor gentleman: a thought that he was fighting with fate in the beloved boy.' This is his fourteenth birthday. Once more his mother had secretly visited him, causing the spying Clare to faint. On this birthday he first meets Lucy, though no significance is attached to the meeting as yet. Richard continues to grow up in the Paradise that Sir Austin has created, a Paradise in which he is kept totally ignorant of the 'meaning' of woman. But while he is kept pure, his father dallies with Lady Blandish and Richard who, unknown to his father, witnesses the flirtation, imitates him in a childish way. Sir Austin, still posing as a suprasexual creature, as perfect 'providence', refuses to see the significance of his own behaviour; he feels all is well with Richard:

> No augury could be hopefuller. The Fates must indeed be hard, the Ordeal severe, the Destiny dark, that could destroy so bright a Spring! But bright as it was, the Baronet relaxed nothing of his vigilant supervision. He said to his intimates: 'Every act, every fostered inclination, almost every thought, in this Blossoming Season, bears its seed for the Future. The living Tree now requires incessant watchfullness (p. 130. 'The Tree' is capitalised as Sir Austin previously referred to Richard as 'a Tree of Eden').

Richard, however, released into a knowledge of sex by seeing Sir Austin kiss Lady Blandish's hand, in his father's absence now falls in love with Lucy Desborough. Meredith's irony is immediately at work: here in Sir Austin's Paradise, the brave new world is actually recaptured. Richard and Lucy, without the knowledge, and against all the efforts of Sir Austin, are 'Ferdinand and Miranda', perfect man and woman, regaining Eden for mankind:

> He had landed on an Island of the still-vexed Bermoothes. The world lay wrecked behind him . . . What splendour in the Heavens! What marvels of beauty about his enchanted head! And, O you Wonder! . . . Radiant Miranda! Prince Ferdinand is at your feet.
>
> Or is it Adam, his rib taken from his side in sleep, and thus transformed, to make him behold his Paradise, and lose it! . . .
>
> The youth looked on her with as glowing an eye. It was the First Woman to him.
>
> And she – mankind was all Caliban to her, saving this one princely youth (pp. 149–50).

The tragic irony is overt – 'The way the System triumphed, just ere it was to fall' – but the more private ironic reversal is also present. As later Richard is 'widow Ann' and Bella Mount Richard III, here Lucy is the more normally educated Ferdinand and Richard, the unique Miranda. This is another aspect of Meredith's turning of the conventional and the expected on its head. It also is an illustration of his use of sexual role-reversal to make thereby an egalitarian statement.

Meredith makes it quite certain that Lucy is the 'right girl'; in the language of the novel, she is the Cinderella that Richard finds by instinct, whilst his father is scientifically trying the glass slipper on ugly sisters. But the instinctual Paradise Lucy and Richard inhabit shares with the scientific concept of Sir Austin the delusion of its nature:

> Pipe, happy sheep-boy, Love! Irradiated Angels, unfold your wings and lift your voices!
>
> They have outflown Philosophy. Their Instinct has shot beyond the ken of Science. Imperiously they know we were made for this Eden: and would you gainsay them who are outside the Gates, and argue from the Fall? (p. 194).

From his own romantic predicament, Richard falls into his father's illusion. Lucy and Richard are spied on by Heavy Benson: 'Enchanted Islands have not yet rooted out their old brood of Dragons. Wherever there is Romance, these Monsters came by inimical attraction.' Beneath this inflated language, Meredith makes it quite clear that Benson is nothing but a dirty old man indulging in voyeurism. (This deflation-technique parallels that employed in making the Apple-Disease at times stand for venereal disease.) Most critics have taken these passages as straight lyricism and consequently seen the tragedy as being caused by Sir Austin's harsh separation of his son from his wife. This is to miss completely the gentle, indulgent and yet precise ironising of romanticism.

It is also to misread the story. Richard, after his illness, does bury his love for Lucy, but, hearing of the possibility of rescuing her from a debasing marriage, his love painfully revives. His subsequent wooing and marriage to her are beset with anti-romantic incidents: he forgets the house where he has lodged her, 'Betrayed by his instincts, the magic slaves of Love!'; he seems to pine for love, 'Lucy wept for the famine-struck hero who was just then feeding mightily' (p. 321); he loses the wedding-ring; his best man, Ripton, becomes grotesquely drunk at the wedding-breakfast and betrays the marriage to Adrian. There is no doubt that Meredith, without therefore condemning it, regards the marriage as a rash one, and Richard as still living in a world of romantic illusion:

> 'The Alps! Italy! Rome! and then I shall go to the East,' the Hero continued. 'She's ready to go anywhere with me, the dear brave heart! Oh, the glorious golden East! . . . I dream I'm Chief of an Arab tribe, and we fly all white in the moonlight on our mares, and hurry to the rescue of my darling! And we push the spears, and we scatter them, and I come to the tent where she crouches, and catch her on my saddle, and away! —' (p. 320).

The Ordeal is shifting from the generic to the personal; Richard's Ordeal is his marriage: 'Complacently [Sir Austin] sat and smiled, little witting that his son's Ordeal was imminent, and that his son's Ordeal was to be his own.' Sir Austin's notion of divine Fate and Meredith's psychological reinterpretation of this coalesce at this climactic point in a chapter entitled 'In which the last act of a comedy takes the place of the first':

> . . . each man has, one time or other, a little Rubicon – a clear or a foul, water to cross . . . Be your Rubicon big or small, clear or foul, it is the same: you shall not return. On – to Acheron! – I subscribe to that saying of THE PILGRIM'S SCRIP:
>
> 'The danger of a little knowledge of things is disputable: but beware the little knowledge of one's self!'
>
> Richard Feverel was now crossing the River of his Ordeal . . . his life was cut in two, and he breathed but the air that met his nostrils. His father, his father's love, his boyhood and ambition, were shadowy . . . And yet the young man loved his father, loved his home: and I dare say Caesar loved Rome: but whether he did or no, Caesar when he killed the Republic was quite bald, and the Hero we are dealing with is scarce beginning to feel his despotic moustache. Did he know what he was made of? Doubtless, nothing at all. But honest passion has an instinct that can be safer than conscious wisdom . . . His audacious mendacities and subterfuges did not strike him as in any way criminal . . . Conscience and Lucy went together (pp. 330–1).

Richard in marrying Lucy is guilty of intensely and unwittingly wounding the devoted Clare. The pain for Clare is brought out with full pathos in the scene where she finds Richard's lost wedding-ring, finds it fits her finger and is teased by her mother and cousins about having found her future husband. Richard is guilty, but his guilt is part of the larger social structure: happiness, says Meredith is like money, the rich take from the poor: 'Who knows the Honeymoon that did not steal somebody's sweetness? Richard Turpin went forth, singing: "Money or life" to the world: Richard Feverel has done the same, substituting "Happiness" for "Money", frequently synonyms. The coin he wanted he would have, and was just as much a highway robber as his fellow Dick . . . His coin chinks delicious music to him. Nature, and the order of things on earth, have no warmer admirer than a jolly brigand, or a young man made happy by the Jews' (p. 386).[6] Meredith treats Lucy's and Richard's marriage realistically. Although they are happy and still in love,[7] Richard is frustrated, ambition has replaced 'Love', and there are minor quarrels and dissatisfactions between them. Adrian, in a semi-seduction of the one through cookery, and Lady Judith Velle, in a semi-seduction of the other through romantic philanthropy, play into the vague dissensions of the couple. It is not just Sir Austin who is responsible for separating the newly-weds and hence indirectly for Richard's infidelity: Fate is other people, but the protagonists make themselves receptive to it. ·

Separated from Lucy, Richard undertakes the reformation of the fallen women of London. He sees them as 'clever, beautiful, but betrayed by Love'. Where his father has seen men as victims of women, Richard sees women as men's victims. Just as he is righting his father's injustice, he is seduced by Bella Mount (the name is a literary and 'earthy' pun) thus proving his father's theory:

> 'When we're young we can be very easily deceived. If there is such a thing as love, we discover it after we have tossed about and roughed it. Then we find the man, or the woman, that suits us:– and then it's too late' [Bella].
> 'Singular!' murmured Richard, 'she says just what my father said' (p. 483).

Of course, what Sir Austin and Bella have in common are their truistic utterances.

Meredith treats Richard's infidelity with as much realism as the marriage; there is no immediate contrition; he writes to Bella: 'Come, my bright Hell-star! . . . You have taught me how devils love, and I can't do without you.' After Bella has refused, and Clare, married to an old but kindly man, has committed suicide, Richard, despairing, leaves for Germany. He has lost none of his romanticism; where once he dreamt of Arabian adventures, of saving the women of London, now he wants to liberate Italy. He is in the company of Lady Judith, who, as Austin Wentworth says, is 'a sentimentalist'.

In the forest thunderstorm, filled with the glory of his newly-discovered paternity, Richard has a supramundane experience. First it is purely physical; it 'communicated nothing to his heart', but penetrated all through his blood. It turns out to be caused by the licking of the leveret he is carrying. Once Richard knows the reason, his *heart* is touched. All Richard's previous glorious moments have been attributed by Meredith simply to instinct, to 'blood'; now he has passed beyond this to the heart,[8] and thence to the spirit – seeing a small forest chapel he is suffused with a sense of universal love:

> Vivid as lightning the Spirit of Life illumined him. He felt in his heart the cry of his child, his darling's touch. With shut eyes he saw them both. They drew him from the depths; they led him a blind and tottering man. And as they led him he had a sense of purification so sweet he shuddered again and again (p. 558).

But Meredith treats this only as momentary inspiration. In London, *en route* home, Richard receives Bella's letter. All his life he has felt subjected to other people's plots, and now he learns that his desertion of Lucy and seduction by Bella was a further plot. After he has challenged Lord Mountfalcon,[9] he delays till evening his return to Raynham. There he discovers his real Ordeal is to abandon his son and wife for possible death:

> O God! what an Ordeal was this! that tomorrow he must face Death, perhaps die and be torn from his darling – his wife and his child (p. 582).

And his father discovers *his* Ordeal in the possible death of his son. Lady Blandish writes:

> His Ordeal is over. I have just come from his room and seen him bear the worst that could be (p. 587).

Love and Death are the Ordeal.

III

> 'There are women in the world, my son!' – Sir Austin Feverel (p. 224).

Women came into the world to tempt men. Sir Austin literalises this conventional concept, thereby making it abnormal and hence available to laughter and ridicule. But Meredith does not simply prove him wrong – love and sex *are* the ordeal, but not exactly as Sir Austin means them.

Who is this woman of ill-omen?

'Mrs Malediction', who visits the child Richard, disturbs Sir Austin by kissing his son:

> Sir Austin had listened with a pleased attention to his boy's prattle. The mention of the Lady changed his face.
> 'Kissed you, my child?' he asked anxiously (p. 23).

'Mrs Malediction' is, in fact Lady Feverel. She visits again before the next crisis. Lady Feverel is the orphan daughter of an Admiral who educated her on his half-pay;[10] her adultery with Diaper Sandoe is discussed at the beginning and near the end of the novel. But Richard, who, until his adulthood, knows nothing of his mother's history, with an uncanny 'fatality' always quotes Sandoe's poems just before he makes some false move. The poems' fatuous sentimentality (praised by Richard) thus runs as a disturbing motif through the novel. Richard has a number of relationships with older women who are seen explicitly as mother-substitutes. Lady Blandish (admirer of Austin Wentworth as well as of Austin Feverel), personified first as 'the Bonnet' then as the 'Autumn Primrose', first awakens Richard to sexuality – 'Emmeline Clementina Matilda Laura, Countess Blandish' he rhapsodises in response to Ralph Norton's love-lorn musings on women's names. But part of her own flirtation with Sir Austin is her assumption of an adoptive parenthood of Richard. When there is the prospect that she might actually become his stepmother, Richard is perturbed with all the jealousy of the boy for his father who has 'won' his 'mother' sexually. Lady Blandish is also linked with Bella Mount: 'She honestly loved the boy. She would tell him: "If I had been a girl, I would have had you for my husband." And he with the frankness of his years would reply: "And how do you know I would have had you?" causing her to laugh and call him a silly boy, for had he not heard her say, She would have had him?

Terrible words, he knew not then the meaning of!' (p. 124).
Lady Judith Velle: 'A second edition of the Blandish',
according to Adrian, 'kissed Lucy protectingly and remarking
on the wonders of the evening, appropriated her husband' (p.
413). Mrs Bella Mount, his seductress, is directly linked with
Lady Feverel (and, of course, with Austin Wentworth's wife,
thereby underlying the parallel roles of the two Austins once
more). Richard decides to rescue his mother from her
adulterous union, in this act making a confidante of Lady
Blandish. He arranges to house his mother with Mrs Berry,
but Mrs Berry has seen Richard with Bella Mount in the Park
and thinks that 'the lady' whom he is to bring is this 'Beller
Donner', as she calls her:

> 'I want you to keep your rooms for me – those [Lucy] had. I
> expect, in a day or two, to bring a lady here—'
> 'A lady?' faltered Mrs Berry . . . 'But I ain't a house of
> Magdalens.' . . . In the evening she heard the noise of wheels
> stopping at the door. 'Never! . . . He ain't rided her out in the
> mornin', and been and made a Magdalen of her afore dark?' . . .
> 'Mr Richard! if that woman stay here, I go forth. My house ain't
> a penitenteary for unfort'nate females Sir—' . . .
> He clapped his hand across her mouth, and spoke words in her
> ear that had awful import to her. She trembled, breathing low:
> 'My God, forgive me! Lady Feverel is it? Your mother, Mr
> Richard?' (p. 469–71).

The evil woman, then, is the sexual mother; and it is against
her that Sir Austin's energies are ultimately, if unconsciously,
directed. A statement in 'The Pilgrim's Scrip' reads: 'To
withstand women, must we first annihilate our Mothers
within us: die half!' It is his child's mother in Lady Feverel that
Sir Austin attempts to annihilate by not allowing her to exist
for Richard. He tries to make a perfect mother of Lucy, his
daughter-in-law, and by his strictures causes her death.
(Richard realises the murderous implications of his father's
position at the time of Clare's death.)
   An important aspect of Meredith's sexual egalitarianism is
his refusal to draw a sharp line between men and women. We

have seen this already in his role-reversal imagery for Lucy
and Richard and Bella and Richard; the women, though
utterly 'feminine', have masculine attributes. In the two
Austins, Meredith displays the importance of femininity in
men. Of Sir Austin he writes: 'The poor gentleman, seriously
believing Woman to be a Mistake, had long been trying to
annihilate his Mother within him. Had he succeeded he
would have died his best half, for his mother was strong in
him' (p. 10). It is Sir Austin's suppression of tenderness and
assumption of a mask that is his undoing, as it is his real
femininity that is his glory and that wins him Meredith's
approval. Mrs Berry, the former indiscreet housemaid, 'Polly
Acton', utters the truth about him late (too late) in the novel:

> '—I'll say his 'art's as soft as a woman's . . . That's where
> everybody's deceived by him . . . It's because he keeps his face,
> and makes ye think you're dealin' with a man of iron, and all
> the while there's a woman underneath. And a man that's like
> a woman he's the puzzle o' life! We can see through
> ourselves . . . and we can see through men, but one o' that sort—
> he's like somethin' out o' natur'. Then I say . . . what's to do is for
> to treat him *like* a woman, and not for to let him 'ave his own way—
> which he don't know himself, and is why nobody else do' (p. 473).

Austin Wentworth is what Sir Austin should have allowed
himself to be: '. . . he was extremely presentable: fair-haired,
with a smile sweet as a woman's: gentle as a child: a face set
with the seal of a courageous calm: so pure a face that looking
on it you seemed to see into his soul' (p. 30). Transparency
versus a mask: both are models for Richard. Austin Wentworth
twice brings spiritual bliss to Richard: first when he enables
him to face the confession of arson ('Feelings he had never
known streamed in upon him, as from an ethereal casement:
an unwanted tenderness: an embracing humour: a
consciousness of some ineffable glory: an irradiation of the
features of humanity' (p. 88)) and for a second time when he
brings the news of Richard's son. There, *nursing* the leveret,
Richard discovers his masculinity in the release of his
femininity. It is, however, too late: he was 'too British to

expose his emotions', the women are killed, Richard has a motherless son, the mask has triumphed:

> Have you noticed the expression in the eyes of blind men? That is just how Richard looks, as he lies there silent in his bed – striving to image her on his brain (p. 592*f*.).

IV

> Alceste is the Jean-Jacques of the Heart.
>
> Meredith, *Essay on Comedy*

Before his wife's adultery, Sir Austin lives in an imagined Golden Age ('He had bid [Lady Feverel and Diaper Sandoe] be brother and sister, . . . and live a Golden Age with him at Raynham'); his educational system is an attempt to regain for his son that lost Eden. He is even tempted towards a prospect of a renewed Utopia on his own account with Lady Blandish:

> . . . was not here a woman worthy the Golden Ages of the world? one who could look upon man as a creature divinely made, and look with a mind neither tempted, nor tainted, by the Serpent! (p.127).

But because he has lost his original Paradise he has sunk into misanthropy: '. . . like Timon, he became bankrupt, and fell upon bitterness'. Meredith later considered *Le Misanthrope* as the greatest comedy written. Sir Austin has much in common with Alceste.

> All are corrupt; there's nothing to be seen
> In court or town but aggravates my spleen.
>
> (*Le Misanthrope*, I, I.)

For Meredith, Molière's Alceste and Molière's great critic, Jean-Jacques Rousseau, have much in common: both are egotistical misanthropists; as Mackay[11] puts it, '*la chute du Misanthrope implique la chute de Jean-Jacques*'. If Sir Austin shares certain characteristics with Timon and Alceste, could it not follow that he bears some resemblance to Rousseau? As yet, there is no absolutely certain evidence that

Meredith was deeply acquainted with Rousseau's work; but his general culture, his education in Germany, where Rousseau was of far greater importance even than in France and England, and a later letter to Morley (1875) congratulating him on his biography of Rousseau, all strongly suggest that he was. Within the novel Austin Wentworth refers with approval to *The Confessions* (p. 85). But of course, if Meredith did have Rousseau in mind as a partial model for Sir Austin, it is as the author of *Emile* that he is most relevant. Sir Austin's basic premise reads almost like a simplified version of Rousseau's position: Man is not born evil (nor absolutely good), but he has only forfeited Paradise through the corruptness of the societies he has formed, he *chooses* evil; his aim should thus be to regain his state of perfection. Both Rousseau and Sir Austin strive towards a Utopia of the future based on a Golden Age in the past. Meredith demonstrates the fundamental Manichaeism involved – he may well have felt this about Rousseau (another 'eulogist of Nature') as well as about Sir Austin:

> . . . A Manichaean tendency, from which the sententious eulogist of Nature had been struggling for years (and which was partly at the bottom of the System), now began to cloud and usurp dominion of his mind. As he sat alone in the forlorn dead-hush of his library, he saw the Devil.
> . . . and the Devil said to him . . . : 'your object now, is to keep a brave face to the world, so that all may know you superior to this human nature that has deceived you. For it is the shameless Deception, not the Marriage, that has wounded you . . . And your System:– if you would be brave to the world, have courage to cast the dream of it out of you: relinquish an impossible project; see it as it is – dead: too good for men!'
> 'Ay!' muttered the Baronet, 'all who would save them perish on the Cross!' (p. 390).

Sir Austin sees Richard as worse than the drunk, pornography-reading Ripton. Meredith, like Molière, believes in the basic good of human nature; what he is criticising in Sir Austin/Rousseau is the romantic, idealist reinterpretation that finds its source and its conclusion in its obverse –

misanthropy. Sir Austin shares with Rousseau his misogyny: Rousseau considers women decidedly inferior and, despite the fact that he does not theoretically regard women as the source of all evil, he makes Sophie's infidelity the cause of Emile's misery, as Lady Feverel was the cause of Sir Austin's.

Many critics of *Richard Feverel* have claimed that Meredith based his notion of the 'System' on Herbert Spencer's contemporary educational theories, published in the *Quarterly Review* (1858). Critics of Spencer thought that he had based his proposals on *Emile*, causing Spencer to claim he had never read a line of Rousseau.[12] Of one thing we can be certain: the cosmopolitan Meredith would not have been guilty of Spencer's complacent philistinism. As there is much in common in the character and in the general theories of Sir Austin and Rousseau, so there is much in common between his 'System' and that of *Emile*.

Rousseau's pupil, Emile, is a boy of pure (upper-class) blood and good health. The father is 'the ideal tutor', but Emile is, in fact, an orphan, so a tutor takes over. He gives the boy apparent freedom, but in fact operates a system of constant espionage. This is exactly the position Sir Austin adopts: 'The possession of his son's secret flattered him. It allowed him to act, and in a measure to feel, like Providence; enabled him to observe and provide for the movements of creatures in the dark' (p. 71). It is precisely this posturing as 'Providence' that Meredith criticises in Sir Austin (while Lucy and Richard are Ferdinand and Miranda, we are told Sir Austin is no Prospero). The basic aim of both Rousseau's and Sir Austin's systems is to combine absolute health of body with truth of soul and thus produce 'Valour' (Sir Austin's aphorisms are the skeleton of Rouseau's decomposed circumlocutions). Both believe in early maternal care and in breast-feeding. Both think of education in essentially 'progressive' terms – the child is not an empty vehicle to be filled, but a growing, developing person; hence the notion of stages of growth. Rousseau divides his pupil's life into four stages: 1 to 5 years, 5 to 12, 12 to 15, and 15 to the early twenties. The first stage is purely physical. Emile learns to eat, walk and talk; the second is 'negative': he is not taught truth, but is shielded from vice; hardihood, strength and courage are developed in the intercourse with Nature; little is learnt; there is no punishing and no rewarding. The next stage concentrates on Emile's intellectual growth, the stress here being on discovery and natural curiosity rather than constraint. Up till this point Emile has been a complete individualist and egotist, for self-love is the source of all passions; now begins his moral and spiritual education: from love and feeling are developed virtue and morality. Emile, who has been brought up entirely in the country, is now shown the town, whilst a bride, as pure as himself, is sought for him. He meets this girl, Sophie, but is then separated from her while he spends two years abroad. The final section of the book is devoted to a description of Sophie's education. But Rousseau wrote a 'misanthropic' sequel, *Sophie and Emile*, in which, after marrying and having children, disaster hits the couple: Sophie is unfaithful and Emile is captured and enslaved by Tunisian pirates.

Sir Austin's 'System' differs in a number of details (Richard, but not Emile, studies history, Emile, but not Richard, learns a manual craft, etc.), but imitates many of the broad outlines of Rousseau's plan. Thus Richard's growth is seen as a series of stages; and stages which, though they have slightly different ages for their demarcation lines (Sir Austin's are more blurred) have a similar educational content though redirected solely to Richard's future relationship with 'Woman'. Many statements are clear echoes:

> In Sir Austin's Note-book was written: 'Between Simple Boyhood, and Adolescence – The Blossoming Season – on the threshold of Puberty, there is one Unselfish Hour: say, Spiritual Seed-time?' (pp. 121—2).

Many aspects seem to bear an extraordinarily strong resemblance: education according to Nature, education for perfection, progressive education through stages, the move from country to town, education right through to marriage, the separation of the lovers and so on. The basic tenets (and the basic character) are far closer to those of Rousseau than to those of Spencer. [13]

Sir Austin follows Rousseau in believing that the primary egotism of man can be transmuted into social conscience and the general will (in Rousseau's case this notion is developed more fully in *The Social Contract* than in *Emile*). There are two ironies deployed by Meredith here: Richard, like Emile, is personally doomed by his efforts at public philanthropy; but above all Rousseau and Sir Austin are arch-egotists. Just as their theoretical Utopia is based on personal misanthropy, so their visions of altruism find their source in an obsession with the self. (The true altruist is, of course, Richard's 'good angel', Austin Wentworth, the man without misanthropy and without a system.)

Sir Austin is not an absolute or a straight portrait of Rousseau, but often he is his essence and his parody. He is also, of course, an 'updated' version. 'Created' in the same year as *Origin of Species*, he is a 'scientific' humanist (in fact, he is neither scientist nor humanist). Rousseau's 'natural man' has been literalised, so that romantic Richard is shocked to discover that in his kinship to the animals is supposed to lie the source of his nobleness.

The upbringing of Richard Feverel is not a direct imitation of the education of Emile, but the overall pattern is strikingly similar and the tone and mood yet more so. In a remarkable review in 1864, Justin McCarthy wrote:

> People in general do not now, I think, read Rousseau's *Emile*; but those who are familiar with that masterpiece of a dead philosophy will probably agree with us as to the profoundly unsatisfactory and disheartening impression which its catastrophe leaves on the mind. Was it for this, the reader is inclined to ask, that science and love do their utmost to make one path smooth, one human existence bright, and noble, and happy? Was Emile from his birth upward trained to the suppression of every selfish thought, to the scorn of all ignoble purpose, to an absolute devotion for truth, courage, purity, and benevolence, only that he might be

deceived in his dearest affections, and that the crowning act of his existence might be the abnegation of self which we can scarcely even regard with admiration? The author had a right to shape his moral and deal with his creations as he would, yet we feel pained and shocked that he should have deemed it right to act thus harshly towards the beloved offspring of his system.

Something of this surprise and disappointment fills the mind when we have reached the close of Richard Feverel's ordeal, and find that he has left his brightest hopes and dearest affections dead and buried behind him. The book closes with a sharp snap or crash; we feel as if something were suddenly wrenched away with pain and surprise; a darkness falls upon the mind. [14]

Is it another of his ironic reversals (and a wish to raise the status of women) that makes Meredith have Richard (Emile) unfaithful and not Lucy (Sophie), and Lucy show an 'abnegation of self which we can scarcely even regard with admiration'? Whether or not this is so, McCarthy certainly captures the subject-matter of the novel and the tone of the tract perfectly: it is tragic without being tragedy; misanthropy passing through idealism has produced a concrete cause for its own disillusionment; egotism has met its just but sad reward in isolation; Utopia may come, but not with the Devil's advocate nor through faith alone.

What Maisie Knew: Portrait of the Artist as a Young Girl

¶ '*What Maisie Knew:* Portrait of the Artist as a Young Girl' was written for a collection edited by a close friend and colleague at Reading University, John Goode. It appeared in *The Air of Reality, New Essays on Henry James* (London, 1972). At the time I was reading psychoanalytic studies of infancy and childhood – Winnicott, Susan Isaacs . . . But the essay also makes some use both of R. D. Laing's early work on the internalisation of interactions within family networks and of other studies along similar lines, then being carried out at the Tavistock Clinic. At the beginning of the 1960s we had published some of this work of Laing's in the *New Left Review*.

Both this and the previous essay, though published in the early 1970s, were written in the latter part of the 1960s. Although *What Maisie Knew* would seem to offer no possible connection with political life, the Student Movement of 1968 formed an important background. For it, too, made great use of the existential, psychological phenomenologies that seemed to explain the predicament of the young. So while writing this literary essay, I was also actively involved in politics and my reflections led to a section on Laing's works and influence in *Psychoanalysis and Feminism* (London, 1974).

171

(All references to *What Maisie Knew* are to the Penguin Modern Classics edition, Harmondsworth, 1969.)

> She wore glasses which, in humble reference to a divergent obliquity of vision, she called her straighteners. . . . (p. 31).

> Mrs Wix gave a sidelong look. She still had room for wonder at what Maisie knew (p. 248).

Cross-eyed Mrs Wix looking sideways through her corrective glasses remains – and surely the odds are against her – one of the sightless amongst the seeing. But for the Jamesian reader, as for the Jamesian heroine, participation in a James novel is a process of initiation into vision. In his *Notebooks*, in his Preface and in the novel, James tells us that the young child Maisie saw more than she understood. For the mature Maisie, and in this precisely does her maturity consist, seeing *is* knowing, vision and knowledge are one. What Maisie knows is what we know, which is what the narrator knows, which is what James knows; and that may be many things from many different angles, but most clearly it is the knowledge that no one else in the novel knows as much as we know about them and us.

> I am not sure that Maisie had not even a dim discernment of the queer law of her own life that made her educate to that sort of proficiency those elders with whom she was concerned. She promoted as it were, their development; nothing could have been more marked, for instance, than her success in promoting Mrs Beale's. She judged that if her whole history, for Mrs Wix, had been the successive stages of her knowledge, so the very climax of the concatenation would, in the same view, be the stage at which the knowledge should overflow. As she was condemned to know more and more, how could it logically stop before she should know Most? It came to her in fact as they sat there on the sands that she was distinctly on the road to know Everything. . . She looked at the pink sky with a placid foreboding that soon she should have learnt All (pp. 194—195).

The content of knowledge is important but so is the stance of the knower. The mature Maisie, of course, shows immaculate taste:

'Sure, you mean, that she'll bolt?'
Maisie knew all about bolting, but, decidedly, she *was* older, and
there was something in her that could wince at the way her father
made the ugly word – ugly enough at best – sound flat and low (p.
135).

At the end of the novel, Maisie has certainly lost her
innocence and her ignorance, but her 'knowledge' is not
corrupt. To suggest, as a number of critics have done, that her
final request to Sir Claude that they should leave and live
together and alone is a sexual proposition, is as absurd as to
suggest that James himself could have been guilty of such
prostitution. Or rather, if you believe one, you have to believe
the other. Maisie has learnt discretion, and in doing so she has
become a discrete, an autonomous person. Like James and
the required reader, having failed in participation she has
gained the autonomy of the observer. But in this novel James
offers us two 'observers', two viewpoints – his 'centre of
consciousness', Maisie, and the governess Mrs Wix. Two
views of the world: the straight and the crooked: 'Make my
point of view, my *line*, the consciousness, the *dim*, scared,
wondering, clinging perception of the child'.[1] 'Don't I best see
the whole thing reflected in the talk, the confidences, the
intercourse of Mrs Wix? . . .[she] thus serves as a sort of a *dim*,
crooked little reflector of the conditions. . . .'[2] The corneal
mist fades from the eyes of the growing child; the aged
governess bursts through her distorting spectacles and earns
the right to her cross-eyed vision: 'The straighteners . . . seemed to crack with the explosion of their
wearer's honesty' (p. 173). Clarity, then a new dimness, the
dimness of distance, can be acquired.

From reflection to reflection: the process of James's art, the
history of his heroine. The pool of the self into which one
gazes first to see others reflected there, then to see oneself and
the others reflected, then to see that the pool is oneself: time
for the thought that is no longer visual but visionary.
Reflection. 'I have ever, in general, found it difficult to write
of places under too immediate an impression . . . the

impression that prevents standing off and allows neither space nor time for perspective. The image has had for the most part to be *dim* if the reflection was to be, as is proper for a reflection, both sharp and quiet.'[3]

The mirror can be seen only as the reflection within it, or it can be seen as a mirror. Or it can be a pane of glass, looked through from either side, but the side of the viewer always dimly reflected in the glass that is being looked through. Or one can see the frame of the glass through which one is looking: the edge of the picture; the proscenium arch. In his theoretical writing James juxtaposes the pictorial and the dramatic technique: the picture and the scene. In *What Maisie Knew* they merge because both are only aspects of the dominant theme of playing with reflections. The novel is not a drama or a painting but it is, in an important sense, a shadow-puppet show or, with its pre-cinema imagery, a film. So is Maisie's view of her world:

> She was taken into the confidence of passions on which she fixed the stare she might have had for images bounding across the wall in the slide of a magic lantern. Her little world was phantasmagoric – strange shadows dancing on a sheet. It was as if the whole performance had been given for her – a mite of a half-scared infant in a great *dim* theatre (p. 21, my italics).

In a theatre one acts plays. Children play-act, play games. Maisie and Mrs Wix don't understand children's games: 'The games were, as [Sir Claude] said, to while away the evening hour; and the evening hour indeed often passed in futile attempts on Mrs Wix's part to master what "it said" on the papers. When he asked the pair how they liked the games they always replied, "Oh immensely!" but they had earnest discussions as to whether they hadn't better appeal to him frankly for aid to understand them' (p. 61). But there isn't one adult in the novel whose main activity is not described as a game: 'I know your game'; 'It was a game like another'; 'It's her ladyship's game'; 'It's a game'; 'I can't make out . . . what game she was playing'. Maisie, in truth, is the instrument, the victim, the ball in these games. James's perception of her growing perception of it is brilliantly rendered; the balance between her metaphor and the 'facts'.

> So the sharpened sense of spectatorship as the child's main support, the long habit, from the first, of seeing herself in discussion and finding in the fury of it – she had had a glimpse of the game of football – a sort of compensation for the doom of a peculiar passivity (p. 83).

> In the course of psychotherapy with this girl, I discovered she was absorbed in a reverie of a perpetual game of tennis. Mixed doubles. Centre Court. Wimbledon. The crowd, the court, the net, the players and the ball, back and forth, back and forth, back and forth. She was all these elements but particularly, at the heart of it all, she was the ball. This ball was served, smashed, volleyed, lobbed, sometimes hit right out of court. . .
>   Now, when one discovered from collateral evidence the nature of her family system, it was found that this reverie was a rather accurate account, from her point of view, of her experience of the family. . . .
>   The family set-up, under one roof, consisted of her father and mother, mother's father and father's mother – mixed doubles. They were in fact ranged against each other, father and his mother against mother and her father. She was the ball in their game, to give one instance of the accuracy of this metaphor. . .[4]

Maisie, of course, remains sane. Indeed for James one of the chief fascinations of the original story was his notion that despite her appalling family circumstances, the child would be preserved, she would come through, triumphant. Perhaps her sanity is also achieved because, from the hints James gives us, the players at some level know they are playing a game: 'The evil they had the gift of thinking *or pretending to think* of each other they poured into her little gravely-gazing soul as into a boundless receptacle' (p. 24, my italics). These relationships then are the games people play.

Maisie starts as the six-year-old daughter of a divorced couple – Beale and Ida Farange. Her impecunious father is granted custody, but for financial considerations relinquishes her for half the time to her mother. At her mother's Maisie has a

governess: Miss Overmore. But Miss Overmore changes sides
and goes over to her father. On her next visit to her mother,
Maisie acquires a new governess, Mrs Wix. During her next
visit to her father Maisie learns that Miss Overmore has
married her father and become Mrs Beale. She also at the
same time learns from the visiting Mrs Wix that her mother is
to marry a handsome young aristocrat, Sir Claude. Sir
Claude, her new stepfather, comes to fetch Maisie from her
father and meets the new Mrs Beale. Slowly, and over Maisie,
they form a relationship with each other. Meanwhile, Ida has
a series of relationships, the main one 'on stage' being with
'The Captain' – at first taken by Sir Claude and Maisie for 'The
Count'. And Beale has a number of relationships, the only
one 'on stage' being with 'The Countess'. Beale takes leave of
Maisie, giving up his responsibility for his daughter,
pretending to be going to America. Sir Claude takes Maisie to
Folkestone. Ida takes leave of Maisie, giving up her daughter
to Sir Claude, and pretends that she is going to South Africa.
Meanwhile Mrs Wix, infatuated with Sir Claude and
scandalised by his relationship with Mrs Beale, tries to save
him (and Maisie) from such an alliance. Mrs Beale tries to get
Sir Claude for herself by asserting that Maisie, who is with
him now in Boulogne, is her stepdaughter, and her right,
therefore. Maisie, after wishfully thinking that perhaps she,
Mrs Wix, Sir Claude and Mrs Beale could all live together,
understands the game and decides she wants to live only with
Sir Claude. She asks first him and then Mrs Beale to give
each other up. He is unable to and she refuses. Maisie 'loses'
and goes off with Mrs Wix, back to England. This is the story:
but what of the metaphorical structure?

> The litigation had seemed interminable and had in fact been
> complicated; but by the decision on the appeal the judgement of
> the divorce-court was confirmed as to the assignment of the child.
> The father . . . was . . . appointed to keep her. . . . He was
> unable to produce the money [he owed Ida] . . . so that after a
> squabble scarcely less public and scarcely more decent than the
> original shock of battle his only issue from his predicament was a

compromise proposed by his legal advisers and finally accepted by hers.

His debt was by this arrangement remitted to him and the little girl disposed of in a manner worthy of the judgement-seat of Solomon. She was divided in two and the portions tossed impartially to the disputants. They would take her, in rotation, for six months at a time . . . the disunited couple had at last grounds for expecting a time of high activity. They girded their loins, they felt as if the quarrel had only begun. They felt indeed more married than ever, inasmuch as what marriage had mainly suggested to them was the unbroken opportunity to quarrel. There had been 'sides' before, and there were sides as much as ever; for the sider too the prospect opened out. . . The many friends of the Faranges drew together to differ about them; contradiction grew young again over teacups and cigars. (p. 17—19).

Maisie's mother is a champion billiard-player. Three balls: two white and one red. Ida has Sir Claude; Beale, Miss Overmore: the two white balls. Maisie is the red ball which everyone uses. 'The player will not obtain an accurate aim until he has learned to keep his eye upon the object ball, and not upon the ball he is striking, especially at the actual moment of the stroke. This is a *sine qua non* of good billiards.'[5] One can certainly see why Ida has 'so often beaten her ex-husband at billiards'. Out with the Captain in Hyde Park Ida meets her husband, Sir Claude, arm-in-arm with Maisie; she confronts Sir Claude head-on, but to hit him hard she offers a sort of side-play with Maisie: 'The next moment [Maisie] was on her mother's breast . . . only to be as suddenly ejected with a push and the brisk injunction: "Now go to the Captain!" . . .Maisie started, moved backward and, looking at Sir Claude, "Only for a moment," she signed to him in her bewilderment. But he was too angry to heed her – too angry with his wife' (pp. 107—8). By the end of the novel Mrs Beale has acquired some of Ida's expertise, and Maisie finds herself once more the most important ball in the game, but not the centre of attention. Mrs Beale has mastered the art of pull and push: '. . . a push at last uncontestably maternal' (p. 210). 'She threw herself upon the child and, before Maisie could resist, had sunk with her upon the sofa, possessed of her, encircling her . . .[then] Maisie's back became aware of a push that vented resentment . . .' (p. 243). Used once more in the confrontation with Sir Claude, Maisie is again pushed aside, this time to go off with Mrs Wix as, long ago, she was pushed off to the Captain by Ida, walking with her lover in Hyde Park when she was supposed to be playing a billiards match in Brussels. In the beginning Maisie 'was divided in two'; in the end 'the child stood there again dropped and divided': the law provides the rules of the game:

> She was still, as a result of so many parents, a daughter to somebody even after papa and mamma were to all intents dead. If her father's wife and her mother's husband, by the operation of a natural or, for all she knew, a legal rule, were in the shoes of their defunct partners, then Mrs Beale's partner was as exactly as defunct as Sir Claude's and her shoes the very pair to which in 'Farange v. Farange and Others', the divorce-court had given priority (p. 208).

Billiards is a sophisticated game from the point of view of the ball, and James adds an ironic twist: the ball escapes, the winner is defeated:

> 'Yes, my dear, I haven't given you up,' Sir Claude said to Mrs Beale at last, 'and if you'd like me to treat our friends here as solemn witnesses I don't mind giving you my word for it that I never will. There!' he dauntlessly exclaimed . . . Mrs Beale, *erect and alive in her defeat*, jerked her handsome face about. . . (pp. 247—8, my italics).

The sets of people in the novel all use Maisie as their 'ball', but they do this in different ways. Ida and Beale use her to toss from one to another, first as a useful missile then as an undetonated bomb that will hopefully go off in the other's court. Mrs Beale reifies her into a precious ball of love, her 'love' for Maisie's fathers, first Beale then Sir Claude: 'Mrs Beale fairly swooped upon her, and the effect of the whole hour was to show the child how much, how quite formidably indeed, after all, she was loved' (p. 93). For Mrs Wix she is an extension of herself, to be held onto through thick and thin, a replacement for the dead child, Clara Matilda, lost in a careless throw (she was crushed beneath a hansom cab in the Edgware Road). Maisie is caught up in a game which is confusingly the same game, and in which the moves – constant acts of possession – seem the same and yet are different. For they all *are* acts of possession. Even Ida and Beale, though eventually they 'drop' her and plan to go off, never in fact leave – they are just explicitly tired of the game: '[Beale's] was the mildness of general indifference [to Ida]'. Their 'death' has the disturbing *presence* to it that also appertains to the 'reincarnated' (in Maisie) Clara Matilda, 'who was in heaven and yet, embarrassingly, also in Kensal Green, where they had been together to see her little huddled grave' (p. 32). James turns on its head the notion that divorce and adultery are in any sense 'desertion' of anyone. Perhaps Maisie's main deprivation as a child is that no one will leave her[6] and thus she has no conception of death until at the end when Sir Claude fails to turn up at the time expected, and James writes: 'She was yet to learn what it could be to recognize in some lapse of a sequence the proof of an extinction, and therefore remained unaware that this momentary pang was a foretaste of the experience of death' (p. 20).

Maisie is confused about the nature of her centrality. Is the ball the victim of the game? Or is it by its very presence the cause of the game? 'She puzzled out with imperfect signs, but with a prodigious spirit, that she had been a centre of hatred and a messenger of insult, and that everything was bad because she had been employed to make it so' (p. 25); '. . . the struggle she appeared to have come into the world to produce' (p. 25). Where does Maisie's responsibility lie? Certainly the presence of the ball *enables* the game to continue. It turns out that Maisie is not responsible where she seems to produce destruction but, alarmingly, she is responsible where apparently she introduces harmony. Her delighted refrain throughout the middle sections of the book is that she brought Mrs Beale and Sir Claude together. The irony is that harmony is chaos, and Maisie *does* divide her parents, not from each other but from their new spouses. This is the responsibility she must face, for creating for herself new parents against her old parents, not in their parental role but in their new marital roles:

> Your mother adored [Sir Claude] at first – it might have lasted. But he began too soon with Mrs Beale. As you say . . . you brought them together (pp. 216—17).

> 'Then my father [Sir Claude] and my mother [Mrs Beale] – !' But she had already faltered and Mrs Wix had already glared back: 'Ought to live together? Don't begin it *again!*' She turned away with a groan, to reach the washing-stand, and Maisie could by this time recognize with a certain ease that that way verily madness did lie (p. 205).

These new 'parents' she must separate if the game is to end, and sanity to triumph over madness. Failing, she leaves them to their own mad world,[7] to face themselves without her, without an excuse, without a daughter.

This is one way in which Maisie learns to decipher her role in the game, and to play it and lose it. There are others, less strategic.

A game seems to demand two or more in opposition. Opposition, polarities. The sides must be opposite each other in order to be sides. But of course they are both 'sides' and in this are disturbingly alike. At moments of intensity, Maisie instinctively glimpses that the divided world is unified. Try as they might to be opposite one another, the contestants are, after all, all contestants. Maisie has a child's knowledge of the congruity of the incongruous; she turns opposition into paradox and finally resolves it by her own *dialectical* act. The child's instincts are the metaphysical artist's formulations:

> . . . her stepmother, so changed – in the very manner of her mother. . . (p. 93).

> The Captain wasn't a bit like [Sir Claude] . . . it finally made our young lady, to classify him further, say to herself that, of all the people in the world, he reminded her most insidiously of Mrs

Wix. He had neither straighteners nor diadem . . . he was sunburnt and deep-voiced and smelt of cigars, yet he marvellously had more in common with her old governess than with her young stepfather (p. 109).

[Beale] gave a small laugh that in the oddest way in the world reminded her of the unique sounds she had heard emitted by Mrs Wix (p. 137).

The Countess stood smiling . . . Maisie felt herself reminded of another smile, which was not ugly . . . the kind light thrown, that day in the Park, from the clean fair face of the Captain (p. 139).

and most importantly of all:

After [Ida] had disappeared Maisie dropped upon the bench again and for some time, in the empty garden and the deeper dusk, sat and stared at the image her flight had still left standing. It had ceased to be her mother only, in the strangest way, that it might become her father, the father of whose wish that she were dead the announcement still lingered in the air. It was a presence with vague edges – it continued to front her, to cover her (p. 160).

While grasping the similarity of the opposing sides, Maisie also tries to comprehend her position in their game. In a beautifully rendered episode, Maisie turns her doll Lisette into herself: 'Was she not herself convulsed by such innocence' as Lisette shows? Of course she finds that she herself becomes her mother: 'She mimicked her mother's sharpness, but she was rather ashamed afterwards, though as to whether of the sharpness or of the mimicry was not quite clear' (p. 37). In this way Maisie learns that she does not want to become like the disputants: she is explicitly scared of being a 'low sneak', which is what her mother calls her father and her father calls her mother.

This method, by which Maisie alternates participants in the game and herself assumes other's roles and projects her own onto another, is a fundamental means of her 'knowledge' which is, after all, as much as anything else, knowledge of the game. But it is, in comparison with another dimension of the struggle for knowledge, elementary. James's description of

Maisie's initiation at the deepest level is profoundly bound up with his method for the whole novel, her progress so much its progress, her art his art.

Maisie's progress is from the 'unseen' centre to the 'seen' and 'seeing' observer. Her move is possible because she comes to see the game in which she is caught up. Her final knowledge is the knowledge of the expert's rejection of the game. But before she gets outside it she has to get fully into it. It is here, in tracing her development, that James's prime images achieve their deep association: the dramatic method of the novel, the drama of the story, the acting of a play, the playing of games, make-believe, the watching of the play, the looking at a picture, the spectacle, the magic-lantern, shadows, the person and his shadow, the inner and the outer self, reflections, the mirror, through the looking-glass, the meeting point of spectator and actor, playing the game, watching the play, writing the play. One could rearrange some of these points (some are parallels), but the chain is the chain of Maisie's life and the chain is the chain of the novel. Glass and shadows are the nodal point; the mirror-image – just look at the story – is crucial.

Maisie, though the centre, is also always outside. At the beginning of the novel this position is forced on her. She is the wrong side of the door:

> She had grown up among things as to which her foremost knowledge was that she was never to ask about them. . . Everything had something behind it: life was like a long, long corridor with rows of closed doors (p. 36).

She can manœuvre her way in the dark passages: 'She had even had in the past a small smug conviction that in the domestic labyrinth she always kept the clue.' But gradually the doors change to glass, become windows, in fact. For safety's sake she still must feel she is a spectator:

> . . . the sharpened sense of spectatorship . . . gave her often an odd air of being present at her history in as separate a manner as if she could only get at experience by flattening her nose against a pane of glass (p. 83).

She was to feel henceforth as if she were flattening her nose upon the hard window-pane of the sweetshop of knowledge (p. 102).

She becomes the window, the window as mirror: '[Ida] postured to her utmost before the last little triangle of cracked glass to which so many fractures had reduced the polished plate of filial superstition' (p. 155); then a two-way mirror, and the glass dissolves. What is the difference between the self and the reflection; between the self and others?

> Then she saw the straighteners all blurred with tears which after a little seemed to have sprung from her own eyes. There were tears in fact on both sides of the spectacles. . . (p. 199).

> [Maisie was] so conscious of being more frightened than she had ever been in her life that she seemed to see her whiteness as in glass. Then she knew that what she saw was Sir Claude's whiteness: he was as frightened as herself (p. 236).

Maisie has spent her childhood being a mirror for others, but the reactions she gets have a terrifying arbitrariness, particularly in the case of her mother. Ida does not reflect her child, which as a 'good' mother she would have done. This is a major deprivation and when it happens, 'the baby gets settled in to the idea that when he or she looks, what is seen is the mother's face. The mother's face is not then a mirror. So perception takes the place of apperception, takes the place of that which might have been the beginning of a significant exchange with the world, a two-way process in which self-enrichment alternates with the discovery of meaning in the world of seen things.'[8] Winnicott's terms certainly coincide with James's – Maisie is, above all, precociously perceptive – the mother was not the mirror she should have been. James claimed that Maisie 'by the play of her good faith' made her mother 'concrete, immense and awful',[9] and Maisie compares her mother to a wild elephant, says her movements are violent like the shutters that fall in front of a shop window. This is indeed the *perceived* mother, the mother as Other and eternally separate.

But Maisie's final relationship with Mrs Wix and with Sir

Claude (the identical tears, the identical fears) reveals in its shared emotion a new 'symbiosis', a oneness characteristic of the newborn baby and its mother, from which an authentic identity can originate. Suddenly acquiring, at thirteen, the symbiotic security that should have been her birthright, Maisie can dispense with it and launch herself into an assertion of self, an understanding of others. Thought-reflection not echo-reflection:

> (Mrs Wix) 'I adore him. I adore him.' Maisie took it well in; so well that in a moment more she would have answered profoundly: 'So do I.' But before that moment passed something took place that brought other words to her lips; nothing more, very possibly, than the closer consciousness in her hand of the significance of Mrs Wix's. Their hands remained linked in unutterable sign of their union, and what Maisie at last said was simply and serenely: 'Oh I know!' (p. 200).

Only from the centre of the game can one get out; it is only unity that one can disrupt, only the heart of a person that one can leave. This finding of the self in others, this taking of the self from others, this is the heart of the matter:

> Now in truth she felt the coldness of her terror, and it seemed to her suddenly she knew, as she knew it about Sir Claude, what she was afraid of. She was afraid of herself (p.232).

> She went about as sightlessly as if he had been leading her blindfold. If they were afraid of themselves it was themselves they would find at the inn (p.234).

At last this watcher of men is sightless: in the moment of vision all is invisible.

Most of the time even words like 'seeing' are used only synecdochally for total sensory and extra-sensory perception. Maisie is alive to the entire kinesics of a person:

> [Beale] clasped her in his arms a moment and rubbed his beard against her cheek. Then she understood as well as if he had spoken it that what he wanted, hang it, was that she should let him off with all the honours (p. 135).

There were things Ida said that she perhaps didn't hear, and there were things she heard that Ida perhaps didn't say (p. 156).

Silence is the language of understanding. It is also a place of retreat from the game, a game in which words are always hurled, a conversation-piece in which Maisie has a major part but few lines:

> Maisie felt the weight of the question; it kept her silent for a space during which she looked at Sir Claude. . .
> 'Nothing,' she returned at last.
> He showed incredulity. 'Nothing?'
> 'Nothing,' Maisie repeated. . . (p. 224)

Maisie has as good a reason as Cordelia for her obstinate silence. Silence is not only the medium in which understanding occurs, it is its precondition – to wait and listen is as essential as to watch: 'She would forget everything, she would repeat nothing. . . She spoiled their fun, but she practically added to her own. She saw more and more; she saw too much' (p. 25). Maisie's technique of stupidity, her refusal actively to participate, comfortably isolates her from the game: 'Her very silence became after this one of the largest elements of Maisie's consciousness; it proved a warm and habitable air, into which the child penetrated farther than she dared ever mention to her companions' (p. 42). This area of silence in a world of talk is a safe but lonely place: 'She had a new feeling, the feeling of danger; on which a new remedy rose to meet it, the idea of an inner self or, in other words, of concealment' (p. 25). An 'inner self' is, in a sense, a false self if we see 'self' as experience, and James, although he tells us that for Maisie concealment is not deception, betrays, by his reiterated use of the term, his own fears that it is. The 'self' that Maisie attains at the end is the assertive, active self in which 'inner' and 'outer' selves are seen to be just her equivalent polarities to those polarities which were the 'siders' in the game. Like the 'opponents', they are merged in her new knowledge.

At the end, Maisie finds her 'discretion' 'shabby'. She starts to ask the taboo questions, both on her own behalf and on behalf of Sir Claude. She also makes her demands: 'She had never yet in her life made any claim for herself, but she hoped that this time, frankly, what she was doing would somehow be counted to her'. 'What helped the child was that she knew what she wanted. All her learning and learning had made her at last learn that' (p. 180). What she wants is Sir Claude, what she gets is Mrs Wix. Why?

Maisie, like everyone else, is enchanted by the fair, young Sir Claude. Among a group of extraordinarily handsome people, he is someone always to be looked at. He is the 'Prince' of the fantasies Mrs Wix relates to Maisie. But all that glitters is not true, and in an inoffensive way Sir Claude lies, evades and 'funks' it. 'His 'princely' qualities show a tarnish in their irresponsible extravagance that Maisie learns to recognise, but that she also learns to love. The most interesting thing about Sir Claude is that his position is strangely analogous to Maisie's own. Like her he is possessed rather than possessing; he plays a part in the game, but it is a reluctant one – he is always trying to 'get out' of it.

Sir Claude and Maisie have a real companionship. He shows not 'a deceitful descent to her years [but] a real indifference to them'. A delicate homosexuality is established as he calls her 'dear boy', 'chap', 'old man'. Hand-in-hand they share a terrible fear of women. Neither is scared of Beale or his associates, but both are terrified of Ida and Mrs Beale, and theirs. Sir Claude is quite explicit about the cause of his fear:

> 'Why, then, did you marry her?'
> 'Just because I *was* afraid.'
> 'Even when she loved you?'
> 'That made her the more alarming. . . Fear, unfortunately, is a very big thing, and there's a great variety of kinds.'
> She took this in with complete intelligence. 'Then I think I've got them all. . . I'm awfully afraid of Mrs Beale.' . . .
> 'I *am* in the same state.'
> 'Oh but she likes you so!' Maisie promptly pleaded.
> Sir Claude literally coloured.'That has something to do with it.'
> Maisie wondered again. 'Being liked with being afraid?' (p. 88).

He is not afraid of Maisie because her love is not possessive, and she is too young to class as a 'woman'. He flirts but he shies away from the adoration he consequently receives.

Apart from his obvious methods of evasion, he has one means of escape that again makes him an interesting parallel to Maisie. He has the child's relationship to reality through fantasy. Treated by others as a 'Fairy Prince', he decides to act the part and refashion the world accordingly. Hyde Park and his adulterous wife are to him the Forest of Arden and fair Rosalind, until Maisie insists on the facts. He 'plays' with Maisie: '. . . if he was to have the credit of perverting the innocent child he might also at least have the amusement'. Poverty-stricken, he cannot give up his luxuries any more than he can give up 'the women'; benign humour covers the dire choices of life, or the dire failure to make choices:

> His fear at all events was there; his fear was sweet to her, beautiful and tender to her, was having coffee and buttered rolls and talk and laughter that were no talk and laughter at all with her; his fear was in his jesting postponing perverting voice; it was just in this make-believe way he had brought her out to imitate the old London playtimes, to imitate indeed a relation that had wholly changed. . . (pp. 223—4).

Sir Claude is in no sense 'childish', but his role is definitely that of a child to a series of grabbing 'mothers'. James uses the same term of him as he uses of the children in *The Turn of the Screw* – 'plastic' – 'poor plastic and dependent male'.

Most interestingly, from my point of view, Sir Claude's relation to the glass-mirror-spectacle image series bears analogies with Maisie's own. He is introduced as a photograph haggled over (as he is, again, at the end) by Maisie, Mrs Wix and Mrs Beale. Maisie gets the photograph and she keeps hold of this perspective of him. He is always 'showman of the spectacle'; he is 'like the single, the sovereign window-square of a great dim disproportioned room'. He is her light in the world and on the world, the lens of the magic lantern, and will take her on his travels. He is an object to be looked at, but also an object to look through. More importantly, in him can she occasionally see herself:

> . . . 'All the same, if you hadn't had the fatal gift of beauty – !'
> 'Well, what?' Maisie asked, wondering why he paused.
> It was the first time she had heard of her beauty (p. 98).

Because he offers her a mirror, it is with him that she can identify herself, and find herself, at the end. Sir Claude is the childhood companion whom Maisie outgrows and whom she wants to save and comfort. Sir Claude can only be happy in her release. Maisie gets free of the game in the way that Sir Claude cannot. The refrain 'you're free' echoes throughout the book. To Ida, Beale and Mrs Beale it means they are released from a marital contract only, ironically, to re-endorse the terms of their captivity. A chaos of 'freedoms' litters the last chapters: to Sir Claude 'to be free' means to escape:

> 'Let her go!' Sir Claude more intensely repeated.
> He was looking at Mrs Beale and there was something in his voice. Maisie knew from a loosening of arms that she had become conscious of what it was; she slowly rose from the sofa, and the child stood there again dropped and divided.
> 'You're free – you're free,' Sir Claude went on. . . (p. 243).

For Mrs Wix 'freedom' is immorality:

> 'Why not, if now she's free?'
> 'Free? Are you imitating *him*? Well, if Sir Claude's old enough to know better, upon my word I think it's right to treat you as if you also were. . .'
> . . . Maisie could guess that she herself had never appeared so wanton. . . Her wantonness meanwhile continued to work upon her friend, who caught again, on the rebound, the sound of deepest provocation.
> 'Free, free, free? If she's as free as *you* are, my dear, she's free enough, to be sure!' (p. 189).

I find the majority of critical reactions to Mrs Wix staggering: to Gale she is 'a homely, good woman', to Edmund Wilson 'the ridiculous old governess', and to Andreas she is, unlike Sir Claude or Mrs Beale, 'complete'. Leavis rebukes

Bewley for his derogation of her with the statement that if she is ugly she is very respectable – she only adores Sir Claude in the sexless way that Maisie does; she is also kind, muddled and conventional and thus will always be so – 'and perhaps – may we not reflect? – it is as well that Maisie, after a childhood that has provided us with James's comedy, should enter adolescence under that kind of respectable tutelage.'[10] This is nonsense. Mrs Wix is quite simply one of James's nastiest characterisations. That she is pathetic in no way detracts from this. It is partly a question of tone: 'She had had a little girl quite of her own, and the little girl had been killed on the spot. She had had absolutely nothing else in all the world, and her affliction had broken her heart. It was comfortably established between them that Mrs Wix's heart was broken' (p. 30); 'Everyone knew the straighteners; everyone knew the diadem and the button, the scallops and satin bands; everyone, though Maisie had never betrayed her, knew even Clara Matilda' (p. 32). There is no gap between James and the mean-minded 'everyone'. This is really dirty writing. When James is explicit he is less nasty, but no less damning: 'the old-fashioned conscience, the dingy decencies, of Maisie's simple instructress' (p. 62); 'She seemed to sit in her new dress and brood over her lost delicacy, which had become almost as doleful a memory as that of poor Clara Matilda' (p. 76). When she tells Sir Claude of Ida's lover it is an 'ugly honesty' – ugly is syntactically ambiguous. One of the high peaks of what Leavis has called her sexless adoration of Sir Claude is surpassingly unpleasant. Sir Claude has just asked why she is so pleased he is 'free':

> Mrs Wix met this challenge first with silence, then with a demonstration the most extraordinary, the most unexpected. Maisie could scarcely believe her eyes as she saw the good lady, with whom she had associated no faintest shade of any art of provocation, actually, after an upward grimace, gave Sir Claude a great giggling insinuating naughty slap. 'You wretch – you *know* why!' And she turned away (p. 179).

Mrs Wix is the ultra-possessive mother and Maisie's

awareness of this is expressed in extravagant metaphors. When she is first separated from her she feels as if she has been 'embedded in Mrs Wix's nature as her tooth had been socketed in her gum'. Mrs Wix penetrates into Maisie's most remote silence, even in her absence. 'Somewhere in the depths of it the dim straighteners were fixed upon her; somewhere out of the troubled little current Mrs Wix intensely waited' (p. 42). Clara Matilda is turned into Maisie's sister with whom Maisie feels as involved as does the child in Wordsworth's 'We are Seven'. Even Sir Claude plays with the notion of Mrs Wix as his mother: 'I don't love *her* . . . she's not my daughter – come, old chap! She's not even my mother, though I daresay it would have been better for me if she had been . . .' (p. 228). The end of the novel is predictable in her first introduction: 'Mrs Wix took her and, Maisie felt the next day, would never let her go'. But if Mrs Wix is possessive, and others are not so much an extension of self as a filling-up of the self, [11] she also requires to be possessed: for example, at one stage she says to Sir Claude:

> You stay here with Maisie, with the carriage and the larks and the luxury; then I'll return to you and we'll go off together – we'll live together without a cloud. Take me, take me (p. 183).

The cry of the desperate virgin. Virgin Mother? '[Mr Wix] had been remarkably absent from his wife's career, and Maisie was never taken to see his grave' (p. 33). This aspect of Mrs Wix prefigures a series of images and notions which James suddenly employs late in the novel. In Boulogne, the long colloquies and the intensest moments that Mrs Wix and Maisie experience take place whilst they are awaiting Sir Claude in a square dominated by a view of a huge gilt Virgin Mary. This symbol is repeated: it picks up previous references to Mrs Wix as a 'prophetess' and 'ardent priestess' to '[her] deep, narrow passion', and it looks forward to her own 'confession' to Maisie that she had 'probably made a fatal mistake early in life in not being a Catholic' – a gaudy religiosity which in its turn connects up with her 'moral sense' and with her romantic fantasies.

When Sir Claude evades through 'make-believe', Mrs Wix compensates for ugliness and poverty by romance. Both make-believe and romantic tales have an appeal to a young child – Mrs Wix makes for Maisie a version of life wondrous 'beyond magic or monsters'. She *is* a good companion for a child in a sense, just as in a sense she is, with her possessiveness, a good mother; despite her 'ugliness and her poverty; she was peculiarly and soothingly safe; safer than anyone in the world' (p. 32). Of course James ironises even this safety – she is as 'safe' as the dead Clara Matilda: she is a permanent feature of the landscape, taken care of, impersonalised; as Maisie comes to say, 'Oh, you're nobody'.

Mrs Wix is also safe because she is firmly part of the world (her fantasising confirms, not denies, this). She has 'sidled and ducked through life' and knows the game. Indeed she teaches it to Maisie:

> There were hours when Mrs Wix sighingly testified to the scruples she surmounted, seemed to ask what other line one *could* take with a young person whose experience had been, as it were, so peculiar. 'It isn't as if you didn't already know everything, is it, love?' and 'I can't make you any worse than you *are*, can I, darling?' (p. 62).

A large aspect of her romantic story-telling about the 'princely' Sir Claude is clearly salacious gossip, as pathetic as that of an aspirant's to a part in this play must be. (Anyone can win her over to their side by kindness.) She initiates Maisie into what she calls a 'moral sense', and this consists precisely in making her understand all the most immoral details of the adults' relationships. In a sequence rich in innuendo, in the middle of Chapter 26, just after Maisie has realised that she must know 'Everything', Mrs Wix completes her enlightenment. The episode runs over two pages and is too long to quote, but a few selections should make the nature of Mrs Wix's action beyond dispute:

> . . . she was visibly at a loss how to make up to such a victim for such contaminations: appealing, as to what she had done and was

doing, in bewilderment, in explanation, in supplication, for reassurance, for pardon and even outright for pity.

'I don't know what I've said to you, my own: I don't know what I'm saying or what the turn you've given my life has rendered me, heaven forgive me, capable of saying. Have I lost all delicacy, all decency, all measure of how far and how bad? . . . What I did lose patience at this morning was at how it was that without your seeming to condemn – for you didn't, you remember! – you yet did seem to *know*. Thank God, in his mercy, at last, *if* you do!' (pp. 195—6).

Maisie tries to put on this 'moral sense' which should go with knowledge of the game. She responds to Mrs Wix's prescription.

(Mrs Wix) 'Has it never occurred to you to be jealous of [Mrs Beale]?'
It never had in the least. . . .
(Maisie) 'If I thought she was unkind to him – I don't know *what* I should do!'
Mrs Wix dropped one of her squints; she even confirmed it by a wild grunt. 'I know what *I* should!'
Maisie at this felt that she lagged. 'Well, I can think of *one* thing.'
Mrs Wix more directly challenged her. 'What is it, then?'
Maisie met her expression as if it were a game with forfeits for winking. 'I'd *kill* her!' That at least, she hoped . . . would guarantee her moral sense (p. 199).

'Why shouldn't I? *You've* come out. Mrs Beale has come out. We each have our turn!' And Maisie threw off the most extraordinary little laugh that had ever passed her young lips (p. 212).

Maisie, of course, tries her hand and gives it up; the tears that she finally sheds lie too deep for a 'moral sense': her knowledge is pure, her freedom complete. 'Mrs Wix spoke not only as if Maisie were not a woman, but as if she would never be one' (p. 216). As far as the women of the novel are concerned, she never will be one of them.

Critical reactions that make Mrs Wix a latter-day Juliet's nurse or a Mrs Micawber (though marginally preferable to those which see her as an 'old dear'), fall far short of the point.

But the point is, of course, a confusing one. It is not only that James evokes sympathy from the reader for Mrs Wix, though this indeed he does: 'Even to the hard heart of childhood there was something tragic in such elation at such humanities' (p. 61). It is also that she *is* his viewpoint. She acts to desperation a role that places herself as object – 'The straighteners, she explained to Maisie, were put on for the sake of others, whom, as she believed, they helped to recognise the bearing, otherwise doubtful, of her regard' (p. 31); but she is also, as gossip, commentator and translator, a window on the world. This wished-for 'looked at' and in fact 'looked with' perspective is an ironic parody on the parallelism of her and Sir Claude, of her and Maisie. It is also a fundamental aspect of James's art.

> The formula from the frump at the end of V *facilitates* my making the child witness the phenomenon in question – prepares the mirror, the plate, on which it is represented as reflected.[12]

Mrs Wix wears glasses to be seen, to see through and as a screen on which the world is reflected, for Maisie and for the readers. If one perspective is innocent (Maisie) and one pornographic (Mrs Wix), what does this make of the novel?

Maisie doesn't give us an innocent view and Mrs Wix a corrupt one: nothing so simple. The wide-eyed guileless child can be a literary 'peeping-Tom' device. When the relationship is growing up between Beale and Miss Overmore we are looking at them and Maisie from the position of a passer-by staring into their carriage; but our viewpoint is also from Maisie, who is seeing the scene in which she is involved reflected in the stare of a passer-by; and then there is James's own window on the scene. This three-way mirror system deeply corrupts the very language of innocence:

> 'Did papa like you just the same while I was gone?' she inquired – full of the sense of how markedly his favour had been established in her absence. . . Papa, on whose knee she sat, burst into one of those loud laughs of his. . . 'Why, you little donkey, when you're

away what have I left to do but just to love her?' Miss Overmore hereupon immediately took her from him, and they had a merry little scrimmage over her of which Maisie caught the surprised perception in the white stare of an old lady who passed in a victoria (p. 35).

Alternatively, in the scene where Mrs Wix fully enlightens Maisie, James shows us only her hysterical feelings about doing so. He doesn't tell us what she tells her: that 'corrupt' knowledge is assumed on behalf of the reader. As Maisie learns, we have to admit that we already know – but what do we know, or rather what *is* there to know? Because James gives us Mrs Wix's horrid horror of it, it assumes those grand proportions of mystery that James felt were the essence of life, and that he was always wanting to portray. Doubtless the Lady of Shalott found Sir Bedivere mysterious as well as handsome; if you look through too many windows and at too many mirrors, or through a telescope, or through corrective glasses, then a clear sense of obscurity is inevitable. Maisie learns, and *What Maisie Knew* is about this lucid vision of obscurity. The mirrors complicate but the vision of multiple reflections is knowledge. But knowledge is also Mrs Wix's gossip. Pornography and vision co-exist – they use the same means. First as the child Maisie, then as the man, Henry James looks through a glass dimly in order that the reflection should be 'sharp' and 'quiet'. Too much light darkens the mind.

Moll Flanders:
The Rise of
Capitalist Woman

¶Almost a decade separates this essay on *Moll Flanders* from the previous literary writings. I was invited, as a feminist I believe, rather than as a literary critic, to edit and introduce a new Penguin edition of Defoe's novel. One critic bylined his review of the edition 'Marxist Moll'. If so, this was due not only to my own Marxist thinking, but (probably more importantly) to the fact that I found E. P. Thompson and Christopher Hill the most interesting writers on the period. In fact, many aspects of *Moll Flanders* fascinated me – least of all its questionable literariness or readability.

As with *Wuthering Heights*, no one notices that it is an 'historical' novel – Defoe and Brontë (two completely different novelists) situate their novels some decades before they are written. Thus they both fit in with my interest in the English novel as developing around a notion of the creation of the self/the character in time.

There is no psychological dimension to Defoe's portrait of Moll but the way he places her in the conditions he depicts offers the possibility whereby such insights could develop. As I emphasise in the essay, here, in this very early novel (1722), we start with childhood. For this collection I have subtitled the essay: 'The Rise of Capitalist Woman'. I find an homology in Defoe's sense of his heroine as a person who grows up and his conception of his society as in the process of development. The English Revolution, to all intents and purposes, was no revolution but a long, prolonged evolution.

(All references to *Moll Flanders* are to the Penguin English Library edition, Harmondsworth, 1978. This text uses the first edition of the novel, set in type in 1721 and published in January 1722.)

Most people have heard of the story of Moll Flanders, even if they have not actually read the novel. Not quite so famous as *Robinson Crusoe*, *Moll Flanders* nevertheless has something of the same mythical status. Probably it is most popularly thought of as a tale of thievery and prostitution, of crime, punishment and worldly success: a lively account of an attractive, independent and wicked woman who eventually makes good – both morally and economically. In fact, *Moll Flanders* is throughout as much about financial investment as about theft, as much about marriage as about prostitution.

In essence, the novel is a vivid dramatisation of the conflicts and confusions over values that took place in one of the most interesting periods of English history – a period of turmoil during the establishment of the moral and legal basis of modern capitalist society. I shall argue that Defoe's novel endures as a profound consideration of the creation of social values and of the relationship of the individual to society.

Published in 1722, *Moll Flanders* was written by an active journalist, a keen observer of the dominant activities of his day. Defoe started his journalistic career at the time of King William as an ardent advocate for the Whigs (broadly speaking the party of change in this period), but became a Tory (broadly speaking a representative of traditional values) under Queen Anne. Brought up a Presbyterian and throughout his life a convinced dissenter, he wrote widely about the politics, practice and spiritual meaning of religion. He ran his own magazine, *The Review*, in which he debated and discussed such issues as marital problems, elections, stock-jobbing, bankruptcy, bribery, atheism, free-thinking, astrology, thieves, pick-pockets, comets, indecent literature, education, dreams and apparitions, sea-monsters, quack doctors, the rights of women and journalism itself.

Defoe, however, was not merely an observer but also a tradesman and speculator; he was steeped in the practical issues of his day. Some of his enterprises brought him bankruptcy and imprisonment – precisely the kind of experience we see reflected in *Moll Flanders*.

Moll, his central character, narrates her own history. In his preface and his synopsis Defoe claims he has only polished her style and refined some of her tales, otherwise it is written entirely 'from her own Memorandums'. Moll plausibly cannot recall anything before her third year – and her third year, only vaguely. She knows, however, that she was born in Newgate Prison to a woman convicted of petty theft who first escaped hanging by 'pleading her belly' and then had her sentence commuted to transportation, leaving Moll alone in the world at the age of six months. After a brief spell with a gypsy tribe, Moll escaped or was abandoned in Colchester at the age of three. Accepted into care by the parish, she was farmed out to a woman who, though she had seen better days, now earned a living by providing for parish orphans until they were old enough to work – in Moll's case at the age of eight. At eight, Moll begs to be allowed to continue living with her adopted 'mother' instead of going into service and this she does until the woman dies leaving Moll a destitute adolescent. But a lady, a member of the local gentry, who had previously taken an interest in her, accepts her as companion to her two daughters. In this house, Moll is first seduced by the elder son and then asked in marriage by the younger one. There is a crisis both because of Moll's secret but very serious attachment to her seducer and because of the family's opposition to a son marrying so far beneath himself socially. Yet Moll and the younger son, Robin, are finally married and live together with their two children for a few years until his death.

Moll is left a young, attractive widow on the look-out for a husband, whom she soon finds. Her new husband – a gentleman-tradesman – turns out a gentleman-rake, spends all her money, is declared bankrupt and to escape arrest flees the country leaving Moll only those few possessions which he had had time to pawn. So as not herself to be charged with the possession of these items, Moll changes her name – to Mrs Flanders – and goes to live in the Mint, a place that because of the royal prerogative acted as a sanctuary for those otherwise liable to prosecution for financial offences. But Moll cannot stand the wicked hypocritical company there and so she goes to live temporarily with a widow who was once in a similar position to herself.

The two women help each other to get new husbands and both seem to do very well for themselves. Moll accompanies her third husband to live on his plantations in Virginia but there, to her utter horror, she discovers that her husband's mother is, in fact, her own mother who had worked out her convict service and married into the Virginian settler community. After a period of great anguish for all of them, Moll insists on leaving her husband/brother and returns to England.

Again on the look-out for a husband, Moll, against her intentions but following her sexual inclination, becomes mistress to a married gentleman whom she meets while she is living in Bath. She is well maintained by him and bears him a son, but after a near fatal illness, he repents of his immoral living and decides to leave her. He takes care of their son and gives Moll a small amount of money. This money Moll places in the private trust of a banker who is wretchedly married to an unfaithful wife and who offers to marry Moll when he has obtained a divorce. Moll says she will consider it only when he is actually free and meanwhile goes to live in Lancashire with a woman she had met earlier.

This woman believes that Moll has a fortune and introduces her to someone whom she claims is her very wealthy brother. Each certain the other is rich, Moll and this man, Jemmy, marry, only to discover their mutual mistake. Jemmy, Moll discovers, is an impoverished gentleman turned highway robber and his 'sister' was an ex-mistress and member of the gang who had promised to find him a wife with a fortune. Though Moll and Jemmy reveal their passionate love for each other, Jemmy decides that their economic circumstances being what they are, they must separate while he sees if he can settle prosperously in Ireland. Meanwhile he absolves Moll from her marriage bonds. Marriage, as we can see from the story as a whole, was a relatively loose contractual arrangement at this period.

Back in London, Moll, who now plans to marry her divorced banker friend, discovers she is pregnant by Jemmy, her 'Lancashire' husband. She has the child at the house of a midwife, a well-disposed woman who becomes Moll's confidante and is later – because her profession is not entirely above-board – known as 'Mother Midnight'. Mother Midnight helps Moll to have her child taken off her hands by a country couple, thus freeing her to marry her banker without his having any suspicions of the marriage she has contracted since he first proposed to her. On their wedding day, to her shock and unbeknownst to either man, Moll sees Jemmy, who is not in Ireland but is being pursued after staging a hold-up.

Moll and the banker live quietly and contentedly for five years until his investments suddenly fail and he dies from the grief of it, leaving Moll destitute and desperate.

More wretched than she has ever been, Moll starts to steal to survive. Gradually she becomes skilled at it but she needs some way to get rid of the things she takes. She finds that her old confidante Mother Midnight has become a pawnbroker and she goes to live with her, planning to earn her living honestly by taking in sewing. But Mother Midnight is a receiver of stolen goods as well as a pawnbroker and Moll gets tempted back into a life of stealing. Defoe spends much time detailing the talents that Moll employs as a thief. She becomes part of a loose fraternity/sorority of thieves, but prefers to work alone as if her colleagues are caught they can save themselves from hanging if they can convict another person. During this period, Moll also earns some money by seducing a drunken gentleman who later, in his sobriety, cannot find it in himself to desist from his sexual relationship with her, despite his intentions. She is also successful at gambling but does not try her luck beyond the first time as she knows it would be a fatal addiction. By now a famous thief, Moll moves with the market – working away from London in the season when the gentry are out of town. Eventually she is caught stealing from a mercer's warehouse by two women and sent to Newgate – the nightmare fate that has haunted her – to end where she began.

In his vivid picture of Newgate, Defoe as author merges (as he does elsewhere) with Moll as narrator. Defoe's eloquent general reflections are indistinguishable from his character, Moll's, own loathing and horror:

> . . . like the waters in the cavities and hollows of mountains, which petrify and turn into stone whatever they are suffered to drop upon, so the continual conversing with such a crew of hell-hounds as I was, had the same common operation upon me as upon other people. I degenerated into stone; I turned first stupid and senseless, and then brutish and thoughtless, and at last raving mad as any of them were; and, in short, I became as naturally pleased and easy with the place as if indeed I had been born there. (p. 262).

Defoe is so inseparable from Moll here – or, rather, vice versa – that in his eloquence he has had a temporary lapse of memory, and forgotten that Moll was in fact born in Newgate.

In Newgate, to her amazement, Moll finds Jemmy. He is living there in more gentlemanly quarters than the lower-class criminals and it is only after some subterfuge that Moll makes herself known to him. It is through her sorrow for his condition that Moll starts to think about her own life and to feel first remorse and then the glimmerings of repentance. In this new penitent frame of mind, Moll, though they are both close to death, manages to get her own and Jemmy's sentence commuted to transportation. With what money and goods she has left in the care of Mother Midnight, Moll manages to purchase her freedom as soon as they arrive in Virginia.

(Jemmy because of his higher social class would have been free to opt for transportation of his own volition – hanging, as he stresses, would have been the more gentlemanly course of action, but Moll dissuades him from it.)

Once in the colony, hoping for some inheritance from her mother, Moll sets about making discreet enquiries about her previous husband/brother but manages instead to secure a most tender encounter with her son by this man. Her son manages property left by his grandmother to his mother and he sees to it that Moll now gets all its revenue. Moll and Jemmy establish a small plantation further down river in Carolina, and by dint of Moll's hard work and the proceeds sent her by her son, they gradually become very rich. In their old age, having worked out the time of their transportation sentences, they return to live the remainder of their lives in prosperous freedom in England. And so end 'the fortunes and misfortunes of the famous Moll Flanders'.

The first decades after the removal of King James in 1688 were in certain senses the most revolutionary in English history. This was the period of bourgeois revolution transcendent, of individualism and capitalism let loose, of the transition from the religion-based ethics of feudalism to the secular ethics of capitalism, of traditional controls removed, of the enclosure movement run rampant. Right and wrong were to be negotiated. The Divine Right of Kings became the Divine Right of Providence. Property became King.

1688 continued the political revolution of 1649 and the power of the new social groupings that had made it. As the failure of the Jacobite rebellion demonstrated, after 1688 there was to be no going back. But the legal and moral framework of the preceding six hundred years did not alter easily. The changes had to be worked through at all levels of society. The old values not only had to be overthrown but also had to be replaced. In a very real way the ground-rules of everyday life and 'common-sense' terms and notions had to be redefined. Thus the period is one of profound value confusion and of unusual social, economic and moral mobility – the like of which has not been seen since in England. It was a time of great uncertainty when different moral and legal codes conflicted in their claims to universal validity. It was a period when the values which today we hold as self-evident were very much up for grabs.

All this is quite clear in Defoe's novel, in which, as has often been pointed out, a major theme is the juxtaposition of contradictory moral elements. Moll is heroine and villain, fair and foul, business woman and thief, wife and prostitute. The critic Arnold Kettle has been one to emphasise this paradox:

> Moll speaks as though she were not implicated in the common lot of criminals. She doesn't think of herself as a criminal. When she learns what the other criminals in Newgate think of her she is morally outraged. Occasionally, for a moment, like Joyce Cary's Sara, she catches sight of herself in some mirror and sees herself, surprised. And she *does* think of herself as . . . a gentle-woman . . .
>
> The underlying tension which gives *Moll Flanders* its vitality as a work of art can be expressed by a contradiction which is at once simple and complicated. Moll is immoral, shallow, hypocritical, heartless, a bad woman: yet Moll is marvellous. Defoe might almost (though he wouldn't have dreamed of it) have subtitled his book 'A Pure Woman'.
>
> Moll's splendour – her resilience and courage and generosity – is inseparable from her badness. The fair and the foul are not isolable qualities to be abstracted and totted up in a reckoning, balancing one against the other. The relationship is far more interesting.[1]

Like Arnold Kettle, a number of sympathetic critics have explained the greatness of Defoe's novel in terms of his ability to display contradictory social and psychic elements which, when perceived in terms of deep structure, attain a unity. This may be so, but in a certain sense it is misleading. For, as I have suggested, what is interesting about early eighteenth-century England and Defoe's novel is that the clear-cut oppositions of crime and good-citizenship, morality and immorality, and the rest, have not yet separated themselves out.

In that period, there was an important shift in the meaning

of right and wrong as regards both morals and the law. Fewer and fewer people were persecuted, as they had been previously, for opinions they held, political or religious; the rapid escalation of the death penalty was for offences against property: 'property and the privileged status of the propertied were assuming, every year, a greater weight in the scales of justice, until justice itself was seen as no more than the outworks and defences of property and of its attendant status', writes the historian E. P. Thompson, discussing this period.[2] In fighting for property and the spoils of power, the society Defoe is presenting has not yet submitted to a stable code of rules. Retrospectively, we can recognise it as a familiar period of commercial capitalism when the system of justice – which is the basis of our own modified version – is struggling to become established; to critical contemporaries it must have seemed an epoch of turmoil. Perhaps, at this level, the poise and serenity of Augustan prose and poetry, the search for order as in Dr Johnson's dictionary, and the high calm of the classical age as we have come to view it were more the aspirations than the reality for men who otherwise felt rootless and unsure. Defoe portrays Moll as a woman of ebullience with the determination to look only to her future: Moll is the new small-time capitalist in the making, she is the pilgrim progressing to what, as sharp-witted child and clear-headed woman, she rightly takes to be the capitalist definition of a gentlewoman – the wife of a prosperous businessman or a self-made woman in her own right. Yet there is plenty of evidence from the novel that Defoe felt the instability of the times as well as their forward-looking fervour: the society was close enough to its own beginnings to feel its rootlessness as well as its brutal determination. In the buried idiom of *Moll Flanders*, Defoe presents it as a society without a father; no traditional God, no traditional law. Moll, the new woman of capitalism, has a mother and is adept at finding surrogate mothers; her paternity is never mentioned. Writing absolutely as though he were Moll, Defoe, likewise, denies the 'fatherhood' (the authorship) of his own novel.

Critics frequently comment on what they see as the confused morality of *Moll Flanders*. It is true that some of the
remarks that Defoe makes in this connection read like the
special pleading of which the days of mass journalism and
pornography have made us rightly suspicious:

> All possible care . . . has been taken to give no lewd ideas, no
> immodest turns in the new dressing up of this story; no, not to the
> worst parts of her expressions. To this purpose some of the vicious
> part of her life, which could not be modestly told, is quite left out,
> and several other parts are very much shortened. What is left 'tis
> hoped will not offend the chastest reader or the modestest hearer;
> and as the best use is made even of the worst story, the moral 'tis
> hoped will keep the reader serious, even where the story might
> incline him to be otherwise. To give the history of a wicked life
> repented of, necessarily requires that the wicked part should be
> made as wicked as the real history of it will bear, to illustrate and
> give a beauty to the penitent part, which is certainly the best and
> brightest, if related with equal spirit and life (pp. 28—9).

Defoe is wrong to claim Moll's repentance is as interesting as
her offences, yet, on the other hand, this is certainly a novel
that is quite unlike Cleland's salacious *Fanny Hill* which was
possibly based on similar actual life-histories. To me it seems
that the gap is not one between Defoe's pretended morality
and his concealed fascination with immorality, but rather
between the crime, punishment and repentance of his story
and the overall moral framework to which he must appeal. It
is not the righteous ending that prevents *Moll Flanders* being a
pornographic tale of wickedness but rather the fact that Moll
is good even while a thief and prostitute and just as bad or just
as good even while she is a wife and investor. It is a question of
the similarity of the crimes and the laws against them, of
'acceptable society' and its 'underside'.

This argument becomes clearer if we ask a concrete question: who were the criminals in Defoe's day? To answer this, I
want to quote once more from the recent interpretations of
E. P. Thompson. Thompson, in considering in great detail
certain social and political aspects of life in Hanoverian
England, comes up with some important general caveats:

. . . since many people have now started to write the history of crime . . . this may be the occasion to object even more strongly to the categories 'gangs' and 'criminal subculture'. Eighteenth-century class prejudice unites here with the anachronistic employment of the (inadequate) terminology of some twentieth-century criminology. Thus Rogers [describes a particular hanging] as 'an unusually full picture of the criminal subculture of Georgian England'. The lamentable thing about this account – and many other accounts . . . – is that they are nothing of the sort; they are simply accounts of the commonplace, mundane culture of plebeian England – notes on the lives of unremarkable people, distinguished from their fellows by little else except the fact that by bad luck or worse judgement they got caught up in the toils of the law . . . If this is a 'criminal subculture' then the whole of plebeian England falls within the category. [3]

What today's criminologists call a 'subculture', eighteenth-century magistrates termed 'gangs'. As Thompson further mentions, there were some real gangs but the wholesale way in which this term was applied is completely misleading.

Defoe's *Moll Flanders* and *Roxana* are likewise usually perceived as novels about criminal subcultures. But in the light of Thompson's strictures, how, in fact, should we classify Moll? Was she a criminal or was she, through bad luck, caught up in the toils of a demonically repressive legal system along with many other unfortunate members of plebeian England?

The seventeenth century had largely condemned people for religious or political opinions. As we have seen, the situation was changing in the early eighteenth century. I suggest that the confusion that surrounds the question of Moll's criminality is the confusion of English society at that period – a topsy-turvy society in which the punishment was often outstandingly more brutal than the offence. Our resolution of the question should indicate how *Moll Flanders* can be both a contemporary documentary fiction and a novel with a larger universal message.

There is considerable evidence that Defoe based his portrait of *Moll Flanders* on an actual person or persons whom he had encountered or heard tell of from first hand. Who this prototype was, has been the subject of speculation (induced by Defoe's own style of narration) since the novel was published. More recently, however, Gerald Howson has come up with a very plausible speculation.[4] Both personally and in his capacity as a journalist, Defoe was very familiar with Newgate prison and its inmates. During most of 1721 he was visiting regularly a close friend who was incarcerated there and his visits would have given him ample opportunity to talk with one woman in particular, Moll King. Moll King was one of the aliases of Mary Godson, a notorious thief and convict. Apart from acquainting Defoe with her own story, Moll King may have recounted the adventures of her friend 'Callico Sarah', a thief and whore with a full and varied life-history of her own. 'Callico' was contraband silk and may have suggested to Defoe the name 'Flanders', which was Flemish lace and likewise usually contraband. As Howson comments: 'It seems likely that Defoe sought [Moll King] out when she was under sentence of death, as a suitable subject for a criminal pamphlet . . . After her reprieve, the pamphlet grew into the novel, the first of its kind in English.'[5]

At one time or another, both Moll King and Callico Sarah worked for and were finally impeached by the notorious gangster, Jonathan Wild. Jonathan Wild was certainly not an ordinary member of plebeian England, but a professional criminal and leader of a genuine subculture. But even here, in identifying a real gang, we must bear Thompson's cautions in mind:

> The categories of 'gang' and 'subculture' might perhaps be rehabilitated if applied, with scrupulous care, to some activities in London, the great ports and the larger fairs, in which certain criminal procedures were professionalized and institutionalized. But we will be examining here less the 'subculture' (the characteristic attitudes, skills transmitted in families and prisons, and cant vocabulary) than the infrastructure to this 'subculture': that is, very specifically, the receivers, the brothels and the pimps, the employers of pick-pockets, the police or thief-takers in profitable symbiosis with these employers, the 'houses of resort', and so on.[6]

Moll King may have worked for Jonathan Wild and thus been part of a gang: but if Defoe used her as a model it was not to document criminality but ordinary life. At times the fictional Moll Flanders is, like Moll King, a professional thief, working – though she does not like doing so – with other thieves. Yet Defoe puts no emphasis on any professional aspect of her work (other than to let her boast about her expertise). Moll steals and prostitutes her body for one reason and one reason alone: she is poor. 'Give me not poverty, lest I steal,' says Moll, and 'the prospect of my own starving . . . hardened my heart'. Or again, 'I wanted to be placed in a settled state of living, and had I happened to meet with a sober, good husband, I should have been as true a wife to him as virtue itself could have formed. If I had been otherwise, the vice came in always at the door of necessity, not at the door of inclination . . .' (pp. 135—6).

Given that it seems he took his models from women who worked for Jonathan Wild, Defoe could have developed his story into a portrait of a genuine criminal underworld, but he did not do so. As Thompson's work illustrates, for most people the line between a criminal class and all plebeian England was a hard one to draw. Moll Flanders is both criminal and plebeian heroine; it is not so much that the combination is plausible as that the distinction is not.

It is not, then, that Defoe is unusually clear-sighted and can see through their superficial differences to the similarity – in Arnold Kettle's Shakespearean phrase – of fair and foul, justice and thief, it is rather that the epoch in which he lived was still struggling to convince itself of the distinction. Defoe is writing from a time in which Moll as wife and Moll as prostitute, Moll as small capitalist and Moll as thief are quite logically the same person: Moll is in all plausibility a moderately good woman caught up from necessity in relatively 'bad' acts; had she been born into better social circumstances it is just as likely that she might have been a bad woman caught up in 'good' acts. In a decade that introduced the death penalty for the theft of a handkerchief or a sapling, good and bad, fair and foul, are not contradictions whose ultimate unity it takes a genius to perceive, but bedfellows whose proximity only subsequent historians have managed to miss.

We can single out here one further theme from the novel that illustrates this proximity as it is played out in Moll's life: what does it mean to be a 'gentlewoman'? Moll, an eight-year-old girl, tells her foster-mother that she does not want to go out into service. A number of wealthy visitors are standing by as, in reply to her foster-mother's teasing, Moll insists that what she wants to be in this life is a 'gentlewoman'. In friendly mockery she becomes known as 'the little gentlewoman':

> Now all this while my good nurse, Mrs Mayoress, and all the rest of them did not understand me at all, for they meant one sort of thing by the word gentlewoman, and I meant quite another; for, alas! all I understood by being a gentlewoman was to be able to work for myself, and get enough to keep me without that terrible bugbear going to service, whereas they meant to live great, rich and high, and I know not what.
>
> Well, after Mrs Mayoress was gone, her two daughters came in, and they called for the gentlewoman too, and they talked a long while to me, and I answered them in my innocent way; but always, if they asked me whether I resolved to be a gentlewoman, I answered Yes. At last one of them asked me what a gentlewoman was? That puzzled me much; but, however, I explained myself negatively, that it was one that did not go to service, to do housework. They were pleased to be familiar with me, and liked my little prattle to them, which, it seems, was agreeable enough to them, and they gave me money too.
>
> As for my money, I gave it all to my mistress-nurse, as I called her, and told her she should have all I got for myself when I was a gentlewoman, as well as now. By this and some other of my talk, my old tutoress began to understand me about what I meant by being a gentlewoman, and that I understood by it no more than to be able to get my bread by my own work; and at last she asked me whether it was not so.
>
> I told her, yes, and insisted on it, that to do so was to be a gentlewoman; 'for,' says I, 'there is such a one,' naming a woman that mended lace and washed the ladies' laced-heads; 'she,' says I, 'is a gentlewoman, and they call her madam.'
>
> 'Poor child,' says my good old nurse, 'you may soon be such a gentlewoman as that, for she is a person of ill fame, and has had two or three bastards' (p. 38).

In Moll's tumultuous society, a gentlewoman is a member of the leisured gentry, or a prostitute: both ends of the social scale meet and are still, today, exemplified by the title 'madam'.

By the mid-nineteenth century, Moll's types of crime will have come to seem eternally sinful and her penitence will appear as a state of grace. In the meantime, Defoe, despite his intentions, cannot make the crimes sinful or the repentance more full of grace than that produced by a full belly. Moll steals because she is poor and leads a moral life because she is prosperous; her social crimes against property have not yet been sufficiently internalised by men to have become so much a part of their unconscious thinking that they seem equivalent to religious sins.

Perhaps this point can be grasped more concretely if we look at those instances in the novel where Defoe really does have Moll convey the abhorrence that he would have us believe he feels for all her offences. I suggest that these instances are incest and murder. The seriousness of Moll's actual incestuous marriage is already foreseen in her reaction to the proposed marriage with Robin, the younger brother of her first lover. She becomes almost fatally ill at the prospect of what seems to her to be such an unnatural marriage and even when she has recovered and consented to the union and been married some years, it is in these terms that she conceives it: '. . . I never was in bed with my husband, but I wished myself in the arms of his brother . . . in short, I committed adultery and incest with him every day in my desires, which, without doubt, was . . . effectually criminal' (pp. 76—7). When, in Virginia, she finds she has unwittingly married her own brother (in fact a half-brother), her revulsion is total. Her brother/husband, after mad rages, declines into a state of presenile dementia which is, in some sense, Defoe's unconscious metaphor for the man's corrupt and unnatural marital state. Moll, unlike her husband, cannot even entertain the notion of concealment:

I was now the most unhappy of all women in the world. Oh! had the story never been told me, all had been well; it had been no crime to have lain with my husband, since . . . I had known nothing of it . . . [However] I was but too sure of the fact, I lived therefore in open avowed incest and whoredom, and all under the appearance of an honest wife; and though I was not much touched with the crime of it, yet the action had something in it shocking to nature, and made my husband, as he thought himself, even nauseous to me . . .

. . . indeed, I mortally hated him as a husband, and it was impossible to remove that riveted aversion I had to him. At the same time, it being an unlawful, incestuous living, added to that aversion, and . . . everything added to make cohabiting with him the most nauseous thing to me in the world; and I think verily it was come to such a height, that I could almost as willingly have embraced a dog as have let him offer anything of that kind to me, for which reason I could not bear the thoughts of coming between the sheets with him (pp. 102, 110).

It is likewise with murder. Despite the violence of her society and the extremities to which she has to go to survive, neither Moll (nor, indeed her highwayman husband, Jemmy) is ever, as far as we know, implicated in murder. In fact, abortion is shocking to her in a way that stealing is not: '. . . I would have been glad to miscarry, but I could never be brought to entertain so much as a thought of endeavouring to miscarry, or of taking anything to make me miscarry; I abhorred, I say, so much as the thought of it' (p. 163).

In a society that valued a person's life less than a teaspoon, the worth of the unborn foetus came into its own. A woman such as Moll's mother could escape hanging if she pleaded pregnancy (and often probably got impregnated by a man making a profession of being a stud); in a society in which many of its most powerful members wanted a rising working population it seems that the only natural relationship that was sacrosanct was that between a mother and her unborn or newborn infant. Moll can soon give up her child for adoption; a woman saved from hanging on account of pregnancy would be executed when her child was six months old.

The society was clearly a sexually lax one that placed small value on human life. In these circumstances, before the new moral codes about property had become sufficiently established to seem wholly natural, thinkers such as Defoe, whether consciously or not, had to fall back for some sure ground onto those social crimes that are so basic to all societies that they are *always* felt to be sins against nature: a certain type of murder and incest. Thompson writes: 'Political life in England in the 1720s had something of the sick quality of a "banana republic",' and indeed it had; but even in this stage of energetic corruption some things had to be too much. As well as being evidence of the immutably social nature of crime, it is a measure perhaps of human desperation that, confronted with mob lynchings and the Newgate hangings, abortion came to seem the only unnatural murder; that faced with what was in all probability a new level in the exploitation of sexuality, incest with a half-brother seemed the only utterly impossible sexual offence.

Moll, then, is criminal and plebeian heroine – they are much the same thing. By the end she has become a prosperous self-made woman; Arnold Kettle calls this a lapse into social conformity. It may be, in one sense, but this is not Defoe's message, nor is it the feeling that the novel leaves us with. Moll is a heroine because she has the courage to be successful, to know what she wants and to go and get it. In the context of the times, for any woman success must have meant to become bourgeois and prosperous. Capitalism in England had developed at this stage into a situation where there was an urban middle class and a growing urban plebeian class – it had not yet developed an industrial working class with a consciousness of itself as a class. Anyone in their right minds who did not want to remain a plebeian, which might easily mean being hanged as a criminal, can only have aspired to be bourgeois. Such an aspiration is still central to our type of society (though the mobility that went with it is not) and so, because of this aspiration, Moll speaks to everything in our culture except our working-class consciousness (if we have one). The history of the novel, in this respect, has been about Moll's type of aspiration – the working-class novel is a rare and not a culturally central form of fiction.

This may get us closer to the question of why *Moll Flanders* can be both a realistic document of its times and have an atemporal, universal appeal. For Defoe's work certainly does have such a generalising impact. Writing of *Robinson Crusoe*, Rousseau considered Defoe's hero to be man in his essence. Coleridge summed up the feelings of many of the Romantic writers when he said: 'He who makes me forget my *specific* class, character, and circumstances, raises me into universal man. Now that is Defoe's excellence. You become a man while you read'.[7] Virginia Woolf became a woman, or rather, in her feminism, a person, when she was re-reading *Moll Flanders* and saw the streets of London through Defoe's eyes.

If, as seems to be the case, Moll, in her courage and determination, speaks to the type of urge to do well for oneself that has been at the heart of the ideology of our society for three hundred years, then she will appear universal to us. Moll is an incarnation of capitalist woman at that moment when the society's ideologists are torn between an awareness that all is new and an effort to make all permanent and changeless. The treatment of marriage and prostitution illustrates this.

Prostitution and theft in this new society are what you do if you cannot get successfully married in the one case, and have no capital in the other. Wife and prostitute, thief and capitalist can be one and the same person at different points of their lives. It is this lack of separation, this easy oscillation that is distinctive of Defoe's society. Prostitution and theft stand to marriage and investment as their necessary other sides. Moll shares thieving or investment with the men of her society; the need for marriage and prostitution for immediate economic reasons are particularly hers as a woman. Defoe joins other writers of his epoch in offering in *Moll Flanders* a treatise on the meaning of the new forms of contractual marriage. For both sexes, though love and looks may be considered, marriage is essentially an economic undertaking and Moll is a heroine because, unlike the majority of her sex (according to Defoe the tradesman), she does not let men get the better of her at a bargain:

> The case was altered with me: I had money in my pocket . . . I had been tricked once by that cheat called love, but the game was over; I was resolved now to be married or nothing, and to be well married or not at all (p. 77).

Defoe believed that women should be educated and allowed to carry on business as men did; in this respect he was a liberal spokesman for the claims for sexual equality that were being made from the middle of the seventeenth century until his own day. But he was also accurate in perceiving that for woman marriage was the passage to the desired state of middle-class security. Moll is an expression of Defoe's particular type of feminism: his notion that everyone who had the energy to fight for it, had a right to an equal bargain. Because of Defoe's feminism writers such as the critic Ian Watt[8] find Moll 'masculine' or, as in the case of Virginia Woolf, not a woman – but 'a person'. She is a woman who is like a man in her economic ambitions and hence her independence. But Defoe's realism means that Moll knows very well that she is a woman and that even if her own life does not entirely illustrate the fact, an aspirant woman's main road to success is marriage, with its concomitant economic support:

> . . . I had no adviser . . . and above all, I had nobody to whom I could in confidence commit the secret of my circumstances to, and could depend upon for their secrecy and fidelity; and I found by experience, that to be friendless is the worst condition, next to being in want, that a woman can be reduced to: I say a woman, because 'tis evident men can be their own advisers, and their own directors, and know how to work themselves out of difficulties and into business better than women (p.135).

Karl Marx thought Robinson Crusoe was not universal man (an impossibility from a Marxist viewpoint) but that in his individualism he was capitalist man at his heroic moment. One of the revolutionary ideologies of the puritanism that went with capitalism was that all people were equal in the eyes of the Lord and this included the equality of men and women. *Moll Flanders* illustrates this concept but also the social reality that was always very different. As the historian Christopher Hill reflects, the doctrine had it that all men were equal but some were more equal than others.[9] Men were certainly more equal than women: 'he for the market only, she for the market through him'. Moll too is capitalist woman at this heroic moment.

But I do not think that this is the only reason why *Moll Flanders* seems to be about something more generally human than early eighteenth-century England. In his novel Defoe presents the problem that a new type of society has in establishing its continuity with the old and how it has to do this, in order to make its particular features seem universal ones. The particular nature of man under commercial capitalism has to appear to be human nature itself. Within *Moll Flanders*, the dilemma of what it means to be a gentleman illustrates this difficulty most pertinently.

Moll is always saying that she doesn't mind marrying a tradesman but he must be able to cut the figure of a gentleman. A gentleman was meant to be a man of dash, bravado and infinite leisure. The concept was a reformulation by a new middle-class society of the person it conceived to be its ancestor in the dominant class of the previous feudal epoch. In fact, the contemporary reality of the dominant middle class was very different from that of feudal times. Jemmy, Moll's Lancashire husband, sums up the predicament of this shift. Too much of a gentleman to turn his hand to a day's work, he likes to spend his time hunting in the forests of America: 'The case was plain; he was bred a gentleman, and by consequence was not only unacquainted, but indolent, and when we did settle, would much rather go out into the woods with his gun, which they call there hunting, and *which is the ordinary work of the Indians* . . .' (p. 304; my italics). As with the 'madam' who is both lady and prostitute, the irony is that Jemmy's gentlemanly habits are likewise those of the lowest possible social group – the American Indian. Top and bottom meet in a society which is still trying to find its way to make its 'middle' group seem uppermost. In the meanwhile, the new dominant man most inappropriately apes the old. Defoe would have agreed with his contemporary, the writer Sir Richard Steele, who observed that 'we merchants are a species of gentry that have grown into this world this last century'.[10] The actual life of the new dominant middle-class man is best embodied in Moll's reflections on the father of her first lover and her first husband. This man leaves the family affair of his son's unsuitable marriage to his wife because he is too busy: '. . . as to the father, he was a man in a hurry of public affairs and getting money, seldom at home, thoughtful of the main chance, but left all those things to his wife' (p. 72). In order to inherit the status of a previous upper class, in the minds of all men, the new bourgeoisie had to be gentlemen, but their commercial enterprises and hard work were a far cry from their inherited image of a feudal nobleman. A 'gentleman' had not yet become indigenous to the middle classes and Defoe bears witness to the difficulty of the transitional moment – how do you preservé (or convert) a continuous imagery about your dominant class (or any class, for that matter) while you change the very social base on which it rests? The new definition of a gentleman mustn't seem to be new. But Defoe is too close to the revolutionary moment itself to have completed such a transformation – his new gentleman-tradesman cannot quite claim a universal status. Defoe does not believe, as the nineteenth century was able to believe, that gentlemen are the same the world and time over. The new gentleman-tradesman that was to represent the dominant social class of this stage of capitalism, Defoe calls an 'amphibious creature, [a] land-water thing' (p. 78). The ideological concept of the gentleman is inherited from the watery feudal past, but it has to adapt to the totally new social conditions of middle-class land.

The particular genius of Defoe is that he does face the fact that the historical conditions of his time are specific, and that he struggles to make them universal in a peculiarly appropriate manner. He does not struggle for universality, as say Swift does, by transferring his contemporary commentary to a timeless realm of allegory, to an early version of a spaceship or a mythical island or a world of near horses and near monkeys. What Defoe does is to place his story in the previous century, implicitly arguing thereby that his own troublesome times are simultaneously over and done with and that all periods are the same – human nature is immutable. But, ironically, it is a mark of Defoe's ability that he only partially succeeds in this 'distancing' venture. For few people realise that *Moll Flanders*, published in 1722, is in this sense an 'historical' novel, its very last words reading 'written in the year 1683'.

Though it was presumably meant to be part of the disguise with which Defoe made out he was hiding the identity of his characters and the events, Defoe's historical dating, I think, alerts us to something else. As a crude generalisation, we can say that a historical sense develops after a major revolution, a change from one type of society to another. Such a change inevitably disrupts previous notions of changeless immutable human nature: if things can alter dramatically, they themselves must have developed out of something else that was a change and so on backwards.

Defoe's pre-dating of *Moll Flanders* should not be compared with later, truly historical novels – there is no question that this novel is about the eighteenth not the seventeenth century. What it should be set beside is Defoe's presentation of his heroine.

If we match the historical dating with the portrayal of the main character it comes to have a different, if unintentional, meaning. It suggests a notion of development.

Pilgrim in Bunyan's *Pilgrim's Progress* travels the journey of his life as a full-grown man; with Moll Flanders, Defoe inaugurates a new tradition which was to become a dominant feature of the English novel. Moll starts as a child and grows progressively older with the pace of the novel. In other words, the novel is structured around her growth. What happens to Moll as a mature woman, indeed, who she is as a woman, depends on the conditions of her birth, her infancy, childhood and adolescence. The child is mother to the woman. As with a concept of social history, an idea of development is a *sine qua non* of a concept of the history of the individual.

Defoe's partial and emergent sense of history does not, then, place his fiction in a timeless void. Even Robinson Crusoe on his island is not like Swift's Houyhnhnms on theirs; he has come from somewhere and is going on to somewhere. Even more so is this the case with *Moll Flanders*. Defoe's historical notion of time and character looks forwards as well as backwards, it is a notion of development. In being this it was peculiarly at one with a notion that is central to capitalist ideology itself: capitalism sees its own universal features in this very quality of growth and development. It is not a type of society that finds, as some do, its rationale in stability, but in expansion and growth. Defoe's very awareness of change helped him to create a new and appropriate universal myth. Furthermore, Defoe's realism, for which he is famous and to which Ian Watt, among others, has devoted some very interesting work, is, I think, a very specific type of realism and one that also explains the balance between the specific historical character of his work and his wish to universalise. Defoe's realism is analogous to the social realism that came out of Russia in the 1920s. In brief, this was an effort in art to portray man as new, socialist man who is simultaneously the image of the truth of all men. Robinsoe Crusoe and Moll Flanders are to bourgeois capitalism what paintings of workers under socialism were to the immediate post-revolutionary Soviet Union: the historically specific struggling for universality.

Because it is Defoe's type of society that we are, despite obvious differences, still living in, we cannot immediately see that what we are witnessing is the genesis of a new 'universal' type born from the chaos of revolutionary change. Critics who dislike Defoe's work find it gauche in style and uncouth in content – they, I suggest, are responding to the imperfections through which Defoe transforms his times. Those who admire Defoe respond to his ability to create a new, 'eternal' and heroic myth out of capitalist society.

Part III   *Psychoanalysis:*
Child Development
and the Question
of Femininity

On Freud and the
Distinction Between
the Sexes

¶ 'On Freud and the Distinction
between the Sexes' was written for Jean Strouse's anthology:
Women and Analysis (New York, 1974). Jean Strouse (whose
book on Alice James I use in the last lecture in the collection)
had been the excellent editor at Pantheon Books of my
book *Psychoanalysis and Feminism*. Her own anthology
brought together essays on women from famous
psychoanalysts and analysts from other schools (Jung,
Horney, Thompson) and followed each with a commentary.
The essay printed here was one of three on Freud; the other
two commentators were Elizabeth Hardwick and Margaret
Mead.

This brief piece demonstrates one aspect of my interest in
psychoanalysis at that time – not an interest I have pursued.
Then I was still hoping it would prove possible to use
psychoanalysis as an incipient science of the ideology of
patriarchy – of how we come to live ourselves as feminine or
masculine within patriarchal societies.

In July 1925, from his holiday house in the Semmering
outside Vienna, Freud wrote to his friend and colleague, Karl
Abraham, in Berlin: 'I have written a few short papers, but

they are not meant very seriously. Perhaps, if I am willing to admit their parentage, I shall tell you about them later.'[1] One of these 'unserious' papers was the highly significant essay clumsily entitled 'Some Psychical Consequences of the Anatomical Distinction Between the Sexes.' Perhaps by September when he asked his daughter, Anna Freud, to present it as his contribution to that year's Psycho-Analytic Congress at Hamburg, Freud had changed his estimation of it. Certainly the essay contains in abbreviated form all Freud's later thoughts on the subject. In itself it marks the first published turning point in his thinking about the psychology of women. Until this point, with decreasing tenacity, he had held to his vague notions of a parallel development of girls and boys – the model being the boy. In the 1925 essay he finally discarded this equilateral theory and tentatively embarked on a new area for the exploration of female psychology and the meaning of female sexuality.

By this date Freud was chronically sick with cancer and he had for some years felt that there was little chance of his discovering anything new of substance. But multiple operations kept him alive for a further fourteen years during which, though less prolifically, he continued to work and write. All his theoretical analyses of women's psychology come during this last period of work. It is perhaps interesting to reflect that Freud, with his reputation as the most honorable misogynist of them all, yet wrote very little (too little) specifically on the question of femininity. If we exclude his early work with Josef Breuer on hysteria, in the twenty-three English volumes of his collected works there are only three brief essays devoted specifically to questions of feminine psychology and three detailed case-histories of women patients. However, there are many discussions of the question scattered throughout his writings on other subjects.

It would seem valid to me to make a rough distinction between those references in the period prior to the 1920s and those that come after the first coherent statement made in 'Some Psychical Consequences of the Anatomical

Distinction Between the Sexes'. Up to about 1920, the comments are isolated observations; after that date their repetition and re-working testifies to a preoccupation with the subject, though this may be due not so much to the specific interest in female psychology as to the type of question this forced him to ask and the new area it led him to explore. The shift in the area of interest was due to some extent to the development of his own work. But, in addition, the problem of feminine psychology was explicitly provoked by the interest of his fellow analysts. During the 1920s and 1930s there was considerable concentration among both men and women practitioners on producing a Freudian analysis of femininity. Before his early death in December 1925, Karl Abraham was one of the pioneers, and the one to whom Freud confessed his ignorance before he went on to make up for his negligence: 'As I gladly admit, the female side of the problem is extra-ordinarily obscure to me. If your ideas and observations on the subject already permit communication, I should very much like to hear about them, but I can wait.'[2] In fact, Freud waited less than six months, not only for further correspondence with Abraham, but also for his own contribution to the subject: the 1925 essay.

'Some Psychical Consequences of the Anatomical Distinction Between the Sexes' can be said to deal with two intimately related but nevertheless distinct themes: the nature of female sexuality and the more general question of feminine psychology to be deduced from interpersonal (socio-sexual) relationships. On this first theme, except as it is influenced by the second, the essay scarcely breaks new ground upon that already explored in the 1905 *Three Essays on Sexuality* (if we include the important footnotes to that treatise that Freud added periodically up until 1924). It is this question of female sexuality and, more specifically, Freud's propo-sition of the two zones of sensitivity – the vaginal and the clitoral – that has received most attention. If I resume Freud's arguments on this aspect here it is for reasons of their popularity – for I consider their interest to lie not in any autonomous value but in their dependence on the second, larger question of feminine psychology. And on this issue the 1925 essay inaugurates a new and crucial analysis to which I shall come later.

There are hints of most of Freud's later theories in his early letters to his one-time great friend, Wilhelm Fliess, with whom he corresponded both profusely and passionately in the late 1880s and 1890s. In 1897, writing to Fliess of his theory of repression, Freud incorporated the following comments:

> . . . we can see that, with the successive waves of a child's development, he is overlaid with piety, shame, and such things. . . These successive waves of development probably have a different chronological arrangement in the male and female sexes. (Disgust appears earlier in little girls than in boys.) But the main distinction between the sexes emerges at the time of puberty, when girls are seized upon by *non*-neurotic *sexual* repugnance and males by libido. For at that period a further zone is (wholly or in part) extinguished in females which persists in males. I am thinking of the male genital zone, the region of the clitoris, in which during childhood sexual sensitivity is shown to be concentrated in girls as well as boys. Hence the flood of shame which overwhelms the female at that period, till the new, vaginal zone is awakened, whether spontaneously or by reflex action. Hence too, perhaps the anaesthesia of women . . . [3]

This position is retained in the *Three Essays* and, more carefully formulated, in the 1925 essay, but this persistence is not for the want of a challenge to it. The letter from Abraham that had so aroused Freud's interest precisely contested the nature of the two-stage theory of female sexuality. But Abraham was concerned with the early prevalence of vaginal feeling not, as recent investigations, with the continued dominance of the clitoris. Freud was sceptical of Abraham's thesis, maintaining that for the small girl the vagina would be psychically fused with the highly responsive anal area. One of Abraham's concerns was to assert that here, as elsewhere, there was a homology between the events of infancy and those of puberty: the adolescent girl, in transferring her orientation from a desire for clitoral stimulation to a wish for vaginal penetration, was repeating in an inverse direction the experience of infancy. Freud's statement that not until puberty is the vagina felt to be the main sexual organ lays greater stress on repression than does Abraham's theory. Most important, it suggests that there is no parallel development in boys and girls. Abraham's suggestion implies an original psychological 'femininity', an infantile receptive vagina as the equal and opposite of the boy's penile masculinity. Freud's contention that in infancy both sexes have a masculine sexuality (the clitoris is the exact equivalent of the penis) and that it is only through a series of repressions that femininity (whose definitional sexual organ is the vagina) can be acquired, is an asymmetrical process rejecting any neat parallel between the sexes and thus by implication rejecting the notion that psychology corresponds in a one-to-one relationship with biology.

Anatomy may, at its point of hypothetical normality, give us two opposite but equal sexes (with the atrophied sex organs of the other present in each), but Freudian psychoanalytic theory does not. Freud's denial of Abraham's suggestion turned out to be neither arbitrary from a theoretical standpoint nor the random result of different empirical observation. Although, as I said earlier, the whole issue is secondary to the greater question of feminine psychology, it is necessary for the consideration of that larger question that the asymmetrical development of boys and girls should be retained in the discussion of both sexuality and psychology.

The post-Masters-and-Johnson restoration of the primacy of clitoral responsiveness claims the opposite of the theory asserted by Abraham; but it too, if applied psychologically, returns us to the dilemma of a law of even development between the sexes. Abraham's notion of an original vaginal receptivity and the opposite thesis of vaginal insensitivity and clitoral dominance may both be correct biologically or neurologically, but they make poor sense psychologically.

Let us pose the problem for the moment at its most basic level: if we live in a patriarchal society in which, from whatever your political standpoint, the sexes are treated at least differently, not to say 'unequally', then is it not highly unlikely that the psychological development of the sexes should be one of parity? Psychology must reflect the social *at least* as much as the biological background – a fact which those who oppose Freud on this question, from whatever perspective, ignore completely.

In a footnote to the *Three Essays*, added in 1915, Freud wrote:

> It is essential to realise that the concepts of 'masculine' and 'feminine', whose meaning seems so unambiguous to ordinary people, are among the most confused that occur in science. It is possible to distinguish at least three uses. 'Masculine' and 'feminine' are used sometimes in the sense of activity and passivity, sometimes in a biological and sometimes, again, in a sociological sense. The first of these three meanings is the essential one and the most serviceable in psycho-analysis. When . . .libido was described . . . as being 'masculine', the word was being used in this sense, for an instinct is always active even when it has a passive aim in view. . . . Activity and its concomitant phenomena (more powerful muscular development, aggressiveness, greater intensity of libido) are as a rule linked with biological masculinity; but they are not necessarily so, for there are animal species in which these qualities are on the contrary assigned to the female. . . Such observation shows that in human beings pure masculinity or femininity is not to be found either in the psychological or biological sense. Every individual on the contrary displays a mixture of the character-traits belonging to his own and to the opposite sex; and he shows a combination of activity and passivity whether or not these last character-traits tally with his biological ones.[4]

Or as he put if fifteen years later, in 1930:

> Sex is a biological fact which, although it is of extraordinary importance in mental life, is hard to grasp psychologically. We are accustomed to say that every human being displays both male and female instinctual impulses, needs and attributes; but though anatomy, it is true, can point out the characteristics of maleness and femaleness, psychology cannot. For psychology the contrast between the sexes fades away into one between activity and

passivity, in which we far too readily identify activity with maleness and passivity with femaleness, a view which is by no means universally confirmed in the animal kingdom.[5]

Freud was concerned over and over again to establish that there was no one-to-one correlation between biology and psychology, that, for example, in psychological terms masculinity and femininity really reduced themselves to activity and passivity and that neither of the sexes held an absolute prerogative over either. Why then did Freud continue to use the terms with sexual connotations rather than those that were more neutral? Clearly not for reasons either of negligence or unconscious male chauvinism, though certainly Freud was capable and guilty of both. In answering the question we get back to the asymmetry of Freud's sexual schema as opposed to the parallel paths tracked out by others working in this field.

If Freud opposed Abraham on his notion of the equilateral opposition of the vagina and the penis and if he criticised other analysts such as Ernest Jones and Karen Horney for their rejection of his crucial notion of psychic bisexuality and of a phallic stage for women, and if he continued to use a male bias in his vocabulary, all this was in terms of a third assumption: the repudiation – by both men and women – of the implications of femininity. The two famous concepts of the castration complex (in men) and penis-envy (in women) are correlatives; they express an identical fear of (and necessity for) the feminine position. Hence, if Freud continued to use the terms 'masculine' and 'feminine' in instances where, by his own admission, activity and passivity would have done as well, it is because it was the *uneven* relationship between the two sexual possibilities, *within* a person as well as *between* persons, that he was trying to decipher. To claim that, say, the 'Wolf-Man' had a 'passive' attitude in this and that respect tells us nothing of the identifications and attachments to persons that he formed; to describe his desire in certain respects as a 'feminine' one locates the identification with, for example, his mother (at least in this particular case-history). Freud's psycho-analytic theories are about sexism; that he himself propagated certain sexist views and that his work has been a bulwark of the ideological oppression of women is doubtless of great importance. But we can understand its significance only if we first realise that it was exactly the psychological formations produced within patriarchal societies that he was revealing and analysing. Opposition to Freud's asymmetrical history of the sexes, whether feminist, humanist, or counter-analytical, may well be more pleasing in the egalitarianism it assumes and sets out to demonstrate but it makes nonsense of the more profound claim that under patriarchy women are oppressed – a claim that Freud's analysis alone can help us to understand.

The 1925 essay is such a landmark precisely because here for the first time Freud gathers together his scattered observations and unpublished arguments on the *different* psycho-sexual history of boys and girls. As he himself admits, all his earlier work had taken the boy as the paradigm, automatically assuming for the girl fairly conventional variations on this male model. Because of this unargued male bias, it was probably inevitable that the first efforts by other analysts to give girls a psychic history of their own should have been either the equilateral ones already mentioned or exaggerations of Freud's own phallocentrism. But in the 1925 essay (and no later writings do more than interestingly elaborate the theories propounded here) Freud establishes both a distinct development for girls and one that is formed within a male-dominated culture.

Up until about this time in Freud's work, the Oedipus complex, a shibboleth on which psychoanalysis stood or fell, had also by and large been the main starting-point of actual analyses. Without detracting from the significance of the Oedipus complex, Freud now established the importance of a new realm – the pre-Oedipal phase, in particular for girls. Hitherto he had assumed a symmetry in the Oedipal moment: boys loved their mothers and consequently wished to get rid of their unfair rivals in love, their fathers; girls desired their fathers, hence directed their jealousy against their mothers. But very early on Freud realised there was no parity here. From the outset he spoke against the proposal to designate the girl's experience the 'Electra complex', which would have accorded it independent and equal mythic weight. The transition that the girl must make from her love for her mother (all babies are attached to the mother) to loving her father could not be brought about by any simple chemical heterosexual attraction (or if it were, then there would be no psychology, which would be tantamount to saying that there was no person), nor could it be a simple physiological response with a homologous psychic structure superimposed – such as is supposed by Abraham's infantile vagina waiting desirously for paternal penetration. A shift of the sort from love of mother to love of father necessitates a complex psychological change. Hence before the girl can move into the positive feminine Oedipus complex (love of father), the pre-Oedipal situation must be crucial; indeed, as Freud says in the essay, the Oedipus complex for girls is only a secondary formation. This pre-Oedipal phase (for boys and girls) was at that point an unexplored region in psychoanalysis, one 'where there are as yet no signposts'. In fact, Freud never really got far beyond an indication of the problems, which is one reason why psychoanalysis maps out the structure of neuroses but not of psychoses, and why it tells us more about the sexual development of men than of women. However, here, in pointing out the territory and the implications of the signs, Freud does the groundwork for an analysis of femininity.

Both boys and girls have feminine and masculine attitudes, both share the identifications and attachments of the pre-Oedipal phase, both have masculine and feminine Oedipus complexes, but in the latter situation the key question is, which wins the day? Here the boy has to learn not to abandon his love for his mother by accepting an identification with her and the girl has to do precisely that; in other words the boy has to repudiate the possibilities of femininity and the girl has to embrace them. If we see then the Oedipus complex not, as it is popularly perceived, as a symmetrical structure, but as an asymmetrical situation, we can get to the heart of the problem. Instead of:

Mother   Father
Girl   loves   loves   Boy

we have both infants loving the mother and abandoning her at the intervention of the father:

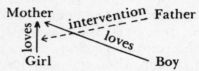

The dual relationship of mother and child is broken into by the father, who prevents the incestuous desires of both his offspring for the mother, whom he alone is allowed to possess.

The father, however, asserts his rights differently in the case of girls and boys. In the 'ideal' case, the boy learns to accept his inferior phallic powers (thus resolving his castration complex) but on the understanding that he will later have the same patriarchal rights and a woman of his own; the girl learns that she has no phallic powers and thus will not now or ever possess her mother or later substitute (a wife) – indeed that she is *like* her mother, without the phallus: she recognises her castration, envies the phallic power, and has to do her best to overcome this envy. (Freud uses the term 'penis-envy' and this has produced a misleadingly biological interpretation.) When the boy accepts the possibility of castration his Oedipus complex is shattered, his sexual love for his mother is abandoned and channelled into other, ostensibly nonsexual pursuits: 'The catastrophe to the Oedipus complex (the abandonment of incest and the institution of conscience and morality) may be regarded as a victory of the race over the individual.'[6] Patriarchal culture prevails, and 'circular' or closed (incestuous) sexuality is subdued.

The girl has another story to learn. Her love of her mother is not, like the boy's, culturally dangerous, just sexually 'unrealistic' within the terms of the culture. If she persists in the belief that she has a penis (a pre-Oedipal supposition based on her phallic, clitoral activity), she will be disavowing reality and this could be the basis of a future psychosis. In the 'ideal' case she will recognise her phallic inferiority, identify with the mother to whom she is to be compared, and then want to take her place with her father: 'Her mother becomes the object of her jealousy. The little girl has turned into a little woman.'[7] No prohibition shatters her love for her mother, but she learns that she possesses nothing with which to implement it. A sense of her inferiority, and closely connected therewith, a repression of masturbation, sets her on the path towards femininity. This repression of the clitoris that can never compete with the phallus as a thrusting and propagating power of patriarchal society foreshadows the later relinquishing of clitoral dominance at puberty and this, in its turn, is a precondition of the transference to vaginal sensitivity. The girl's positive Oedipus complex (love of the father) is entered into only by default; it is not as strong as the boy's Oedipus complex nor is there any reason fully to give it up – on the contrary, its acquisition is the first triumph of her feminine destiny under patriarchy. If we might elaborate on Freud here, we could say that where the boy's resolution and abandonment of his Oedipus complex is his entry into his cultural heritage, the girl, on the contrary, finds her cultural place in patriarchal society when she finally manages to achieve her Oedipal love for her father. This difference must have enormous implications.

I have given a schematic presentation of the central thesis of 'Some Psychical Consequences of the Anatomical Distinction between the Sexes'; there are other suggestions therein that lead in other but related directions. It seems to me that in Freud's psychoanalytical schema, here as elsewhere, we have at least the beginnings of an analysis of the way in which a patriarchal society bequeaths its structures to each of us (with important variations according to the material conditions of class and race), gives us, that is, the cultural air we breathe, the ideas of the world in which we are born and which, unless patriarchy is demolished, we will pass on to our children and our children's children. Individual experimentation with communes and so forth can do no more than register protest. For whether or not the actual father is there does not affect the perpetuation of the patriarchal culture within the psychology of the individual; present or absent, 'the father' always has his place. His actual absence may cause confusion, or, on another level, relief, but the only difference it makes is within the terms of the overall patriarchal assumption of his presence. In our culture he is just as present in his absence. The Oedipus complex, then, expresses in miniature the power of the father or that of the name-of-the-father, but father it is. All feminist accounts that I have read or encountered misrepresent patriarchal society as one embodying the power of men in general; in fact, it is quite specifically the importance of the *father* that *patriarchy* signifies. Freud's 1925 essay is a key to the understanding of the oppression of women under patriarchy.

Psychoanalysis: A Humanist Humanity or a Linguistic Science?

¶ 'Psychoanalysis: A Humanist Humanity or a Linguistic Science?' is a draft of a lecture I gave at the Rockefeller Conference on the Humanities, held at Bellagio, Italy, in the late spring of 1977. By this time I was in the middle of my psychoanalytic training. I had been interested in Lacan's work since the mid-1960s but now, in my training, I was confronted with a very different tendency within psychoanalysis: the British school of object-relations theory. I had read some of these writings previously as aids and inspirations for my literary interests. But experience of a personal analysis is an altogether different event. This paper is my musing at the time on the two opposite positions of Lacan and of object-relations theorists.

It is a problematic pleasure to consider the relationship of psychoanalysis to the Humanities. Psychoanalysis illustrates the double connotation of a Humanity. It is concerned with human culture and its theory and practice is (or should be) humane in the deepest sense of the word. Beneath this, within the term 'Humanity' and within psychoanalysis, is the implication of a humanist philosophy.

233

If the term 'Humanities' is cognate with Terence's '*Homo sum; humani nil a me alienum puto*', then psychoanalysis is almost an ideal type. Freud's self-analysis taught him the pains and pleasures of his own human nature and their extremities left him convinced that nothing felt, spoken or acted by people should be classified as outside the arena of human experience. Thus psychoanalysis reclaimed mental illness from the extra-human territory of moral or physical condemnation: it brought the 'unknown' down from the skies and located it within the human unconscious. For instance, hysteria is rescued from classification as obstinate malingering; abundant female sexuality from its nineteenth-century implications of moral degeneracy; schizophrenia from twentieth-century biochemical determinism, and so on.

A system of thought that is about human nature, must also have somewhere within it, and despite protestations to the contrary, an image of man. Within the terms of psychoanalysis as a Humanity Lionel Trilling has, perhaps, best expressed Freud's humane vision of human nature:

> The Freudian man is, I venture to think, a creature of far more dignity and far more interest than the man which any other modern System has been able to conceive. Despite popular belief to the contrary, man as Freud conceives him, is not to be understood by any simple formula (such as sex) but is rather, an inextricable tangle of culture and biology. And not being simple, he is not simply good; he has, as Freud says somewhere, a kind of hell within him from which arise everlastingly the impulses which threaten his civilisation. He has the faculty of imagining for himself more in the way of pleasure and satisfaction than he can possibly achieve. Everything he gains he pays for in more than equal coin, compromise and compounding with defeat constitute his best way of getting through the world. His best qualities are the result of a struggle whose outcome is tragic. Yet he is a creature of love; it is Freud's sharpest criticism of the Adlerian psychology that to aggression it gives everything and to love nothing at all. One is always aware in reading Freud how little cynicism there is in his thought. His desire for man is only that he should be human, and to this end his science is devoted.[1]

Nurtured as he was on Sophocles, Shakespeare, Goethe

and Ibsen, Freud's concept of man is not optimistic or utilitarian nor, on the other hand, mystical or religious. He was gentle but emphatic with opponents on both these issues. Thus he defends to the end his notion of man's death drive against those who found its pessimism unpalatable and thus, at the opposite extreme, he writes to his friend, the Swiss Pastor, Pfister, how he will leave to him the higher spiritual realms whilst he toils in the basement. Freud's concern is man formed among men.

Psychoanalysis is not only a theory about human nature and a concept of man, it is also a therapy that aims to help man. All aspects are interdependent. Freud, who thought health was an ideal fiction, nevertheless subscribed to a loose description of satisfactory living as the ability to love and to work well. The therapeutic aim of psychoanalysis as a Humanity differs somewhat in its manifestations according to the different psychoanalytic tendencies but all of these operate within this framework. Some analysts stress that aspect of the work which hopes to bring under the individual's conscious control the drives and desires whose strength and prohibition are tormenting him. Others aim for a more harmonious balance of the polar forces of love and aggression whose lack of equilibrium has caused the distress or disorientation. Perhaps most simply, the aim of this 'know thyself' endeavour is some never-complacent 'accept thyself so that thou can accept thy neighbour': a proposition that brings us back full circle to Terence.

Many accusations are made against Freud and subsequent psychoanalysts for failure to conform to Terence's ideal. These are accusations that claim psychoanalysts do not practise what psychoanalysis preaches. They accept the humanist tenets but argue they are not implemented. Freud, for example, is charged with antagonism to women and intolerance of homosexuality, yet Freud knew the great extent of his own femininity and the psychological significance of his important male friendships. It is not my intention here to counteract these accusations nor to submit that a man may have his prejudices but as a psychoanalyst he should not. I would suggest that standing as an ideal type does not mean one practises that type ideally. In this field, doubtless psychoanalysis has much malpractice to answer for. An example, however, from the country which is usually accused of housing its worst offenders, indicates that the Terence tradition is not *only* honoured in the breach. I quote from a review of *Splitting*, a lengthy case history by the American psychoanalyst, Robert Stoller:

> The patient, Mrs G., was a most unusual woman. She broke almost all of society's rules: she shot several men. . . She committed armed robbery. . . She stole three cars. . . wrote bad cheques. . . was the subject of two pornographic movies; had innumerable sexual relations with men (including family members such as her grandfather and an uncle); had over 20 homosexual affairs; four marriages. . . five illegitimate pregnancies. . . addiction to amphetamine. . . with two drug psychoses; mainlining and sniffing of heroin. . . association with motor cycle gangs, criminals, drug pushers and corrupt policemen; over 30 moving traffic violations, drag racing and many serious vehicle accidents (with no driver's licence). . . [Yet to Dr Stoller] she was a likeable person, a fact which emanates from the verbatim reports and is corroborated by Dr Stoller's statements about his relationship with her.[2]

There are other criticisms of psychoanalysis which charge that its basic propositions are neither humanist nor humane. In this respect, and for the purposes of this argument, we can reduce the prevalent radical criticisms of psychoanalysis to two broad themes. They come from radical therapy groups, left-wing and largely phenomenological and existentialist in their own approach, and from feminist and gay groups which share and dispute a concern with psychoanalysis over definitions of gender formation and sexuality. Both these groups fault psychoanalysis for propagating conformism to bourgeois ideology and for ignoring social reality in the construction of psychological material.

An important aspect of the claim of conformism to bourgeois ideology is the supposed superiority of the analyst and the demand that the patient identify with him and his values. Practices involving the complete parity of patient and therapist or of all members of a consciousness-raising group are designed to counteract these possibilities. The notion that psychoanalytic practice subtly coerces adaptation to an inhumane conservative society is counteracted by a radical alternative that reverses the postulates: sanity is madness; madness sanity. Behind the fundamental misunderstanding about social reality we can clearly glimpse the presupposition that psychoanalysis is inhumane. So the argument goes: Why cannot it see that the nuclear family scapegoated and drove into schizophrenia that adolescent boy? That of course women envy the penis when men have all the power?

I think that these criticisms of psychoanalysis are based on misapprehension; but psychoanalysis itself cannot avoid some responsibility for the misunderstandings. Before acknowledging the pertinence of criticisms of psychoanalysis as a 'humanity', in this its humanist sense, let us pay it due tribute. This aspect of psychoanalysis is, in the best sense of the term, a part of the liberal humanist tradition. A future for it that is worth having will criticise and transform but not lose the gains that it has accrued to itself here. It is, indeed, in part, for the abuses of its humanism that its humanism must be criticised.

Furthermore, whatever the criticisms of its humane and humanist practice, and whatever may be the validity of its own claim to be a science, in one limited sense, psychoanalysis will always be a 'humanity': it is about the human being within human culture. In attempting to reconstruct the history of the individual, the point to which psychoanalysis returns is to the inception of the human animal as a social being – to the origin and source of its humanity. Beneath that is what Freud called the 'biological bedrock', ever-present but impenetrable by psychoanalysis. The human being of psychoanalytic inquiry is the individual within culture. He is not, nor can he be, an isolate or a 'natural' man.

Undoubtedly then, the predominant tradition of psycho-analysis has been as one of the humanities, within this, at its best, it has been both humane and humanist. But Freud always insisted that it was a science. He tried to root its scientificity in analogies with the natural sciences and this has led the subsequent debate as to its scientific status up some grotesque blind alleys.

At times Freud pondered on the implications of the biology of the human being. Subsequently, his comparison of the psychoanalytic method with that of other sciences has been confused with his interest in biology to produce a situation in which the biological bedrock – not the psychoanalytical one of psychical reality – is tested as the yardstick of psychoanalysis' claim. (A typical example is the notion that Master's & Johnson's gadgets have disproved part of Freud's theories of sexuality.) Caught between this misunderstanding and the contemporary fetishism of measurement as the means to scientific verifiability, psychoanalysis can have had little hope as a science and may well have wanted to count its blessings as a Humanity. But I suspect that Freud would have rejected this classification much as when Havelock Ellis gallantly offered it the title of Art: he thanked him but declined. The problem, then, is twofold: a Humanity or a Science, humanist or anti-humanist?

An implication of humanism is that not only is man at the centre of his own world ('man makes history'), but also at the centre of himself; that he has the possibility of choice, of being master of his own actions. Where psychoanalysis is concerned, the generous postulates of humanism have been taken to extremes and hence distorted in the philosophy that underlies that branch of it which is known as ego-psychology.

Within ego-psychology the function of the ego is to master, integrate and adapt, its task is to take control of as much of what is out of its control as it can. Such an ego, standing supreme, is the individualist triumphant. When Freud originally wrote that the therapeutic aim was that 'Where id was there should ego come to be', his intention was clearly the humanist one of putting a man's sense of self as far as possible at the centre of himself. Ego-psychology takes this to extremes and ignores another immensely important and seemingly contradictory remark of Freud's: that the ego is never master even in its own house.

With ego-psychology we reach both the dead end of humanism and its death. For this ego is a master confronting other masters, an 'identity' recognising only other 'identities'. It gets trapped in knowing the other only as other than itself (i.e. not being able to know it), or as the same as self (i.e. not knowing that it is other). Its method of understanding is only empathic understanding which banishes scientific, that is, analytical, understanding. The magnificence of Terence's statement gets stuck on the horns of this dilemma.

In presenting the case against psychoanalysis as a humanistically inclined Humanity, I am going to turn to the French psychoanalytic school of Jacques Lacan. Lacan made a complete break with ego-psychology, denouncing it as the ideology of free enterprise. He continued to attack what he saw as the humanist nucleus of ego-psychology. His work, therefore, was a persistent effort to read Freud in Freud's own anti-humanist utterances. I do not intend here to try and even cursorily survey the vast difficulties of Lacan's work, only to select one or two themes of pertinence to our question about psychoanalysis as a Humanity with humanist implications.

Lacan has taken his own conception of the ego from Freud's work on narcissism, mourning and melancholia. This ego is *not* centred in itself – as is that of the ego-psychologists – but is formed in alienation. The small human infant forms its ego in an identification with an other (person) who is a whole object. It is thus in its very formation other than itself and it is constantly threatened by its own otherness. We can see how this gets us out of the humanist dilemma of self and other and, indeed, into frightening possibilities in which the ego far from being a master, is instead a slave to its own illusion of wholeness and mastery. 'Man', in no way the centre-piece of the humanist world, has moved into the margins of 'himself'.

The thrust of Lacan's attack is against the biologism of

prevalent psychoanalytic theory. If the ego is not at one with itself, neither is man in harmony with his biology. Lionel Trilling admired Freud for his vision of man as a complex intermix of culture and biology. For the French psychoanalysts of the Lacanian school, the human being is human precisely at those points where he is *severed* from his biology. For instance: the human animal needs food and with the taking of food goes pleasure. (The psychoanalytic exemplary instance is the sucking infant.) When the biological need is satisfied, the breast is removed but the wish for pleasure continues. If we see this pleasure as erotic, then human sexuality comes into being at the moment of the absence of the natural object and at that moment desire is created by becoming detached from biological need. The removal of the natural object leaves the infant with a 'memory trace' of it, an ideational representation that has come about in this inter-subjective setting of mother and infant. This memory-trace signifies loss – it is not an image of the missing object but a signifier which fits into a system of signifiers. This is the transition from the biological individual to the human unconscious – a structure of signifiers. It is the transformation too of the biologically present object to the social and psychological object known only by its absence. Once more we can see the undercutting of Terence's dictum. We could almost rewrite it as: I am human, therefore I myself am alien to myself.

When Lacan writes: 'The unconscious is a concept forged on the trace of that which operates to constitute the subject', he is referring to this moment of the creation both of the social and of the self as social (the unconscious is always social – Jung's collective unconscious is tautologous, redundant) in the inscription of absence. He therefore reformulates Freud's task 'where id was, there shall ego come to be' as 'there where the gap was, must I come to be'. There is no question of the ego mastering more of the terrifying primary processes, rather the task is to re-found one's subjectivity in the gap.

This gap, which is neither the self nor the other but is one in which both are constituted and both are alienated, is the field of communication or 'language'. What people share, therefore, is this field of language (which Lacan calls the 'Other') and their own otherness to themselves. It is for this reason that psychoanalysis is a linguistic exercise and that the pathological condition which it addresses 'resolves itself wholly in a language-analysis, because the symptom is itself linguistically structured, because it is itself a language the utterance of which must be brought to birth'. The analyst in his otherness and as representative of the 'Other' which is human language must facilitate this utterance. If we forget this linguistic dimension and regard the analytic cure as an identification with the analyst's ego or as the establishment of a more positive identity (the ego-psychologist's project), then, implies Lacan, we reify both the self and the other and induce in the patient a masochistic wish for approbation from the analyst as master. These latter criticisms of Lacan's do indicate for us the weakness at the heart of humanist psychoanalysis, the distortion of which is the strength of ego-psychology. They show us, too, why such a practice can become a relevant target for the banal attacks of radical therapy or anti-psychoanalytic feminism. In its ego-psychology abuses humanism reveals its flaw.

The Lacanian school, then, would rescue psychoanalysis from the impasse of humanism by re-establishing it as a linguistic science. To do this Lacanians read a motif in Freud's work that counterpoints his humanism, that de-centres man from himself and makes him part of a text. This clearly has huge implications both for psychoanalysis and for the understanding of the human being. It affects our concept of what it means to be a person.

I want to look briefly at some of the implications of this radical shift within psychoanalysis by a brief glance at the question of the psychological distinction between the sexes. This is because it is a field that interests me particularly and because it is crucial to our concept of the human being.

What follows are really notes that I hope can be taken up in discussion:

All human societies make a social mark of the distinction

between the sexes. This is a structural distinction, placing people on one side or other of an imagined line – it has nothing to do with content or quality. Societies name the people on either side men and women and their attributes masculinity and femininity; these are not fixed qualities but the mark that distinguishes them means that each is the condition of the other and at no point can they occupy the same place. They are, if you like, vehicles for meaning but have no meaning of themselves. (Freud was very aware of this, calling them 'meanings of uncertain content'.) Because all societies make this distinction between the sexes, femininity and masculinity are universal signifiers, signifying only their relationship to each other, which means their difference from each other.

A baby becomes human at that moment when the natural object of his biological need is absent and his desire for it is created. At that moment when his biological ground-plan comes only to underpin his psyche in the very act of its establishment by its severance from it, the baby acquires his first signifying element: the mark of what is missing. In all cases, the baby is born into a society that has already marked the distinction between the sexes and has, as part of its essential structure, therefore, the signifying terms, masculinity and femininity. As the baby enters the human world of signifiers it enters into a structure in which somewhere along the chain are the terms 'masculine' and 'feminine', signifiers that are – so to speak – lying in wait to be filled with their meaning, what it is they signify. The baby enters the signifying chain at the moment of absence of the object, but this object is not what is signified. The baby has a memory-trace signifying satisfaction but it is left to satisfy itself from its own phantasies.

In psychoanalytic terminology, a phantasy is an imaginary scene in which the subject is the protagonist and in which, in distorted manner, a wish is fulfilled. Phantasy is the setting for the desire (wish) which came into being with its prohibition (absence of object). The baby, or any human subject of whatever age, places himself as actor somewhere in the scene. (One can easily verify this structure from one's own day-dreams.) The place the subject occupies is unfixed or even invisible being de-subjectivised as often in dreams. Phantasies are scripts capable of dramatisation, usually in visual form.

Laplanche and Pontalis write:

> . . . the primary function of fantasy [is] to be a setting for desire . . . But as for knowing who is responsible for the setting, it is not enough for the psychoanalyst to rely on the resources of his science, nor on the support of myth. He must also become a philosopher.[3]

At this point I wish to depart from the French psychoanalysts to whom my observations are so far indebted.

I, too, do not know who is responsible for the setting that is phantasy, but would like to hazard a suggestion. Just as the biological function underpins the desire which exists by virtue of its separation from that function (see above), so it may be that the external world is the support for the phantasy which likewise comes into being at that moment when it is, through its absence, clearly differentiated from it.

Of the coming into being of sexuality and phantasy at the moment of their split from biology (the moment of Lacan's memory-trace), Laplanche and Pontalis write:

> It is known that erogeneity can be attached to predestined zones of the body (thus, in the activity of sucking, the oral zone is destined by its very physiology to acquire an erogenous value), but it is also available to any organ (even internal organs), and to any region or function of the body. In every case the function serves only to support, the taking of food serving, for instance, as a model for fantasies of incorporation. Though modelled on the function, sexuality lies in its difference from the function: in this sense its prototype is not the act of sucking, but the enjoyment of going through the motions of sucking . . . the moment when the external object is abandoned, when the aim and the source assume an autonomous existence with regard to feeding and the digestive system.[4]

I am suggesting that just as it is at this moment of separation from biology that the human animal becomes a human being, so also it is at this moment that the natural object becomes (in its absence) a human object. All the 'things' – the people, sounds, sights and smells, and so on – that were there in the outside world surrounding the baby before its humanisation, provide the support (or underpin) for the phantasy scenario which comes into being with their absence.

Hence we could say that phantasy is modelled on the external world but comes into being with its difference from it. Elsewhere Laplanche and Pontalis write: '[Fantasy] is not an *object* that the subject imagines and aims at, so to speak, but rather a *sequence* in which the subject has his own part to play and in which permutations of roles and attributions are possible.'[5] The external world with its many roles and attributions *before* it is (for the baby) an external world (a material world) would offer, I would think, an underpinning for this sequence. (At this point one should remind oneself that neither the substructural biology, nor the substructural external reality are the object of psychoanalytic enquiry.)

The human baby, then, is now a phantasising sexual human being inserted into a structure of signifying terms. In other words, he has, like the rest of humanity, an unconscious. It will be some time before the baby acquires all the signifying terms – the basic structure of language. When it does, two of these terms are masculinity and femininity, related as signifying terms by their difference. As they are related by their difference, some further signifying term must mark the difference – a difference that says they can never be the same as each other. It is the phallus – with all the connotations of such a term as are found in its ancient usage – that is the signifying mark of the distinction between the sexes. (The speculative reasons for the privileged position of the phallus would take me too far afield from my general topic here.) It is the mark of difference and as such is 'discovered' by the infant when it is found to be *absent* in the mother.

Here the relevant signifying terms, then, are: masculinity,

femininity and the mark of their difference: the phallus. They are unfilled by any signified object but at some point will come to have some such content and the baby, as it more fully takes its place within the human order, will have to 'know' what it is that is signified in his particular society by the terms. It is here, I suggest, in filling these signifying terms, that phantasy and the external world which, in its severance from it, underpins phantasy, come into play to occupy the place left open by the signifier, to become what is signified. Whatever their anatomical sex, all babies will form their sexed identifications with whatever is signified on either side of the line that is drawn by the presence or absence of the phallus.

The external world acts only as a support to the content of the phantasy, to the actors in the dramatisation. The phantasy, using this world as a support, supplies the story and what is to be signified by the various terms. Thus, for instance, the penis and he who possesses it (the father) come to be signified by, but they are not identical with, the phallus which as a signifying term can move around giving us such important concepts and observations as the unconscious phallic mother. This inconstant relationship between the signifying term and its content is witnessed by the bisexuality of all people and by the more extreme possibilities, such as transsexualism.

My purpose in this brief and very partial presentation has been to illustrate how far removed from the humanist implications of psychoanalysis as a humanity is this re-reading of it as a science of language, in which the fundamental social order is a chain of signifying terms wherein the baby must be inserted. The ego is formed in an imaginary identification with another whole (person) and is thus other than itself; basic identifications, as are those of sex, are made not by identifying with actual people – mother or father – but by insertion into a symbolic order in which the key signifier of the difference, the phallus, can shift around over what is signified.

In opposition to this version, a humanist understanding

would – and in the case of humanistic psychoanalysis does – treat the human being as though he were, or at least could come to be, at the centre of himself, and those with whom one was or was not identifying, as themselves – as meaning what they stand for. In this philosophy there is no tension between the signifier and the signified. But it should be stressed that the humanist vision of man is no less complex for it is as varied and diverse as all the innumerable differences and permutations of which man is capable.

Lacan has set up his psychoanalytic linguistic science in explicit opposition to psychoanalysis as a humanist discipline featuring as a humanity. Because this latter dimension of psychoanalysis is so varied and so much more prevalent, I have not illustrated it here, only described it.

The Lacanian school argues against the empiricism of the humanist method, a method which involves the accumulation of ever more various case histories. We can easily see that the humanist argument would presuppose such an accumulation. The humanist position goes for the texture of the ever more diverse and this in its turn establishes its humane approach – there is nothing that anyone can say, know or feel that does not touch a resonance somewhere in oneself. If it stopped there, such understanding would only be empathy, but it does not, for in its turn this approach wants to establish its scientific status. Its understanding is not empathy but systematic knowledge because what is observed is not infinitely various, it is only the combinations, the complex totalities that make up the whole, that are so.

The Lacanians argue that the humanist position is pure ideology and the ego which poses as strong is the supreme ideologue trapped in a frightening illusion of strength. This may be true, but the material for psychoanalysis comes from the person in the consulting room. We all live within ideology, both the general ideology of all human society and the specific ideologies of our times. It may well be the case that the humanist ideology is in itself only the liberal side of the capitalistic, free-enterprise coin – but we cannot escape it:

must live ourselves (indeed, be ourselves) within its meanings while we are in such a society. The psychoanalyst cannot discard or disregard the fact that we want to feel as though we are or could be at the centre of ourselves and that we have this as our (doubtless, never-accomplished), endeavour. His clinical work, and *therefore* his theory, must be not only a scientific knowledge of the human being who, as it were, is free from the specific ideologies of his society and inserted only in the biggest ideology – the universal human Order itself – but a science that works with both propositions.

The humanist aspect of psychoanalysis offers much greater freedom within the specific ideology; it speaks, therefore, to the person embedded within that ideology – as all of us in the west are. The Lacanian method would seem to cut through this as an illusion, situating the person only in the larger human Order. The danger of the humanist approach is that it may propagate a more tolerant version of the present state of things and thereby confirm them; the danger of the Lacanian method is that it may subvert it only by not noticing it.

Lacan's reading of Freud develops one motif of his work; the humanist another. Lacan would regard the humanist Freud as the pre-scientific, the pre-Freud, Freud; the Freud who was unable to use a linguistic science because he lived before its proper development but who nevertheless prefigured it. I would suggest, on the contrary, that it was important that there were 'two Freuds' and that a humane science of psychoanalysis as theory and therapy, will try to bring them together not 'again', but anew.

Freud and Lacan: Psychoanalytic Theories of Sexual Difference

¶ 'Freud and Lacan' was published in *Feminine Sexuality: Jacques Lacan and the Ecole Freudienne* (London, 1982). Jacqueline Rose and myself first conceived and embarked on the project in 1977. Our original aim had been to gather together the dispersed thinking on the question of femininity from Lacan's works and then set this together with post-Lacanian and anti-Lacanian French feminist psychoanalytic essays on the subject. In the end it seemed both more feasible as a task of scholarship and more coherent as a political project to produce a volume only of Lacan and Lacanian contributions.

Jacqueline Rose translated and annotated all the essays she had discovered and selected. We wrote separate but complementary introductions. Mine – reprinted here – was on the psychoanalytic background to Lacan and Jacqueline Rose's was on the movement of the concept of femininity within Lacan's own writings. She also reflected on the French feminist objections to Lacan's theories. We worked closely together on every aspect of the volume. Lacan's psychoanalytic ideas about femininity return direct to the Freud who wrote: 'femininity is a concept of uncertain content'. Lacan, in emphasising the uncertainty, the illusory, delusive nature of the subject (the ego or 'I'), in stressing that this 'I' is a construction that the unconscious shows to disappear, demonstrated how sexual identity partakes of the same uncertainty, how it too is a construction. Its disappearance in the unconscious proves it is such. Lacan's work interested me for many reasons. Feminism discovered women as a distinct social group – a group whose identity was as women. But there is another side to that description, there is the point where femininity disappears, where it is nothing other – neither more nor less – than the various places where it is constructed. In very different idiom and speaking to very different questions, the interest in Lacan in this essay has some echoes of my interest in Althusser in 'Women: The Longest Revolution'. There women were nothing other than the different social and economic structures in which they were created; there was no essential category: 'women'. Lacan's work sets up that realisation at the very heart of the question of the construction of femininity.

> I object to all of you [Horney, Jones, Rado, etc.,] to the extent that you do not distinguish more clearly and cleanly between what is psychic and what is biological, that you try to establish a neat parallelism between the two and that you, motivated by such intent, unthinkingly construe psychic facts which are unprovable and that you, in the process of doing so, must declare as reactive or regressive much that without doubt is primary. Of course, these reproaches must remain obscure. In addition, I would only like to emphasize that we must keep psychoanalysis separate from biology just as we have kept it separate from anatomy and physiology . . .
>   (Freud, letter to Carl Müller-Braunschweig 1935)

Jacques Lacan dedicated himself to the task of re-finding and re-formulating the work of Sigmund Freud. Psychoanalytic theory today is a variegated discipline. There are contradictions within Freud's writings and subsequent analysts have developed one aspect and rejected another, thereby using one theme as a jumping-off point for a new theory. Lacan conceived his own project differently: despite the contradictions and impasses, there is a coherent theorist in Freud whose ideas do not need to be diverged from; rather they should be set within a cohesive framework that they anticipated but which, for historical reasons, Freud himself could not formulate. The development of linguistic science provides this framework.

It is certainly arguable that from the way psychoanalysis has grown during this century we have gained a wider range of therapeutic understanding and the multiplication of fruitful ideas, but we have lost the possibility of a clarification of an essential theory. To say that Freud's work contains contradictions should not be the equivalent of arguing that it is heterogeneous and that it is therefore legitimate for everyone to take their pick and develop it as they wish. Lacan set his face against what he saw as such illegitimate and over-tolerant notions of more-or-less peacefully coexistent lines of psychoanalytic throught. From the outset he went back to Freud's basic concepts. Here, initially, there is agreement among psychoanalysts as to the terrain on which they work: psychoanalysis is about human sexuality and the un-conscious.

The psychoanalytic concept of sexuality confronts head-on all popular conceptions. It can never be equated with genitality nor is it the simple expression of a biological drive. It is always psycho-sexuality, a system of conscious and unconscious human fantasies involving a range of excitations and activities that produce pleasure beyond the satisfaction of any basic physiological need. It arises from various sources, seeks satisfaction in many different ways and makes use of many diverse objects for its aim of achieving pleasure. Only with great difficulty – and then never perfectly – does it move from being a drive with many component parts – a single 'libido' expressed through very different phenomena – to being what is normally understood as sexuality, something which *appears* to be a unified instinct in which genitality predominates.

For all psychoanalysts the development of the human

subject, its unconscious and its sexuality go hand-in-hand, they are causatively intertwined. A psychoanalyst could not subscribe to a currently popular sociological distinction in which a person is born with their biological gender to which society – general environment, parents, education, the media – adds a socially defined sex, masculine or feminine. Psychoanalysis cannot make such a distinction: a person is formed *through* their sexuality, it could not be 'added' to him or her. The ways in which psycho-sexuality and the unconscious are closely bound together are complex, but most obviously, the unconscious contains wishes that cannot be satisfied and therefore have been repressed. Predominant among such wishes are the tabooed incestuous desires of childhood.

The unconscious contains all that has been repressed from consciousness, but it is not co-terminous with this. There is an evident lack of continuity in conscious psychic life – psychoanalysis concerns itself with the gaps. Freud's contribution was to demonstrate that these gaps constitute a system that is entirely different from that of consciousness: the unconscious. The unconscious is governed by its own laws, its images do not follow each other as in the sequential logic of consciousness but by condensing onto each other or by being displaced onto something else. Because it is *unconscious*, direct access to it is impossible but its mani-festations are apparent most notably in dreams, everyday slips, jokes, the 'normal' splits and divisions within the human subject and in psychotic and neurotic behaviour.

Lacan believed that though all psychoanalysts subscribe to the importance of the unconscious and to the privileged position of sexuality within the development of the human subject, the way in which many post-Freudians have elaborated their theories ultimately reduces or distorts the significance even of these fundamental postulates. To Lacan, most current psychoanalytic thinking is tangled up in popular ideologies and thus misses the revolutionary nature of Freud's work and replicates what it is its task to expose:

psychoanalysis should not subscribe to ideas about how men and women do or should live as sexually differentiated beings, but instead it should analyse how they come to be such beings in the first place.

Lacan's work has always to be seen within the context of a two-pronged polemic. Most simply he took on, sometimes by explicit, named reference, more often by indirect insult or implication, almost all analysts of note since Freud. Both internationally and within France, Lacan's history was one of repeated institutional conflict and ceaseless opposition to established views. Outside France his targets were the theories of American dominated ego-psychology, of Melanie Klein and of object- relations analysts,[1] most notably, Balint, Fairbairn and Winnicott. Lacan was more kindly disposed to the clinical insights of some than he was towards those of others but he argued that they are all guilty of misunderstanding and debasing the theory inaugurated by Freud.

The second prong of Lacan's polemic relates to a mistake he felt Freud himself initiated: paradoxically, while cherishing the wounds of his rejection by a lay and medical public, Freud strove to be easily understood. The preposterous difficulty of Lacan's style is a challenge to easy comprehension, to the popularisation and secularisation of psychoanalysis as it has occurred most notably in North America. Psychoanalysis should aim to show us that we do not know those things we think we do; it therefore cannot assault our popular conceptions by using the very idiom it is intended to confront; a challenge to ideology cannot rest on a linguistic appeal to that same ideology. The dominant ideology of today, as it was of the time and place when psychoanalysis was established, is humanism. Humanism believes that man is at the centre of his own history and of himself; he is a subject more or less in control of his own actions, exercising choice. Humanistic psychoanalytic practice is in danger of seeing the patient as someone who has lost control and a sense of a real or true self (identity) and it aims to help regain these. The matter and manner of all Lacan's work challenges this notion of the human subject: there is none such. In the sentence structure of most of his public addresses and of his written style the grammatical subject is either absent or shifting or, at most, only passively constructed. At this level, the difficulty of Lacan's style could be said to mirror his theory.

The humanistic conception of mankind assumes that the subject exists from the beginning. At least by implication, ego-psychologists, object-relations theorists and Kleinians, base themselves on the same premise. For this reason, Lacan considers that in the last analysis, they are more ideologues than theorists of psychoanalysis. In the Freud that Lacan uses, neither the unconscious nor sexuality can in any degree be pre-given facts, they are constructions; that is, they are objects with histories and the human subject itself is only formed within these histories. It is this history of the human subject in its generality (human history) and its particularity (the specific life of the individual) as it manifests itself in unconscious fantasy life, that psychoanalysis traces. This immediately establishes the framework within which the whole question of female sexuality can be understood. As Freud put it: 'In conformity with its peculiar nature, psychoanalysis does not try to describe what a woman is – that would be a task it could scarcely perform – but sets about enquiring *how she comes into being*' (my italics).[2]

Lacan dedicated himself to reorienting psychoanalysis to its task of deciphering the ways in which the human subject is constructed – how it comes into being – out of the small human animal. It is because of this aim that Lacan offered psychoanalytic theory the new science of linguistics which he developed and altered in relation to the concept of subjectivity. The human animal is born into language and it is within the terms of language that the human subject is constructed. Language does not arise from within the individual, it is always out there in the world outside, lying in wait for the neonate. Language always 'belongs' to another person. The human subject is created from a general law that comes to it from outside itself and through the speech of other people, though this speech in its turn must relate to the general law.

Lacan's human subject is the obverse of the humanists'. His subject is not an entity with an identity, but a being created in the fissure of a radical split. The identity that seems to be that of the subject is, in fact, a mirage arising when the subject forms an image of itself by identifying with others' perception of it. When the human baby learns to say 'me' and 'I' it is only acquiring these designations from someone and somewhere else, from the world which perceives and names it. The terms are not constants in harmony with its own body, they do not come from within itself but from elsewhere. Lacan's human subject is not a 'divided self' (Laing) that in a different society could be made whole, but a self which is only actually and necessarily created within a split – a being that can only conceptualise itself when it is mirrored back to itself from the position of another's desire. The unconscious where the subject is not itself, where the 'I' of a dream can be someone else and the object and subject shift and change places, bears perpetual witness to this primordial splitting.

It is here, too, within the necessary divisions that language imposes on humans, that sexuality must also find its place. The psychoanalytic notion that sexual wishes are tabooed and hence repressed into the unconscious is frequently understood in a sociological sense (Malinowski, Reich, Marcuse . . .). The implication is that a truly permissive society would not forbid what is now sexually taboo and it would thus liberate men and women from the sense that they are alienated from their own sexuality. But against such prevalent notions, Lacan states that desire itself, and with it, sexual desire, can only exist by virtue of its alienation. Freud describes how the baby can be observed to hallucinate the milk that has been withdrawn from it and the infant to play throwing-away games to overcome the trauma of its mother's necessary departures. Lacan uses these instances to show that the object that is longed for only comes into existence *as an object* when it is lost to the baby or infant. Thus any satisfaction that might subsequently be attained will always contain this loss within it. Lacan refers to this dimension as 'desire'. The baby's need can be met, its demand responded to, but its desire only exists because of the initial failure of satisfaction. Desire persists as an effect of a primordial absence and it therefore indicates that, in this area, there is something fundamentally impossible about satisfaction itself. It is this process that, to Lacan, lies behind Freud's statement that 'We must reckon with the possibility that something in the nature of the sexual instinct itself is unfavourable to the realisation of complete satisfaction'.[3]

This account of sexual desire led Lacan, as it led Freud, to his adamant rejection of any theory of the difference between the sexes in terms of pre-given male or female entities which complete and satisfy each other. Sexual difference can only be the consequence of a division; without this division it would cease to exist. But it must exist because no human being can become a subject outside the division into two sexes. One must take up a position as either a man or a woman. Such a position is by no means identical with one's biological sexual characteristics, nor is it a position of which one can be very confident – as the psychoanalytical experience demonstrates.

The question as to what created this difference between the sexes was a central debate among psychoanalysts in the 1920s and 1930s. Lacan returned to this debate as a focal point for what he considered had gone wrong with psychoanalytic theory subsequently. Again Lacan underscored and re-formulated the position that Freud took up in this debate. Freud always insisted that it was the presence or absence of the phallus and *nothing else* that marked the distinction between the sexes. Others disagreed. Retrospectively, the key concept of the debate becomes transparently clear: it is the castration complex. In Freud's eventual schema, the little boy and the little girl initially share the same sexual history which he terms 'masculine'. They start by desiring their first object: the mother. In fantasy this means having the phallus which is the object of the mother's desire (the phallic phase). This position is forbidden (the castration complex) and the differentiation of the sexes occurs. The castration complex ends the boy's Oedipus complex (his love for his mother) and inaugurates for the girl the one that is specifically hers: she will transfer her object love to her father who seems to have the phallus and identify with her mother who, to the girl's fury, has not. Henceforth the girl will desire to have the phallus and the boy will struggle to represent it. For this reason, for both sexes, this is the insoluble desire of their lives and, for Freud, because its entire point is precisely to be insoluble, it is the bedrock beneath which psychoanalysis cannot reach. Psychoanalysis cannot give the human subject that which it is its fate, as the condition of its subjecthood, to do without:

> At no other point in one's analytic work does one suffer more from an oppressive feeling that all one's repeated efforts have been in vain, and from a suspicion that one has been 'preaching to the winds', than when one is trying to persuade a woman to abandon her wish for a penis on the ground of its being unrealisable.[4]

There was great opposition to Freud's concept of the girl's phallic phase and to the significance he eventually gave to the castration complex. Lacan returns to the key concept of the debate, to the castration complex and, within its terms, the meaning of the phallus. He takes them as the bedrock of subjectivity itself and of the place of sexuality within it. The selection of the phallus as the mark around which subjectivity and sexuality are constructed reveals, precisely, that they are constructed, in a division which is both arbitrary and alienating. In Lacan's reading of Freud, the threat of castration is not something that has been done to an already existent girl subject or that could be done to an already existent boy subject; it is, as it was for Freud, what 'makes' the girl a girl and the boy a boy, in a division that is both essential and precarious.

The question of the castration complex split psycho-analysts. By the time of the great debate in the mid-1920s, the issue was posed as the nature of female sexuality but underlying that are the preceding disagreements on castration anxiety. In fact, all subsequent work on female sexuality and on the construction of sexual difference stems from the various places accorded to the concept of the castration complex. It stands as the often silent centre of all the theories that flourished in the decades before the war; the effects of its acceptance or rejection are still being felt.

The arguments on female sexuality are usually referred to as the 'Freud–Jones debate'. In the presentation that follows I have not adhered to the privileging of Jones' work because the purpose of my selection is to draw attention to the general nature of the problem and present Freud's work from the perspective to which Lacan returns. I shall leave aside details of differences between analysts; rank those otherwise different on the same side; omit the arguments of any analyst, major or minor, whose contribution in this area does not affect the general proposition – the selection will seem arbitrary from any viewpoint other than this one. Individual authors on the same side differ from one another, are inconsistent with themselves or change their minds, but these factors fade before the more fundamental division around the concept of castration. In the final analysis, the debate relates to the question of the psychoanalytic understanding both of sexuality and of the unconscious and brings to the fore issues of the relationship between psychoanalysis and biology and sociology. Is it biology, environmental influence, object-relations or the castration complex that makes for the psychological distinction between the sexes?

Freud, and Lacan after him, are both accused of producing phallo-centric theories – of taking man as the norm and woman as what is different therefrom. Freud's opponents are concerned to right the balance and develop theories that explain how men and women in their psycho-sexuality are equal but different. To both Freud and Lacan their task is not to produce justice but to explain this difference which to them uses not the man, but the phallus to which the man has to lay claim, as its key term. But it is because Freud's position only clearly became this in his later work that Lacan insists we have to 're-read it', giving his theory the significance and coherence which otherwise it lacks.

Although Lacan takes no note of it, there is, in fact, much in Freud's early work, written long before the great debate, that later analysts could use as a starting-point for their descriptions of the equal, parallel development of the sexes. Divisions within writings on the subject since, in many ways, can be seen in terms of this original divergence within Freud's own work.

Freud's work on this subject can be divided into two periods. In the first phase what he had to say about female sexuality arises in the context of his defence of his theory of the fact and the importance of infantile sexuality in general before a public he considered hostile to his discoveries. This first phase stretches from the 1890s to somewhere between 1916 and 1919. The second phase lasts from 1920 until his final work published posthumously in 1940. In this second period he is concerned with elaborating and defending his understanding of sexuality in relation to the particular question of the nature of the difference between the sexes. By this time what he wrote was part of a discussion within the psychoanalytic movement itself.

In the first phase there is a major contradiction in Freud's work which was never brought out into the open. It was immensely important for the later theories of female sexuality. In this period Freud's few explicit ideas about female sexuality revolve around his references to the Oedipus complex. The essence of the Oedipus complex is first mentioned in his published writings in a passing reference to *Oedipus Rex* in *The Interpretation of Dreams* (1900); in 1910 it is named as the Oedipus complex and by 1919, without much theoretical but with a great deal of clinical expansion (most notably in the case of Little Hans), it has become the foundation stone of psychoanalysis. The particular ways in which the Oedipus complex appears and is resolved characterise different types of normality and pathology; its event and resolution explain the human subject and human desire. But the Oedipus complex of this early period is a simple set of relationships in which the child desires the parent of the opposite sex and feels hostile rivalry for the one of the same sex as itself. There is a symmetrical correspondence in the history of the boy and the girl. Thus in 'Fragment of an Analysis of a Case of Hysteria' (1905) Freud writes: 'Distinct traces are probably to be found in most people of an early partiality of this kind – on the part of a daughter for her father, or on the part of a son for his mother',[5] and the entire manifest interpretation of Dora's hysteria is in terms of her infantile Oedipal love for her father, and his substitute in the present, Herr K. Or, in 'Delusions and Dreams in Jensen's *Gradiva*': 'It is the general rule for a normally constituted girl to turn her affection towards her father in the first instance'.[6] And so on. At the root of Freud's assigning parallel Oedipal roles to girls and boys lies a notion of a natural and normative heterosexual attraction; a notion which was to be re-assumed by many psychoanalysts later. Here, in Freud's early work, it is as though the concept of an Oedipus complex – of a fundamental wish for incest – was so radical that if one was to argue at all for the child's incestuous desires then at least these had better be for the parents of the opposite sex. Thus it was because Freud had to defend his thesis of infantile incestuous sexuality so strenuously against both external opposition and his own reluctance to accept the idea, that the very radicalism of the concept of the Oedipus complex acted as a conservative 'stopper' when it came to understanding the difference between the sexes. Here Freud's position is a conventional one: boys will be boys and love women, girls will be girls and love men. Running counter, however, to the normative implications of sexual symmetry in the Oedipal situation are several themes. Most importantly there is both the structure and the argument of the *Three Essays on the Theory of Sexuality*

(1905). Lacan returns to this work reading the concept of the sexual drive that he finds latent there through the light shed on it in Freud's later paper on 'Instincts and Their Vicissitudes' (1915).

The *Three Essays* is the revolutionary founding work for the psychoanalytic concept of sexuality. Freud starts the book with chapters on sexual aberration. He uses homosexuality to demonstrate that for the sexual drive there is no natural, automatic object; he uses the perversions to show that it has no fixed aim. As normality is itself an 'ideal fiction' and there is no qualitative distinction between abnormality and normality, innate factors cannot account for the situation and any notion of the drive as simply innate is therefore untenable. What this means is that the understanding of the drive itself is at stake. The drive (or 'instinct' in the Standard Edition translation), is something on the border between the mental and the physical. Later Freud formulated the relationship as one in which the somatic urge delegated its task to a psychical representative. In his paper, 'The Unconscious', he wrote:

> An instinct can never become an object of consciousness – only the idea that represents the instinct can. Even in the unconscious, moreover, an instinct cannot be represented otherwise than by an idea . . . When we nevertheless speak of an unconscious instinctual impulse or of a repressed instinctual impulse . . . we can only mean an instinctual impulse the ideational representative of which is unconscious.[7]

There is never a causal relationship between the biological urge and its representative: we cannot perceive an activity and deduce behind it a corresponding physical motive force. The sexual drive is never an entity, it is polymorphous, its aim is variable, its object contingent. Lacan argues that the *Three Essays* demonstrate that Freud was already aware that for mankind the drive is almost the *opposite* of an animal instinct that knows and gets its satisfying object. On the other hand, object-relations theorists contend that Freud suggested that the sexual drive was a direct outgrowth of the first satisfying relationship with the mother; it repeats the wish to suck or be held. The baby thus has a first 'part-object' in the breast and later an object in the mother whom it will love pre-Oedipally and then as a 'whole object' Oedipally. Later the sexual drive of the adult will seek out a substitute for this which, if it is good enough, can and will satisfy it.

Though the lack of clarity in some parts of the *Three Essays* could, perhaps, be held responsible for this diversity of interpretation and for the new dominant strand of humanism that Lacan deplores, there is absolutely nothing within the essays that is compatible with any notion of natural heterosexual attraction or with the Oedipus complex as it is formulated in Freud's other writing of this period. The structure and content of the *Three Essays* erodes any idea of normative sexuality. By deduction, if no heterosexual attraction is ordained in nature, there can be no genderised sex – there cannot at the outset be a male or female person in a psychological sense.

In the case of 'Dora', Freud assumed that had Dora not been an hysteric she would have been naturally attracted to her suitor, Herr K, just as she had been attracted to her father when she was a small child. In other words, she would have had a natural female Oedipus complex. But the footnotes, written subsequently, tell another story: Dora's relationship to her father had been one not only of attraction but also of identification with him. In terms of her sexual desire, Dora is a man adoring a woman. To ascribe the situation to Dora's hysteria would be to beg the whole founding question of psychoanalysis. Hysteria is not produced by any innate disposition. It follows that if Dora can have a masculine identification there can be no natural or automatic heterosexual drive.

Until the 1920s Freud solved this problem by his notion of bisexuality. 'Bisexuality' likewise enabled him to avoid what would otherwise have been too blatant a contradiction in his position: thus he argued that the too neat parallelism of the boy's and girl's Oedipal situations, the dilemma of Dora, the presence of homosexuality, could all be accounted for by the fact that the boy has a bit of the female, the girl of the male. This saves the Oedipus complex from the crudity of gender determinism – but at a price. If, as Freud insists, the notion of bisexuality is not to be a purely biological one, whence does it arise? Later analysts who largely preserved Freud's early use of the term, did relate bisexuality to the duplications of anatomy or based it on simple identification: the boy partly identified with the mother, the girl partly with the father. For Freud, when later he reformulated the Oedipus complex, 'bisexuality' shifted its meaning and came to stand for the very uncertainty of sexual division itself.

Without question during this first period, Freud's position is highly contradictory. His discovery of the Oedipus complex led him to assume a natural heterosexuality. The rest of his work argued against this possibility as the very premise of a psychoanalytic understanding of sexuality. There is no reference to the Oedipus complex or the positions it assumes in the *Three Essays* and by this omission he was able to avoid recognising the contradiction within his theses, though the essays bear its mark within some of the confusing statements they contain.

By about 1915 it seems that Freud was aware that his theory of the Oedipus complex and of the nature of sexuality could not satisfactorily explain the difference between the sexes. Freud never explicitly stated his difficulties (as he did in other areas of work), but in 1915, he added a series of footnotes to the *Three Essays* which are almost all about the problem of defining masculinity and femininity. Other writers – notably Jung – had taken Freud's ideas on the Oedipus complex as they were expressed at the time to their logical conclusion, and in establishing a definite parity between the sexes had re-named the girl's Oedipal conflict, the Electra complex. Whether it was this work – Freud rejected the Electra complex from the outset – or whether it was the dawning awareness of the unsatisfactory nature of his own position that provoked Freud to re-think the issue, cannot be established; but something made him look more intensively at the question of the difference between the sexes.

One concept, also added in 1915 to the *Three Essays*, marks both the turning point in Freud's own understanding of the differences between men and women, and also the focal point of the conflict that emerges between his views and those of most other analysts on the question. This concept is the castration complex.

During the first phase of Freud's work we can see the idea of the castration complex gradually gain momentum. It was discussed in 'On the Sexual Theories of Children' (1908), crucially important in the analysis of Little Hans (1909), yet when he wrote 'On Narcissism: An Introduction' in 1914, Freud was still uncertain as to whether or not it was a universal occurrence. But in 1915 it starts to assume a larger and larger part. By 1924, in the paper on 'The Dissolution of the Oedipus Complex', the castration complex has emerged as a central concept. In his autobiography of 1925, Freud wrote: 'The *castration complex* is of the profoundest importance in the formation alike of character and of neurosis'.[8] He made it the focal point of the acquisition of culture; it operates as a law whereby men and women assume their humanity and, inextricably bound up with this, it gives the human meaning of the distinction between the sexes.

The castration complex in Freud's writings is very closely connected with his interest in man's prehistory. It is unnecessary to enumerate Freud's dubious anthropological reconstructions in this field; what is of relevance is the importance he gave to an *event* in man's personal and social history. It is well known that before he recognised the significance of fantasy and of infantile sexuality, Freud believed the tales his hysterical patients told him of their seductions by their fathers. Although Freud abandoned the particular event of paternal seduction as either likely or, more important, causative, he retained the notion of an event, prehistorical or actual. Something intruded from without into the child's world. Something that was not innate but came from outside, from history or prehistory. This 'event' was to be the paternal threat of castration.

That the castration complex operates as an external event, a law, can be seen too from a related preoccupation of Freud's. Some time around 1916, Freud became interested in the ideas of Lamarck. This interest is most often regarded, with condescension, as an instance of Freud's nineteenth-century scientific anachronism. But in fact, by 1916, Lamarck was already outmoded and it is clear that Freud's interest arose not from ignorance but from the need to account for something that he observed but could not theorise. The question at stake was: how does the individual acquire the whole essential history of being human within the first few short years of its life? Lamarckian notions of cultural inheritance offered Freud a possible solution to the problem. In rejecting the idea of cultural inheritance, Freud's opponents may have been refusing a false solution but in doing so they missed the urgency of the question and thereby failed to confront the problem of how the child acquires so early and so rapidly its knowledge of human law. Karen Horney's 'culturalist' stress – her emphasis on the influence of society – was an attempt to put things right, but it failed because it necessitated an implicit assumption that the human subject could be set apart from society and was not constructed solely within it: the child and society were separate entities mutually affecting each other. For Horney there are men and women (boys and girls) already there; in this she takes for granted exactly that which she intends to explain.

Freud's concept of the castration complex completely shifted the implications of the Oedipus complex and altered the meaning of bisexuality. Before the castration complex was given its full significance, it seems that the Oedipus complex dissolved naturally, a passing developmental stage. Once the castration complex is postulated, it is this alone that shatters the Oedipus complex. The castration complex institutes the superego as its representative and as representative thereby of the law. Together with the organising role of the Oedipus complex in relation to desire, the castration complex governs the position of each person in the triangle of father, mother and child; in the way it does this, it embodies the law that founds the human order itself. Thus the question of castration, of sexual difference as the product of a division, and the concept of an historical and symbolic order, all begin, tentatively, to come together. It is on their interdependence that Lacan bases his theories in the texts that follow.

When Freud started to elevate the concept of castration to its theoretical heights, resistance started. It seems that infantile sexuality and the Oedipus complex were un-palatable ideas for many outside the psychoanalytical movement, yet it would appear that there was something even more inherently unacceptable about the notion of a castration complex and what it assumed in the girl child, penis envy, even for psychoanalysts. After this point, Freud's emphasis on the importance of the castration complex comes not only from his clinical observations, his growing awareness of the contradictions of his own work, and his increasing interest in the foundations of human history, but to a degree as a response to the work of his colleagues.

Lou Andreas-Salomé, van Ophuijsen, then Karl Abraham and Auguste Starcke in 1921 initiate the response to the notion. Franz Alexander, Otto Rank, Carl Müller-Braunschweig, and Josine Müller continue it until the names that are more famous in this context – Karen Horney, Melanie Klein, Jeanne Lampl-de Groot, Helene Deutsch, Ernest Jones – are added in the mid-1920s and 1930s. Others join in: Fenichel, Rado, Marjorie Brierley, Joan Rivière, Ruth Mack Brunswick, but by 1935 the positions have clarified and the terms of the discussion on sexual differences do not change importantly, though the content that goes to fill out the argument does so.

Karl Abraham's work is crucial. He died before the great debate was in full flow, but his ideas, though often not acknowledged, were central to it – not least because most of Freud's opponents believed that Abraham's views were representative of Freud's. As Abraham is ostensibly amplifying Freud's work and writing in support of the concept of the castration complex, this was an understandable but completely mistaken assumption. In their letters Freud and Abraham are always agreeing most politely with one another and this makes it rather hard to elucidate the highly significant differences between them. One difference is that Freud argues that girls envy the phallus, Karl Abraham believes that both sexes in parallel fashion fear castration – which he describes as lack of sexual potency.[9] In Abraham's thesis, boys and girls – because they are already different – respond differently to an identical experience; in Freud the same experience distinguishes them. By implication for Abraham, but not for Freud, by the time of the castration complex there must already be 'boys' and 'girls'. This important distinction apart, the real divergence between Abraham's arguments and those of Freud can best be glimpsed through the shift of emphasis. In the work of both writers incest is taboo ('castration'); but only for Freud must there be someone around to forbid it: prohibition is in the air.

In Freud's work, with its emphasis on the castration complex as the source of the law, it is the father who already possesses the mother, who metaphorically says 'no' to the child's desires. The prohibition only comes to be meaningful to the child because there are people – females – who have been castrated in the particular sense that they are without the phallus. It is only, in other words, through 'deferred action' that previous experiences, such as the sight of female genitals, become significant. Thus, for Freud, contained within the very notion of the castration complex is the theory that other experiences and perceptions only take their meaning from the law for which it stands. In Abraham's work, to the contrary, the threat of castration arises from an actual perception that the child makes about a girl's body: no one intervenes, there is no prohibiting father whose threat is the utterance of a law; here it is the 'real' inferiority of the female genitals that once comprehended initiates the complex in both sexes.

Here, however, within Freud's work, we come across a further and most important contradiction; it was one he did not have time fully to resolve. It is a contradiction that explains subsequent readings of Abraham's and Freud's work as coincident. Freud is clear that the boy's castration complex arises from the penis being given significance from the father's prohibition; but sometimes he suggests that the girl's penis envy comes from a simple perception that she makes; she sees the actual penis, realises it is bigger and better and wants one. Clearly such inequity in girls' and boys' access to meaning is untenable: why should the girl have a privileged relationship to an understanding of the body? In fact, there is evidence that Freud was aware of the discrepancy in his account; his published statements tend to be confusing, but in a letter he wrote: 'The sight of the penis and its function of urination cannot be the motive, only the trigger of the child's envy. However, no one has stated this'.[10] Unfortunately neither Freud nor any subsequent analyst stated this clearly enough in their published writings.

Freud referred to Abraham's article on the female castration complex (1920) as 'unsurpassed'. But absolutely nothing in the theoretical framework of Freud's writing confirmed Abraham's perspective. Freud certainly talks of the woman's sense of 'organ-inferiority' but this is never for him the *motive* for the castration complex or hence for the dissolution of the Oedipus complex; it is therefore not causative of female sexuality, femininity or neurosis. For Freud the absence of the penis in women is significant only in that it makes meaningful the father's prohibition on incestuous desires. In and of itself, the female body neither indicates nor initiates anything. The implication of the different stress of Freud and Abraham is very far-reaching. If, as in Abraham's work, the actual body is seen as a motive for the constitution of the subject in its male or female sexuality, then an historical or symbolic dimension to this constitution is precluded. Freud's intention was to establish that very dimension as the *sine qua non* of the construction of the human subject. It is on this dimension that Lacan bases his entire account of sexual difference.

If Freud considered that the actual body of the child on its own was irrelevant to the castration complex, so too did he repeatedly urge that the actual situation of the child, the presence or absence of the father, the real prohibition against masturbation and so on, could be insignificant compared with the ineffable presence of a symbolic threat (the 'event') to which one is inevitably subjected as the price of being human. Unable to accept the notion of cultural inheritance, other analysts, agreeing with Freud that an actual occurrence could not account for the omnipresent castration anxiety they found in their clinical work, had to look elsewhere for an explanation. In all cases, they considered the castration complex not as something essential to the very construction of the human subject but as a fear that arises from the internal experiences of a being who is already, even if only in a primitive form, constituted as a subject. As a consequence, in none of these alternative theories can castration have any fundamental bearing on sexual difference.

Thus Stärcke found the prevalence of castration anxiety in the loss of the nipple from the baby's mouth, so that daily weaning accounted for the universality of the complex. As a further instance he proposed the baby's gradual ability to see itself as distinct from the external world: 'The formation of the outer world is the original castration; the withdrawal of the nipple forms the root-conception of this'.[11] Franz Alexander and Otto Rank took castration back to the baby's loss of the womb, which was once part of itself. Freud took up his colleague's ideas on separation anxiety (as he termed it) most fully in *Inhibitions, Symptoms and Anxiety* written in 1925, but two years earlier he had added this footnote to the case of Little Hans:

While recognising all of these roots of the complex, I have

nevertheless put forward the view that the term 'castration complex' ought to be confined to those excitations and consequences which are bound up with the loss of the *penis*. Any one who, in analysing adults, has become convinced of the invariable presence of the castration complex, will of course find difficulty in ascribing its origin to a chance threat – of a kind which is not, after all, of such universal occurrence; he will be driven to assume that children construct this danger for themselves out of the slightest hints . . . [12]

There is a fundamental distinction between recognising that the castration complex may refer back to other separations and actually seeing these separations as castrations. To Freud the castration complex divided the sexes and thus made the human being, human. But this is not to deny the importance of earlier separations. Freud himself had proposed that the loss of the faeces constituted the possibility of a retrospective referral; the castration complex could use it as a model. Freud's account is retroactive: fearing phallic castration the child may 'recollect' previous losses, castration gives them their relevance. In the other accounts it is these separations that make castration relevant; here the scheme is prospective: early losses make the child fear future ones. For Freud, history and the psychoanalytic experience is always a reconstruction, a retrospective account: the human subject is part of such a history. The other explanations make him grow developmentally. If one takes castration itself back to the womb, then the human subject was there from the outset and it can only follow that what makes him psychotic, neurotic or 'normal' is some arbitrarily selected constitutional factor or some equally arbitrary environmental experience.

Once more, Lacan underlines and reformulates Freud's position. The castration complex is *the* instance of the humanisation of the child in its sexual difference. Certainly it rejoins other severances; in fact, it gives them their meaning. If the specific mark of the phallus, the repression of which is the institution of the law, is repudiated then there can only be psychosis. To Lacan, all other hypotheses make nonsense of psychoanalysis. For him they once again leave unanswered the question whence the subject originates, and, he asks, what has happened to the language and social order that distinguishes him or her from other mammals – is it to have no effect other than a subsidiary one, on formation? Above all, how can sexual difference be understood within such a developmental perspective?

If it is argued that there is nothing specific about the threat of phallic castration; if birth, weaning, the formation of the outer world are all castrations, then something else has to explain the difference between the sexes. If castration is only one among other separations or is the same as the dread of the loss of sexual desire common to men and women alike (Jones' *aphanisis*), then what distinguishes the two sexes? All the major contributors to this field at this period, whether they supplemented or opposed Freud, found the explanation in a biological predisposition. This is the case with Freud's biologistic defender, Helene Deutsch, as it is with his culturalist opponent, Karen Horney.

The demoting of the castration complex from its key role in the construction of sexual difference, and the subsequent reliance on biological explanations, was accompanied by a further change. In the mid-1920s the focus of discussion shifted and a new epoch began. The crisis of the concept of the castration complex may well have contributed to a change of emphasis away from itself and towards a preoccupation with female sexuality. When the well-known names associated with the discussion – Horney, Deutsch, Lampl-de Groot, Klein, Jones – join in, their concern is less with the construction of sexual difference than it is with the nature of female sexuality. It is from this time that we can date what has become known as the 'great debate'. The debate was to reach its peak when in 1935, Ernest Jones, invited to Vienna to give some lectures to elucidate the fast growing differences between British and Viennese psychoanalysts, chose as his first (and, as it turned out, only) topic, female sexuality. While female sexuality is of course central to our concerns, we can see that something highly important was lost in the change of emphasis. Retrospectively one can perceive that the reference point is still the distinction between the sexes (the point of the castration complex) but by concentrating on the status and nature of female sexuality, it often happens that this is treated as an isolate, something independent of the distinction that creates it. This tendency is confirmed within the theories of those opposed to Freud. The opposition to Freud saw the concept of the castration complex as derogatory to women. In repudiating its terms they hoped both to elevate women and to explain what women consisted of – a task Freud ruled as psychoanalytically out-of-bounds. But from now on analysts who came in on Freud's side also saw their work in this way. Women, so to speak, had to have something of their own. The issue subtly shifts from what distinguishes the sexes to what has each sex got of value that belongs to it alone. In this context, and in the absence of the determining role of the castration complex, it is inevitable that there is a return to the very biological explanations from which Freud deliberately took his departure – where else could that something else be found?

For Freud it is, of course, never a question of arguing that anatomy or biology is irrelevant, it is a question of assigning them their place. He gave them a place – it was outside the field of psychoanalytic enquiry. Others put them firmly within it. Thus Carl Müller-Braunschweig, assuming, as did others, that there was an innate masculinity and femininity which corresponded directly with the biological male and female, wrote of a 'masculine and feminine id'. There is now not only an original masculinity and femininity but a natural heterosexuality. In 1926, Karen Horney spoke of the 'biological principle of heterosexual attraction' and argued from this that the girl's so-called masculine phase is a defence against her primary feminine anxiety that her father will violate her. Melanie Klein elaborated the increasingly prevalent notion that because of her primordial infantile feminine sexuality, the girl has an unconscious knowledge of the vagina. This naturalist perspective, exemplified in the work of Ernest Jones, posits a primary femininity for the girl based on her biological sex which then suffers vicissitudes as a result of fantasies brought into play by the girl's relations to objects. The theorists of this position do not deny Freud's notion that the girl has a phallic phase, but they argue that it is only a reaction-formation against her natural feminine attitude. It is a secondary formation, a temporary state in which the girl takes refuge when she feels her femininity is in danger. Just as the boy with his natural male valuation of his penis fears its castration, so the girl with her natural femininity will fear the destruction of her insides through her father's rape. The presence or absence of early vaginal sensations becomes a crucial issue in this context – a context in which impulses themselves, in a direct and unmediated way, produce psychological characteristics. Freud argued strenuously against such a position. In a letter that, read in this context, is not as cryptic as it at first appears, he wrote to Müller-Braunschweig:

> I object to all of you [Horney, Jones, Rado, etc.], to the extent that you do not distinguish more clearly and cleanly between what is psychic and what is biological, that you try to establish a neat parallelism between the two and that you, motivated by such intent, unthinkingly construe psychic facts which are un-provable and that you, in the process of doing so, must declare as reactive or regressive much that without doubt is primary. Of course, these reproaches must remain obscure. In addition, I would only like to emphasise that we must keep psychoanalysis separate from biology just as we have kept it separate from anatomy and physiology . . .[13]

However, there were those opponents of Freud's position who did not want to lean too heavily or too explicitly on a biological explanation of sexual difference; instead they stressed the significance of the psychological mechanism of identification with its dependence on an object. In both Freud's account and those of these object-relations theorists, after the resolution of the Oedipus complex, each child hopefully identifies with the parent of the appropriate sex. The explanations look similar – but the place accorded to the castration complex pushes them poles apart. In Freud's schema, after the castration complex, boys and girls will more or less adequately adopt the sexual identity of the appropriate parent. But it is always only an adoption and a precarious one at that as Dora's 'inappropriate' paternal identification had proved long ago. For Freud, identification with the appropriate parent is a *result* of the castration complex which has already given the mark of sexual distinction. For other analysts, dispensing with the key role of the castration complex, identification (with a biological prop) is the *cause* of sexual difference. Put somewhat reductively, the position of these theorists can be elucidated thus: there is a period when the girl is undifferentiated from the boy (for Klein and some others, this is the boy's primary feminine phase), and hence, when both love and identify with their first object, the mother; then, as a result of her biological sex (her femininity) and because her love has been frustrated on account of her biological inadequacy (she has not got the phallus for her mother and never will have), the little girl enters into her own Oedipus complex and loves her father; she then fully re-identifies with her mother and achieves her feminine identity.

It can be seen from this that the question of female sexuality was itself crucial in the development of object-relations theory. This understanding of femininity put a heavy stress on the first maternal relationship; the same emphasis has likewise characterised the whole subsequent expansion of object-relations theory. When the 'great debate' evaporated, object-relations theorists concentrated attention on the mother and the sexually undifferentiated child, leaving the problem of sexual distinction as a subsidiary that is somehow not bound up with the very formation of the subject. This is the price paid for the reorientation to the mother, and the neglect of the father, whose prohibition in Freud's theory, can alone represent the mark that distinguishes boys and girls. The mother herself in these accounts has inherited a great deal of the earlier interest in female sexuality – her own experiences, the experiences of her, have been well documented, but she is already constituted – in all her uncertainty – as a female subject. This represents an interesting avoidance of the question of sexual difference.

Freud acknowledged his serious inadequacies in the area of the mother-child relationship. In fact, his blindness was dictated not so much by his personal inclinations or his own masculinity – as he and others suggested – but by the nature of psychoanalysis as he conceived it. To Freud, if psychoanalysis is phallo-centric, it is because the human social order that it perceives refracted through the individual human subject is patro-centric. To date, the father stands in the position of the third term that *must* break the asocial dyadic unit of mother and child. We can see that this third term will always need to be represented by something or someone. Lacan returns to the problem, arguing that the relation of mother and child cannot be viewed outside the structure established by the position of the father. To Lacan, a theory that ignores the father or sees him embodied within the mother (Klein) or through her eyes, is nonsense. There can be nothing *human* that pre-exists or exists outside the law represented by the father; there is only either its denial (psychosis) or the fortunes and misfortunes ('normality' and neurosis) of its terms. Ultimately for Kleinian and non-Kleinian object-relations theorists (despite the great differences between them) the distinction between the sexes is not the result of a division but a fact that is already given; men and women, males and females, *exist*. There is no surprise here.

The debate with his colleagues also led Freud himself to make some crucial reformulations. Again these can be said to stem from his stress on the castration complex. Time and again in the last papers of his life he underscored its significance. In rethinking his belief that the boy and the girl both had a phallic phase that was primary, and not, as others argued, reactive and secondary, he re-emphasised, but more importantly, reformulated his earlier positions. The Oedipus complex as he had originally conceived it led to what he considered the impasses and mistakes of the arguments he opposed. The natural heterosexuality it assumed was untenable but a simple reversal with the stress on the first maternal relation was equally unsatisfactory. Without an ultimate reliance on a biologically induced identificatory premise, such a position does not account for the difference between the boy and the girl. Lacan would argue that it is at this juncture that Freud – his earlier positions now seen to be leading in false directions – brings forward the concept of desire. 'What,' asks Freud, 'does the woman [the little girl] want?' All answers to the question, including 'the mother', are false: she simply *wants*. The phallus – with its status as potentially absent – comes to stand in for the necessarily *missing* object of desire at the level of sexual division. If this is so, the Oedipus complex can no longer be a static myth that reflects the real situation of father, mother and child; it becomes a structure revolving around the question of where a person can be placed in relation to his or her desire. That 'where' is determined by the castration complex.

In his 1933 essay 'Femininity', Freud puts forward the solutions of his opponents on the issue of female sexuality as a series of questions. He asks 'how does [the little girl] pass from her masculine phase to the feminine one to which she is biologically destined?'[14] and contrary to the answers of his opponents, he concludes that: 'the constitution will not adapt itself to its function without a struggle',[15] and that though 'It would be a solution of ideal simplicity if we could suppose that from a particular age onwards the elementary influence of the mutual attraction between the sexes makes itself felt and impels the small woman towards men . . . we are not going to find things so easy . . . '.[16] The biological female is destined to become a woman, but the question to which psychoanalysis must address itself, is *how*, if she does manage this, is it to happen? His colleagues' excellent work on the earliest maternal relationship, from a psychoanalytic point of view, leaves unanswered the problem of sexual differentiation. As Freud puts it: 'Unless we can find something that is specific for girls and is not present or not in the same way present in boys, we shall not have explained the termination of the attachment of girls to their mother. I believe we have found this specific factor . . . in the castration complex'.[17]

Freud ended his life with an unfinished paper: 'Splitting of the Ego in the Process of Defence' (XXIII, 1940). It is about the castration complex and its implication for the construction of the subject. It describes the formation of the ego in a moment of danger (of threatened loss) which results in a primary split from which it never recovers. Freud offers the reaction to the castration complex when a fetish is set up as its alternative, as an exemplary instance of this split. In this paper we can see clearly the position of Freud's to which Lacan is to return. A primordially split subject necessitates an originally lost object. Though Freud does not talk of the object as a lost object as Lacan does, he is absolutely clear that its psychological significance arises from its absence, or as he put it in the essay on 'Femininity' from the fact that it could never satisfy: ' . . . the child's avidity for its earliest nourishment is altogether insatiable . . . it never gets over the pain of losing its mother's breast'.[18] Even the tribal child, breast-fed well beyond infancy, is unsatisfied: pain and lack of satisfaction are the point, the triggers that evoke desire.

Freud's final writings are often perceived as reflecting an old man's despair. But for Lacan their pessimism indicates a clarification and summation of a theory whose implications are and must be, anti-humanist. The issue of female sexuality always brings us back to the question of how the human subject is constituted. In the theories of Freud that Lacan redeploys, the distinction between the sexes, brought about by the castration complex and the different positions that must subsequently be taken up, confirms that the subject is split and the object is lost. This is the difficulty at the heart of being human to which psychoanalysis and the objects of its enquiry – the unconscious and sexuality – bear witness. To Lacan, a humanist position offers only false hopes on the basis of false theories.

It is a matter of perspective – and Lacan would argue that the perspective of post-Freudian analysts is ideological in that it confirms the humanism of our times. In the view of Kleinians and other object-relations theorists, whether it is with a primitive ego or as an initial fusion with the mother from which differentiation gradually occurs, the perspective starts from an identification with what seems to be, or ought to be, the subject. The problem these theorists address is: what does the baby/person do with its world in order for it to develop? Then the question is inverted: has the human environment been good enough for the baby to be able to do the right things? In these accounts a sexual identity is first given biologically and then developed and confirmed (or not) as the subject grows through interaction with the real objects and its fantasies of them on its complicated road to maturity.

Lacan takes the opposite perspective: the analysand's unconscious reveals a fragmented subject of shifting and uncertain sexual identity. To be human is to be subjected to a law which decentres and divides: sexuality is created in a division, the subject is split; but an ideological world conceals this from the conscious subject who is supposed to feel whole and certain of a sexual identity. Psychoanalysis should aim at a destruction of this concealment and at a reconstruction of the subject's construction in all its splits. This may be an accurate theory, it is certainly a precarious project. It is to this theory and project – the history of the fractured sexual subject – that Lacan dedicates himself.

Psychoanalysis and
Child Development

¶ The following review of Victoria Hamilton's *Narcissus and Oedipus: The Children of Psychoanalysis* (London, 1982), appeared in the *New Left Review*, Summer 1983.

In *Narcissus and Oedipus: The Children of Psychoanalysis*, Victoria Hamilton challenges Freud's theories of infantile and child development. She deploys psychoanalytic theories other than Freud's, mainly those of object-relations analysts, and she also uses some Kleinian and fewer Anna Freudian insights. She joins these with ethnological observations, theories of attachment behaviour and cybernetics to build an alternative model. In this she stresses the infant's and child's positive capacity for relationships, curiosity, play and creativity. She backs her thesis from direct observation of infant behaviour and her clinical experience of psychotherapy. The book is most sensitive, thoughtful and erudite. For me it is also highly problematic. In this review I am going to focus on the problems and not do justice to the book's creative insights. This is because it seems to me significant that a book as good as this one should nevertheless reflect a prevalent trend which exists on the outer edges of psychoanalysis – or rather of the use to which psychoanalysis

278

is put in various psychodynamic psychotherapies. This trend undermines the difficult and disturbing centre of psychoanalysis, turning it ultimately into a sociology of the emotions. It returns to the empirical observations from which psychoanalysis took its departure at the end of the last century. It produces a phenomenology where Freud strove for a science exactly as a way out of the impasses of phenomenology.

In brief, Hamilton proposes that where Freud has a concept of a neonate for whom the external world is experienced only as part of itself (primary narcissism), we should instead stress how from birth a baby engages in the mutuality of a two-person relationship. She considers that from the very beginning the baby is enough of a person to relate to its mother curiously and happily as someone other than itself. In her schema, narcissism is a pathology set up by something going wrong in the actual mother-child interaction. Likewise she sees Freud's concept of the Oedipus complex as being about an unnecessary pathology. Where Freud sees infantile sexual curiosity as being prohibited and then redirected – the Oedipus complex in which incestuous desires and their attendant questions are forbidden, repressed and later sublimated – Hamilton believes in a natural 'holy curiosity' which is only repressed or misdirected in malign conditions: Oedipus was an adopted child kept (like the Victorian children surrounding Freud) excessively in the dark. Hamilton offers subtle and moving re-readings of the two Greek myths to illustrate her argument.

The problem, I believe, is that though there is much overlap, in essence, Freud and Hamilton are talking about different things. In her introduction, Hamilton writes: 'in this book, it is Freud's view of relationship as a *secondary* development which is challenged. I do not attempt as Freud so valuably did, to characterise early relationships by reference to the *infant's unconscious accompanying phantasies*'[1] (my italics). But Freud's work is only ever about the unconscious however much that may and must interact with other modes of mental life. It is nowhere about child development as such.

Despite all the major psychoanalytic developments during and since Freud's time, psychoanalysis both as theory and therapy has always remained about the unconscious. It is not that there is nothing else to talk about; it is just that this is what psychoanalysis is about. Hamilton writes of Melanie Klein: 'Klein ignored the child's interactional context and his powers of cognition, perception and problem-solving outside the realm of "phantasy"';[2] and that Freud's 'tragic vision of knowledge omits the other side of curiosity – the "mystery" of reality of which one may "comprehend a little . . . each day"'.[3] But as Freud answered in another context: '[the] opposition accuses psychoanalysis of one-sidedness . . . Our one-sidedness is like that of the chemist, who traces all compounds back to the force of chemical attraction. He is not on that account denying the force of gravity; he leaves that to the physicist to deal with.'[4] I believe that any ultimately fruitful integration of the many theories of child development and of psychoanalysis must recognise their differences before it begins.

When Freud first used hypnosis and listened to the stories of his hysterical patients, he realised that the body symptom – the cough, the paralysed leg, the blindness which had no known physiological cause – expressed an idea not available to consciousness. There was another 'place' where the Cartesian division between mind and body did not apply. In the Freudian schema there are 'instincts' or 'drives' which are hypothetical entities existing on this borderland between the biological and the psychological, they exist prior to any distinction that could be made between unconscious and conscious. As they are on this borderline they cannot – except as a hypothesis – exist in a 'pure' state; ideas must have become attached to them. It is these mental representations of instincts that are contained within the unconscious – again these are only posited as a deduction back from the symptoms that confront us. The unconscious is set up by the refusal of these mental representations to consciousness – they cannot emerge except distorted by the censorship that prohibits them. They take the various routes into expression of neurotic symptom-formation, the many psychopathologies of everyday life, the psychosis of dreaming, of joking and so on. Psychoanalytic therapy is about the interpretation of these manifestations and the reconstruction of the hypothesised unconscious meanings latent beneath them.

During this century there has been a growing interest in the transference relationship within the clinical psychoanalytic setting as a means for understanding unconscious communications in the 'here and now'. The analysand transfers unconscious feelings and modes of communication onto and into the analyst. With the increasing stress on 'analysing the transference' a shift took place in the gravitational centre of psychoanalytic theory and therapy. Right up until his final writings in 1939, Freud himself remained committed to giving priority to interpreting what had been repressed into the unconscious. As repression proper only takes place with the prohibition on infantile desires (the Oedipus complex and the law against it: the castration complex), Freud's orientation was towards understanding the neuroses. As theory and therapy, Freud's thesis is always only of a reconstruction of the hypothetical unconscious infantile phantasies of the subject. Primary narcissism comes as a postulate within this framework. Clinically it was indicated by the withdrawal of the self during, for example, moments of acute ill-health. The sick person cannot afford to consider others – whence does this psychic possibility in all of us arise?

Object-relation theorists and Melanie Klein and those who followed her, felt that through the transference relationship, the therapist could experience more primitive forms of unconscious communication – the projections, introjections, splitting mechanisms, for instance, of the pre-verbal infant or of the psychotic. With the stress on the transference, the way was open to an emphasis on the *relationship* between analyst and analysand.

It is here that the psychoanalytic pole of Hamilton's work must be situated. Once the emphasis is not on the subject's construction of him or herself within history (Freud) but on the analytical relationship, the theories of infancy must shift accordingly. Because the transference repeats the past; the transference relationship repeats a past relationship. For Michael Balint, the major theorist here, there is no primary narcissism – only primary love: the patient is only a patient by definition of the relationship to the therapist, without a therapist he would be something else than a patient. The neonate cannot be a baby without a mother. Winnicott's contribution was to explore the dynamics of the relationship, the movement of the baby (and the baby in the adult analysand) from self to other via transitional phenomena and experiences. For the implications of Hamilton's theories, Klein's assertion of a primitive and primary ego which the neonate brings with it into the world – an unorganised but existent self – is of importance. It is only from the basis of such a proposition that the baby can be seen as an active partner of a relationship. But it is here, at this juncture, I would argue, that we slip away from the origins of Hamilton's theories within object-relations psychoanalysis and move onto very different terrain. She is proposing ultimately not an alternative psychoanalytic theory and practice, but something else. This, of course, does not invalidate it; though I believe that while the ideas are creative, the confusion behind them is not.

Balint, Klein and their followers are always talking about the unconscious. It is beside the point to accuse them, as is done here, of not sufficiently understanding cognition, perception or social interactions. This is not their task. When object-relations theorists are not talking about the unconscious, they do not believe that they are practising psychoanalysis: 'I wish to emphasise,' writes Winnicott in the introduction to his book, *Therapeutic Consultations in Child Psychiatry*, 'that my aim in presenting these consultations is not to give a series illustrating symptomatic cure. I am rather aiming to report examples of *communication with children*[5] (my italics).

When Hamilton describes her own and others' observations of infants and children and her therapeutic sessions, and constructs her theory, she is using some important psychoanalytic insights but she is not talking about anything psychoanalytical. Obviously much more than the symptoms of the unconscious come into a psychoanalytic therapeutic set-up; but if these 'other things' become the focus then a new therapy is produced and a new theory about these other aspects of mental life obviously will have to be forthcoming.

The emphasis in Hamilton's work is that her patients come for treatment because of their response to perturbing social and emotional conditions. Their behaviour, their expressions, their symptoms and their dreams are all seen to reflect these disturbing conditions and their responses to them, and they are interpreted as such. Because the clinical situation is not, despite the transference, the *same* as the original situation, in time the disturbed way of responding to disturbing conditions will change, and a 'cure' will be effected. However, for a psychoanalyst, what is relevant are not *social* or emotional conditions that are perturbing, but the very desires of the analysand themselves which are disturbing, even unbearable – hence they are unconscious. When Hamilton interprets a dream, she interprets the manifest content as a direct reflection or communication about an emotional situation; a psychoanalytic interpretation would use the patient's symptomatic associations, slips, elisions, omissions to see what it was that was too difficult to be expressed, what was hidden (latent) behind the manifest content.

If I say that Hamilton's clinical sessions always sound pleasant, I am not suggesting that they are not hard work. The pain and problems that patient and therapist experience are certainly there, but they come from elsewhere; they are brought from outside. A psychoanalytic session on the contrary is often, indeed usually, painful and arduous and difficult *in and of itself*. In Melanie Klein's uncompromising words: 'Analysis is not in itself a gentle method: it cannot spare the patient *any suffering*, and this applies equally to children.'[6] As one patient said to me at a mid-way point in the analysis: 'I used to come here feeling miserable and leave the session feeling better; now I come here feeling alright and leave miserable'. As analysand, one just does not want to know. The work, the challenge, the assignment taken on, is to know what one does not want to.

Using all the evidence of Bowlby, Bateson, Tinbergen and many others (which I do not dispute), Hamilton argues that the infant and, therefore, the child and adult naturally want to move out, relate, change. Yes, but this is not the infant or the infantile part that psychoanalysis addresses; that part, which is represented in the unconscious, is in conflict. It is outward-seeking, there are drives, 'the libido', but it is also deeply and definitionally conservative. The psychoanalytic notions of resistance, the death drive, and the negative therapeutic reaction fit in here. Usually misunderstood as being about their manifestations as aggression, they are, in essence, about this conservatism. The symptom is the radical part; the psychoses or neuroses are themselves efforts at cures – the repression is not working well enough and the mental representation of the drive (the forward-directed element) is breaking through. Analysis aims to help the symptom to rephrase itself, the delusion to express what it was originally about, not what it has become displaced onto.

Like others before her, Hamilton disputes the tragic nature of Freud's vision. Yet it has always seemed to me that psychoanalysis is an exemplary instance of Gramsci's 'pessimism of the intellect, optimism of the will'. Its practice is about the immense difficulty and the immense determination to change (the will); its theory is about the difficulty.

The model proposed by Hamilton must perforce not only be different, but opposite to that of psychoanalysis. For her, we start in health. Just as the problems come from the social situation outside a clinical setting, so too does the definition of health. The 'good-enough mother' will facilitate the necessary degree of healthy dependence and independence and the normal curiosity of the child:

> . . . the central theme of the book is that development proceeds from the intensely social to the personal. Problems of differentiation are emphasised more than those of object- or person-relating. In normal circumstances, attachment and object-relating may be taken for granted, being the secure base out of which differentiation occurs. The developing 'ego' may be thought of as an internal governor which functions, like the mother, as a secure base and as the regulator of the child's rapidly shifting, emotional field. The eager search for knowledge about the external world and one's self is seen more as the natural fruit and accompaniment of differentiation than the product of predominantly negative experiences such as pain, absence, or the frustration of sexual wishes.[7]

In this perspective, mental illness is a mistake, an unnecessary misdirection on a hilly but otherwise satisfactory road. But for psychoanalysis, normality is an 'ideal fiction', illness and health are on a continuum. The neurotic more often than the adjusted citizen will seek treatment simply because the pain of an aspect of life has come to seem greater than the pain of changing this aspect, but there is no *essential* difference between the two: '. . . a healthy person, too, is virtually a neurotic. . . The distinction between nervous health and neurosis is thus reduced to a practical question and is decided by the outcome – by whether the subject is left with a sufficient amount of capacity for enjoyment and efficiency'[8]; and 'Psychoanalytic research finds no fundamental, only quantitative distinctions between normal and neurotic life.'[9] The unconscious is universal, we are all and each of us Narcissus and Oedipus. These myths are not about pathological errors of mothering or adoption but about the untenable, the illicit and the wished-for within all of us.

There is a tendency at present, well represented by *Narcissus and Oedipus: The Children of Psychoanalysis*, to question the methodology that moves from the abnormal to the normal: Darwin's interest in mutations, Freud's in neurosis and psychosis. In this tendency it is argued: why should the canker tell us about the rose? For me, there are problems with reversing the methodology as there are problems with the allied notion of an optimism of the intellect. As I see it there is a kind of pleonasm present in proceeding from the normal. By what yardstick do we measure it? Hypothetically, if pathologies need not exist – they are unnecessary disturbances of a natural process, deformations alien to it – what is the natural process? We can tell a rose apart from a bluebell, genre from genre, but how can we begin to understand what it means for it to grow aright until it has gone wrong? Darwin's mainland finches would have gone on being distinguishable from tortoises, but only their isolated island variants gave the clue to the birdiness of the so-called normal finch. What is normality until it isn't? Or, perhaps, put another way: health, neurosis and psychosis are simultaneously the same and different. For Freud we are all Narcissus, we are all Oedipus; some of us get more stuck on these particular rocks than others. But normality is a 'fiction' we can only create from our position of disturbance. Simplifying matters greatly, Freud 'discovered' a phantasy of primary narcissism through withdrawals of the self into itself, the Oedipus complex through the symptomatic surfacing of desires in his own and others' hysteria. The terms narcissist and hysteric do not define separate categories of people; they are past presences, present potentialities, moments in the histories – past and present – of all of us.

Victoria Hamilton's Narcissus and Oedipus are not children nor even adopted children of psychoanalysis. They are the offspring of a sensitive and perceptive account of child development. There is plenty of room for such an account. As Freud commented: 'Psychoanalysis has never claimed to provide a complete theory of human mentality in general.'[10] The areas addressed by psychoanalysis and theories of child development have many points of contact and overlap but their objects of investigation are very different indeed.

Femininity,
Narrative and
Psychoanalysis

     ¶ While I was acting as a consultant
to the Humanities faculty of Deakin University, Victoria,
Australia (1982), I was invited to participate in an
interdisciplinary, all-Australia conference on *Narrative*.
'Femininity, Narrative and Psychoanalysis' is a transcription of
a tape-recording of my contribution.

    The focus, once more, is on my long-standing interest in the
questions of femininity, in stories and, once again – by now, for
more than thirty years – *Wuthering Heights*! But these old
preoccupations came up in a new context and my contribution
related directly to the issues that others spoke of at the
conference. There was great interest in the avant-
garde, in 'deconstruction', and in forms of literature and
art that eroded the norms by being transient, imagistic,
carnivalesque.

After some initial remarks on narrative in psychoanalytic
practice I shall say a little about women in the early history of
the novel, and turn from that to psychoanalytic theory; finally
I shall illustrate some of my concerns with reference to
Wuthering Heights.

As everybody knows, psychoanalysis is a talking cure. Obviously the analyst is male or female, the patient is male or female. If, as we frequently hear, language itself is phallocentric, what happens within the psychoanalytic practice? If language is phallocentric, what is a woman patient doing when she is speaking? What is a woman analyst doing when she is listening and speaking back? These stark questions are relevant to the type of work one can do on a literary text.

Psychoanalysts, at one level, are hearing and retelling histories. The patient comes with a story of his or her own life. The analyst listens; through an association something intrudes, disrupts, offers the 'anarchic carnival' back into that history, the story won't quite do, and so the process starts again. You go back, and you make a new history. Simultaneously with that, the analyst, in analysing his or her own countertransference, performs the same process on himself or herself, listens to a history, asks, 'Why am I hearing it as that?': something from the analyst's own associations disrupts, erupts into that narrative – the analyst asks a question from a new perspective, and the history starts all over again.

I bring this up here because I think it relates to questions about the role of carnival, about the role of disruption. What can you do but disrupt a history and re-create it as another history? Of course, you have multiple histories, though you can only live within one at a time.

I want to look very briefly at one kind of history: that pre-eminent form of literary narrative, the novel. Roughly speaking, the novel starts with autobiographies written by women in the seventeenth century. There are several famous men novelists, but the vast majority of early novels were written by large numbers of women. These writers were trying to establish what critics today call the 'subject in process'. What they were trying to do was to create a history from a state of flux, a flux in which they were feeling themselves in the process of becoming women within a new bourgeois society., They wrote novels to describe that process – novels which said: 'Here we are: women. What are our lives to be about? Who are we? Domesticity, personal relations, personal intimacies, stories . . . ' In the dominant social group, the bourgeoisie, that is essentially what a woman's life was to become under capitalism. The novel is that creation by the woman of the woman, or by the subject who is in the process of becoming woman, of woman under capitalism. Of course it's not a neat homogeneous construction: of course there are points of disruption within it; of course there are points of autocriticism within it. *Wuthering Heights,* for example, is a high point of autocriticism of the novel from within the novel. I shall discuss it soon in that light.

As any society changes its social structure, changes its economic base, artefacts are re-created within it. Literary forms arise as one of the ways in which changing subjects create themselves as subjects within a new social context. The novel is the prime example of the way women start to create themselves as social subjects under bourgeois capitalism – create themselves as a category: women. The novel remains a bourgeois form. Certainly there are also working-class novels, but the dominant form is that represented by the woman within the bourgeoisie. This means that when contemporary Anglo-Saxon feminist critics turn to women writers, resurrect the forgotten texts of these women novelists, they are, in one sense, being completely conformist to a bourgeois tradition. There is nothing wrong with that. It is an important and impressive tradition. We have to know where women are, why women have to write the novel, the story of their own domesticity, the story of their own seclusion within the home and the possibilities and impossibilities provided by that.

This tradition has been attacked by critics such as Julia Kristeva as 'the discourse of the hysteric'. I believe that it has to be the discourse of the hysteric. The woman novelist must be an hysteric. Hysteria is the woman's simultaneous acceptance and refusal of the organisation of sexuality under patriarchal capitalism. It is simultaneously what a woman can do both to be feminine and to refuse femininity, within patriarchal discourse. And I think that is exactly what the novel is; I do not believe there is such a thing as female writing, a 'woman's voice'. There is the hysteric's voice which is *the woman's masculine language* (one has to speak 'masculinely' in a phallocentric world) talking about feminine experience. It's both simultaneously the woman novelist's refusal of the woman's world – she is, after all, a novelist – and her construction from within a masculine world of that woman's world. It touches on both. It touches, therefore, on the importance of bisexuality.

I will say something very briefly about the psychoanalytical theories behind this position of the woman writer who must speak the discourse of the hysteric, who both refuses and is totally trapped within femininity. Then I'll lead on to some of the things that were said earlier about how to disrupt this.

There is much current interest in re-reading Freud in terms of the moment at which sexual division is produced within society: the moment of the castration complex, the moment when the heterogeneously sexual, polymorphously perverse, carnivalesque child has imposed on it the divisions of 'the law'; the one law, the law of patriarchy, the mark of the phallus. At that moment two sexes are psychologically created as the masculine and the not-masculine. At the point in which the phallus is found to be missing in the mother, masculinity is set up as the norm, and femininity is set up as what masculinity is not. What is not there in the mother is what is relevant here; that is what provides the context for language. The expression which fills the gap is, perforce, phallocentric.

In Lacanian thinking this is called the moment of the symbolic. The symbolic is the point of organisation, the point where sexuality is constructed as meaning, where what was heterogeneous, what was not symbolised, becomes organised, becomes created round these two poles, masculine and not-masculine: feminine.

What has gone before can be called the pre-Oedipal, the

semiotic, the carnivalesque, the disruptive. Now one can take two positions in relation to that. Either the pre-divided child, the heterogeneous child, the pre-Oedipal child, exists with its own organisation, an organisation of polyvalence, of poly-phony. Or alternatively that very notion of heterogeneity, of bisexuality, of pre-Oedipality, of union in a dyadic possibility of child with mother, that image of oneness and heterogeneity as two sides of the same coin, is, in fact, provided by the law, by the symbolic law itself. The question to me has a political dimension to it. If you think that the heterogeneous pre-Oedipal polyvalent world is a separate structure in its own right, then the law is disruptable, the carnival can be held on the church steps. But if this is not the case, if the carnival and the church do not exist independently of each other, the pre-Oedipal and the Oedipal are not separate, discrete states – if, instead, the Oedipal with the castration complex is what defines the pre-Oedipal, then the only way you can challenge the church, challenge both the Oedipal and its pre-Oedipal, is from within an *alternative symbolic universe*. You cannot choose the imaginary, the semiotic, the carnival as an alternative to the symbolic, as an alternative to the law. It is set up by the law precisely as its own ludic space, its own area of imaginary alternative, but not as a symbolic alternative. So that politically speaking, it is only the symbolic, a new symbolism, a new law, that can challenge the dominant law.

Now this does have relevance for the two alternative types of feminist literary criticism which exist today. It was suggested in another paper at this conference that this area of the carnival can also be the area of the feminine. I don't think so. It is just what the patriarchal universe defines as the feminine, the intuitive, the religious, the mystical, the playful, all those things that have been assigned to women – the heterogeneous, the notion that women's sexuality is much more one of a whole body, not so genital, not so phallic. It is not that the carnival cannot be disruptive of the law; but it disrupts only within the terms of that law.

This suggests a criticism of the French school associated with Kristeva, and to me it explains why that school is essentially apolitical. One needs to ask why Kristeva and her colleagues, while producing very interesting ideas, choose exclusively masculine texts and quite often proto-fascist writings as well. Disruption itself can be radical from the right as easily as from the left. This type of disruption is contained within the patriarchal symbolic. To me this is the problem.

I shall just mention some things about *Wuthering Heights* here so that we can use it if we like as a text on which to hang some ideas. I do not want to offer a psychoanalytic reading of this novel; I want to use *Wuthering Heights* simply to illustrate some of the points that I have tried to make here.

Emily Brontë is not writing a carnivalesque query to the patriarchal order; she is clearly working within the terms of a language which has been defined as phallocentric. Yet she is, through a kind of irony, posing questions about patriarchal organisation, and I'll sketch in some of the questions that I think are asked by the novel. First, who tells the story? Emily Brontë's manuscript was stolen from her and presented to a publisher by her sister, Charlotte. It was eventually published under a male pseudonym: Ellis Bell. The author is a woman, writing a private novel; she is published as a man, and acquires some fame and notoriety. She uses two narrators – a man, Lockwood, and a woman, the nurse, Nelly Dean. The whole novel is structured through those two narrators. Lockwood is a parody of the romantic male lover. He is set up as a foppish gentleman from the town who thinks he loves all the things the romantic gentleman is supposed to love, such as solitude, or a heart of gold beneath a fierce exterior. These things are criticised from within the novel, particularly through the character of Isabella, who thinks that Heathcliff is a dark, romantic Gothic hero who will prove to be the true gentleman beneath all his cruelty.

The story of Catherine and Heathcliff is a story of bisexuality, the story of the hysteric. Catherine's father had promised he would bring her back a whip from his visit to Liverpool. Instead he picks up a gypsy child who is fatherless, who never has had and never will have a father's name, who is given just one name: Heathcliff, the name of a brother of Catherine's who had died in infancy. Catherine looks in her father's pocket, finds the whip broken; instead of this whip she gets a brother/lover: Heathcliff.

Heathcliff is what Cathy wants all the rest of her life. She, in fact, makes the conventional feminine choice and marries somebody with whom she cannot be fully united – Edgar Linton. Edgar provides only an illusion of complementarity. I do not mean that they do not have a sexual relation; they have a child whose birth in one sense – the most unimportant – causes Catherine's death. The person that Catherine wants to be 'one' with is Heathcliff. Breaking the incest taboo, she says, 'I *am* Heathcliff, he's more myself than I am.' And Heathcliff says the same of Catherine. Each is the bisexual possibility of the other one, evoking a notion of oneness which is the reverse side of the coin of diverse heterogeneity. This type of 'oneness' can only come with death. Catherine dies; she haunts Heathcliff for twenty years, which is the date when the novel opens: it opens with Lockwood, who is given Heathcliff's dream, thinking (because he is the parodic romantic figure) that he can also get oneness. Heathcliff himself waits the whole stretch of the novel to have his own dream, which is to get back to Catherine. He dies getting back to her. 'Oneness' is the symbolic notion of what happens before the symbolic; it is death and has to be death. The choices for the woman within the novel, within fiction, are either to survive by making the hysteric's ambiguous choice into a femininity which doesn't work (marrying Edgar) or to go for oneness and unity, by suffering death (walking the moors as a ghost with Heathcliff).

I want to end with my beginning, and with a question. I think the novel arose as the form in which women had to construct themselves as women within new social structures; the woman novelist is necessarily the hysteric wanting to repudiate the symbolic definition of sexual difference under patriarchal law, unable to do so because without madness we are all unable to do so. Writing from within that position can be conformist (Mills and Boon romantic novels) or it can be critical (*Wuthering Heights*). I think the novel starts at a point where society is in a state of flux, when the subject is in the process of becoming a woman (or man) as today we understand that identity. If we are today again talking about a type of literary criticism, about a type of text where the subject is not formed under a symbolic law, but within what is seen as a heterogeneous area of the subject-in-process, I would like to end with asking a question: *in the process of becoming what*? I do not think that we can live as human subjects without in some sense taking on a history; for us, it is mainly the history of being men or women under bourgeois capitalism. In deconstructing that history, we can only construct other histories. What are we in the process of becoming?

The Question of Femininity and the Theory of Psychoanalysis

¶ A somewhat different version of a part of this paper was given as a talk to the Scientific Meeting of the Institute of Psychoanalysis in London in the spring of 1983. In all respects, it represents work-in-progress; incomplete, uncertain. It is about how the concept of femininity, and the problem it presents, provokes the development of Freud's psychoanalytic theory – this is a different question from that of the various analytical theories of femininity though eventually the two dimensions cannot be separated.

This talk, like the one I gave at Bellagio, is also a musing on different tendencies within psychoanalysis; this time, those of Freud and Melanie Klein. Although this piece is tentative and unfinished, I have included it here as it seems to echo so many of the preoccupations of the other essays in this volume. Although I did not realise it at the time of writing, it now appears to me, on looking back over the last twenty years, that it shows both the continuities and shifts in my previous thinking.

This talk is not about psychoanalytic concepts of femininity; it is about the connection between the question of femininity and the construction of psychoanalytic theory. I suggest that for Freud, 'femininity' sets the limits – the starting- and the end-point – of his theory, just as its repudiation marked the limits of the possibility of psychotherapeutic cure:

> We often have the impression that with the wish for a penis and the masculine protest we have penetrated through all the psychological strata and have reached bedrock, and that thus our activities are at an end. This is probably true . . . The repudiation of femininity can be nothing else than a biological fact . . .[1]

This intimate relationship between the problem of femininity and the creation of theory has not characterised other psychoanalytic work. This is largely to do with the shifting orientation: from neuroses to their underlying psychoses; from Oedipal to pre-Oedipal. In part it is to do with a difference in the nature of the theoretical constructions. After Freud the theoretical concepts belonging to psychoanalysis were there to be added to, repudiated, confirmed. By and large, alterations and alternatives emanate directly from the clinical work. But Freud had a different task: it was to make *other* concepts psychoanalytical.

For Freud the notion of the unconscious is there, an idea waiting in the circumambient literature; it is transformed into a theory by his application of it to the material he observed. Freud's patients, correct, repudiate or confirm his concepts which remain always larger, wider in application than their particularity in the clinical setting. But if we take Melanie Klein as an example we can see a different intellectual process. When she starts her work the theory and practice of psychoanalysis is already established. Immersed in her practice she comes to question specific aspects of the existent psychoanalytic theory. Her patients do not lead her back into an overarching theory but forward to a new description which relates only to what is observed and experienced. There is no preoccupation with the nature of theory as such, or with the nature of science, or with making psychoanalysis scientific. This is assumed. Not so for Freud.

What did Freud consider to be the nature of theory? I am going to give two quotations which will mark the framework. First, from the *New Introductory Lectures*:

> We cannot do justice to the characteristics of the mind by linear outlines like those in a drawing or in a primitive painting, but rather by areas of colour melting into one another as they are represented by modern artists. After making the separation we must allow what we have separated to merge together once more.[2]

and in 'Why War?', his address to Einstein:

> It may perhaps seem to you as though our theories are a kind of mythology and, in the present case, not even an agreeable one. But does not every science come in the end to be a kind of mythology like this? Cannot the same be said today of your own Physics?[3]

Lines drawn to communicate what we know is only a blurred merging. Myths – symbolical stories set up to explain other stories.

When he first used hypnosis with patients, Freud (like others) was aware that the treatment echoed an important hypnoid state within the hysterical attack itself. At least within Freud's psychonalytic theory, there remains, I believe, always this homologous structure: a characteristic element of the illness is taken up and repeated in the treatment and then, in its turn, finds a place at the centre of the theoretical construction. The famous reflection at the end of the Shreber case is an indication:

> Since I neither fear the criticism of others nor shrink from criticizing myself, I have no motive for avoiding the mention of a similarity which may possibly damage our libido theory in the estimation of many of my readers. Schreber's 'rays of God' which are made up of a condensation of the suns rays, of nerve fibres, and of spermatozoa, are in reality nothing else than a concrete representation and projection outwards of libidinal cathexes, and they thus lend his delusions a striking conformity with our

theory . . .It remains for the future to decide whether there is more delusion in my theory than I should like to admit, or whether there is more truth in Schreber's delusion than other people are as yet prepared to believe.[4]

And later:

I have not been able to resist the seduction of an analogy. The delusions of patients appear to me to be the equivalent of the constructions which we build up in the course of analytic treatment – attempts at explanations and cure. . . [5]

If for Freud a scientific theory was a myth (there is nothing pejorative in this), then we should remember both how his case histories read like *romans à clef* and how, if uneasily, he was well aware of this:

I have not always been a psychotherapist. Like other neuropathologists, I was trained to employ local diagnosis and electro-prognosis, and it still strikes me myself as strange that the case histories I write should read like short stories and that, as one might say, they lack the serious stamp of science.[6]

If the theory is a myth, the case history a short story, then of course the essence of the illness is in some way a story too. As one commentator has put it: 'Charcot sees, Freud will hear. Perhaps the whole of psychoanalysis is in that shift.'[7] I don't believe that this particular transition is the whole of psychoanalysis; but I do feel that it is important. Rather than stress language, the talking cure, I would emphasise here the listening treatment. Hysterics are creative artists, they suffer from reminiscences, they have heard something that has made them ill:

The point that escaped me in the solution of hysteria lies in the discovery of a new source from which a new element of unconscious production arises. What I have in mind are hysterical phantasies, which regularly, as it seems to me, *go back to things heard* by children at an early age and only understood later. The age at which they take in information of this kind is very remarkable – from the age of six to seven months onwards.[8]

In these early papers – before *The Interpretation of Dreams* and an interest once more in the visual and in perception – the stress is on the aural and its connection with the formation of unconscious phantasies. Charcot saw and classified and dismissed what he heard:

> You see how hysterics shout. Much ado about nothing . . . [She is said to talk] of someone with a beard, man or woman . . . Whether man or woman is not without importance, but let us slide over that mystery.[9]

But Freud decided that these tales of sound and fury did signify something. The move from seeing to hearing, from Charcot to Freud, is the move away from observation and the attendant blindness of the seeing eye.

Stories have two dimensions: what they are about and who tells them. Freud first believed that the stories were true and then that they were true as stories. Hysterics tell tales and fabricate stories – particularly for doctors who will listen. At first Freud was over-credulous. He thought they were about what they said they were about on a realistic plane, he then realised his patients were telling stories. The stories were about psychic reality: the object of psychoanalysis. What they are about then, is first seduction and then phantasy; who tells them – this is the beginning of psychoanalysis as a theory and therapy of subjectivity.

Social historians of western Europe and America consider that hysteria reached epidemic proportions during the nineteenth century. It was primarily a disease of women. Alice James, sister of the novelist Henry and philosopher William James, will do to illustrate my theme here. Like Dora, Alice's conversion symptoms seem mainly to have been constructed from an identification with her father: an hysterical paralysis of the leg for his amputation. No one doubted that Alice was as able as her brothers; but she made her illness into her career, writing her diaries to parallel the communications of her body. She described her own feelings:

> As I used to sit immovable reading in the library with waves of violent inclination suddenly invading my muscles taking some

one of their myriad forms such as throwing myself out of the window, or knocking off the head of the benignant pater as he sat with silver locks, writing at his table, it used to seem to me that the only difference between me and the insane was that I had all the horrors and suffering of insanity but the duties of doctor, nurse and strait-jacket imposed upon me, too. Conceive of never being without the sense that if you let yourself go for a moment you must abandon all, let the dykes break and the flood sweep in, acknowledging yourself abjectly impotent before immutable laws.[10]

She also commented:

When I am gone pray don't think of me simply as a creature who might have been something else, had neurotic science been born.[11]

Many nineteenth-century doctors got furious with their hysterical patients, finding themselves locked in a power struggle in which their opponent's best weapon was the refusal to be cured. Freud and subsequent analysts are familiar with the problem. Freud's understanding of this – in characteristic fashion – moved from the notion of a social gain in illness (removal of middle-class women from intolerable situations) to a psychological one where it bifurcated. It became on the one hand, the theories of resistance, the negative therapeutic reaction, and, particularly, after the case of Dora, of transference and counter-transference. On the other hand, after a difficult trajectory which I am going to try to trace here, it led to the concept of a fundamental human repudiation of femininity – a repudiation which, for Freud, was the bedrock of psychoanalysis both as theory and therapy.

I think – and I want to be tentative here – that psychoanalysis had to start from an understanding of hysteria. It could not have developed – or certainly not in the same way – from one of the other neuroses or psychoses. Hysteria led Freud to what is universal in psychic construction and it led him there in a particular way – by the route of a prolonged and central preoccupation with the difference between the sexes. The sexual etiology of hysteria spoke to Freud from the symptoms, stories and associations of his patients and the otherwise unattended to, accidental comments of his colleagues. But the question of sexual difference – femininity and masculinity – was built into the very structure of the illness.

There are two aspects to Freud's interest in Charcot's work that I think should be stressed. They are separate, but I suggest Freud brought them together. Charcot emphasised the existence of male hysteria. He also organised the disease. When Freud returned from Paris to Vienna the first paper he presented was on male hysteria. In his report, he commented of Charcot's work:

> Hysteria was lifted out of the chaos of the neuroses, was differentiated from other conditions with a similar appearance, and was provided with a symptomatology which, though sufficiently multifarious, nevertheless makes it impossible any longer to doubt the rule of law and order.[12]

At the same time, when Freud's friendship with Fliess was at its height, he wrote to him congratulating him on his work on menstruation with these words: '[Fliess had] stemmed the power of the female sex so that it bears its share of obedience to the law.'[13] The search for laws, lines to sort out the blurred picture; laws that in the end are anyway only myths.

The laws about the human psyche will be one and the same thing as the laws about sexual difference. Hysteria was the woman's disease: a man could have it. In Freud's hands hysteria ceases to be a category pertaining to any given sector of the population, it becomes a general human possibility. And a possibility not only in the sense that anyone can have it, but in that it provides the clues to the human psyche itself.

We can see Freud stumbling from the specificity of hysteria to the construction of subjectivity in the general human condition in these early writings from the 1880s and 1890s. Always it is via the dilemma of sexual difference.

Conditions related *functionally* to sexual life play a great part in the

> aetiology of hysteria . . . and they do so on account of the high psychical significance of this function especially in the female sex.[14]

> Hysteria necessarily presupposes a primary experience of unpleasure – that is, of a passive nature. The natural sexual passivity of women explains their being more inclined to hysteria. Where I have found hysteria in men, I have been able to prove the presence of abundant sexual passivity in their anamnesis.[15]

> Her hysteria can therefore be described as an acquired one, and it presupposed nothing more than the possession of what is probably a very widespread proclivity – the proclivity to acquire hysteria.[16]

Freud tried all sorts of explanations as to why an illness so clearly found predominantly in women, should also occur in men. But it was a cry of Eureka! when he wrote enthusiastically to Fliess: 'Bisexuality! I'm sure you are right!' Bisexuality was a postulate of something universal in the human psyche. But while bisexuality explained why men and women could be hysterics it did not account for why it was their femininity that was called into play.

At the level of the story, the tale Freud heard was of paternal seduction. After holding on to this information with conviction he writes to Fliess that something is hindering his work. The obstacle has something to do with Freud's relationship to Fliess – the relationship of a man to a man which, by 1937, was to be the other expression of the bedrock of psychoanalytic theory and therapy, once more, a repudiation – this time, on the man's side – of femininity, of passivity in relation to a man.

Many commentators, including Freud himself, have observed that it was Freud's femininity that predominated in this relationship with Fliess; it is possible that it was his femininity that rendered that friendship eventually untenable. Freud referred on several occasions to his own neurosis as 'my mild hysteria'. He did so frequently at the time when he was blocked in his work on hysteria. He has a breakthrough: 'I no longer believe in my neurotica'. Hysterics are not suffering the trauma of paternal seduction, they are expressing the phantasy of infantile desire. Is this true of hysterics or of everyone? Freud's clinical listening and his self-analysis come together:

> One single thought of general value has been revealed to me. I have found, in my own case too, falling in love with the mother and jealousy of the father, and I regard it as a universal event of early childhood, even if not so early as in children who have been made hysterical . . . If that is so, we can understand the riveting power of *Oedipus Rex* . . . [17]

Hysteria, the Oedipal illness; source of the concept of the Oedipus complex, discovered through the hysteria of Freud, a male analyst. Universal bisexuality; universal Oedipus complex; hysteria the most Oedipal neurosis, the one that most utilises bisexuality. Women more Oedipal, more bisexual, more hysterical. These connections were to remain for many years in search of a theory that explained them. What was universal, what specific to hysteria, what to femininity?

Something else that came to be connected was going on with Freud's investigations. These early texts are preoccupied with two aspects of hysteria: the absences or gaps in consciousness and the splitting of consciousness. Anna O's illness reveals the absences, Miss Lucy R's the splitting.

> [The] idea is not annihilated by a repudiation of this kind, but merely repressed into the unconscious. When this process occurs for the first time there comes into being a nucleus and centre of crystallisation for the formation of a psychical group divorced from the ego – a group around which everything which would imply an acceptance of the incompatible idea subsequently collects. The splitting of consciousness in these cases of acquired hysteria is accordingly a deliberate and intentional one. At least it is often *introduced* by an act of volition; for the actual outcome is something different from what the subject intended. What he wanted was to do away with an idea, as though it had never appeared, but all he succeeds in doing is to isolate it psychically. [18]

The splitting of consciousness, the disappearance of meaning, the unconscious – these cease to be confined as characteristics of hysteria and again become universalised. Freud finally distinguishes his theory of hysteria from Pierre Janet's on the grounds that Janet argues that hysteria's defining feature was splitting and Freud that it was conversion. For Freud, splitting was a general condition. Freud came back to the question at the end of his life. In the fragmentary paper on 'Splitting of the Ego in the Process of Defence' he is uncertain whether, in 1938, he is on to something new or merely saying again what he has said before. It is a return to the preoccupation with splitting that had marked his work on hysteria fifty to sixty years before. I shall argue that what he says at the end is both old and new. What is new is that by the end of the 1930s he has brought it into line with the problem of sexual difference. In the early days, it went only side by side with that question – he had not yet established the point of their connection.

Not yet connected with splitting, then, in the early work on hysteria there remained the problem of the division into masculinity and femininity. In the 1890s Freud came very close to sexualising repression. Fliess offered one version of this argument, the other was to be Adler's mistake. In a draft entitled 'The Architecture of Hysteria', Freud wrote: 'It is to be expected that the essentially repressed element is always what is feminine. What men essentially repress is the paederastic element.'[19] How close and yet how different is this to the repudiation of femininity as the bedrock of psychoanalysis in *Analysis Terminable and Interminable* in 1937. But sexualising repression was not an idea that Freud held on to for long. Six months later, in the letter to Fliess in which he tells of the hold-up in his self-analysis, he comments: 'I have also given up the idea of explaining libido as the masculine factor and repression as the feminine one . . .'[20] And yet – with all the difference in the world – in Freud's theory libido remains 'masculine' and it is not that repression is feminine, but that femininity is repudiated.

The concept that brought together Freud's observation of splitting and the dilemma of sexual difference as it was posed in hysteria, was the castration complex. I don't want to go into details of the concept here – merely to note whence it arose, what it explained and how forcefully it was (and maybe still is), rejected by other analysts. It came from Freud's pursuit of the internal logic of what he needed to describe. He used both Fliess's biological and Adler's sociological accounts as buffers from which his theory needed to bump away. In a fascinating two pages at the end of the paper on 'A Child is being Beaten', he explains why these accounts fail. The concept of castration arose, too, from a listening ear tuned to the problem in the case histories, in particular, in that of Little Hans. What it explained was briefly this: how the formation of the human psyche was inextricably linked with the construction of a psychological notion of sexual difference.

For Freud, the child's first question is hypothesised as 'where do babies come from?' The second (or maybe chronologically the other way round for girls) is: 'what is the difference between the sexes?' The theoretician in Freud reformulated his own hypothesis – the child's imagined questions – as the myth (or theory) of the Oedipus complex and the myth (or theory) of the castration complex: lines around blurred fields of colour.

The splitting that set up the unconscious is repeated in a split that sets up the division between the sexes. For this reason, the 1938 paper on the splitting of the ego uses as its exemplary instance the conscious acceptance of the castration complex and the simultaneous unconscious repudiation of the possibility of its implications (femininity) as expressed in the setting up of a fetish object.

For Freud the final formation of the human psyche is coincident with the psychological acquisition of the meaning of sexual difference. In Freud's theory this is not there from the beginning, it has to be acquired:

> If we could divest ourselves of our corporeal existence, and could view the things of this earth with a fresh eye as purely thinking beings, from another planet for instance, nothing perhaps would strike our attention more forcibly than the fact of the existence of

two sexes among human beings, who, though so much alike in other respects, yet mark the difference between them with such obvious external signs. But it does not seem that children choose this fundamental fact in the same way as the starting-point of their researches into sexual problems . . . A child's desire for knowledge on this point does not in fact awaken spontaneously, prompted perhaps by some inborn need for established causes.[21]

The story told is about the acquisition and repudiation of this knowledge.

Sexual difference – but why should it be femininity that is repudiated? Before Freud, many doctors and commentators thought that hysterics were women trying to escape or protest their female role; Freud toyed with the possibility that all that was feminine was repressed, the repressed feminine would thus have been the content of the unconscious itself. We are all familiar with how often women are thought to be more in touch with the unconscious, more intuitive, nearer the roots of nature – in Ezra Pound's words:

> . . . . the female
> Is an element, the female
> Is a chaos
> An octopus
> A biological process

Freud's answer was: no, 'we must keep psychoanalysis separate from biology'; repression must not be sexualised. But femininity *does* come to represent this point where meaning and consciousness vanish. Because this point is chaos, that which has been made to stand in for it – made to indicate the gap – is unbearable and will be repudiated. In the loss of balance, something to fill the gap will be hallucinated, a breast; produced as fetish, envied – a penis. The clinical experience of splitting and of castration is horror – penis-envy, hallucination, fetishism are quick relief.

It is commonly held that castration rests on deprivation – what is taken away from one, as, for instance, in weaning. I would suggest, however, that what it rests on and organises into its sexual meanings is, on the contrary, splitting. It only then 'subsequently' uses deprivation. One cannot experience absence, a gap – mankind, like nature, abhors a vacuum – one can only experience this unexperienceable as something taken away. One *uses* deprivation to describe the indescribable – the indescribable are splitting and the castration complex.

Freud talks of splitting where Klein perceives 'split off parts' which can be communicated to the analyst by projection. The similarity of vocabulary conceals essential differences. I am not sure that the splitting of which Freud talks could be experienced in the transference. It can be witnessed in fetishism, but on the other side of the fetish object there is nothing there: no object, therefore, no subject. In my limited experience all the analyst can do is bear witness; all the patient can do is experience the most intense horror, a horror that is about absence but which can become filled with phantasmagoria. The emptiness of chaos made carnate, a plethora of unorganised feelings and objects.

In splitting, the subjectivity of the subject disappears. The horror is about the loss of oneself into one's own unconscious – into the gap. But because human subjectivity cannot ultimately exist outside a division into one of two sexes, then it is castration that finally comes to symbolise this split. The feminine comes to stand over the point of disappearance, the loss. In popular imagery, castration is usually thought of as something cut off, missing, absent, a wound, a scar. Analytically, I believe it is experienced not only in these pallid indicators of absence but as something appallingly out of place: something there which should not be there. The trauma captured in splitting is that one isn't there; the same trauma that castration comes to symbolise is that one is incomplete; the trauma that can be lived over and over again in the endless by-ways of life's failures and imperfections. The loss can only be filled up:

> If one of the ordinary symbols for a penis occurs in a dream doubled or multiplied, it is to be regarded as a warding off of castration.[22]

Because human subjectivity cannot ultimately exist outside a division between the sexes – one cannot be no sex – then castration organises the loss of subject-hood into its sexual meanings. Something with which the subject has identified, felt to be his or herself (something that satisfies the mother, the phallic phase – *being* the phallus for the mother – completing her), disappears, is missing. Castration is 'discovered' in the mother who is no longer perceived as whole, complete – something is missing, the baby has left her. The baby goes absent – vanishes from the mirror. Bisexuality is a movement across a line, it is *not* androgyny. For Freud there is no sexual distinction symbolised before the castration complex has done its organising of the desires expressed within the Oedipal situation. There are male and female, active and passive, multifarious *behavioural* distinctions between boy and girl infants, but no notion in the psyche that one is not complete; that something can be missing.

The castration complex is not about women, nor men, but a danger, a horror to both – a gap that has to be filled in differently by each. In the fictional ideal type this will be for the boy by the illusion that a future regaining of phallic potency will replace his totality; for a girl this will be achieved by something psychically the same: a baby. Phallic potency and maternity – for men and women – come to stand for wholeness.

Hysteria was, and is – whatever the age or generational status of the man or woman who expresses it – the daughter's disease: a child's phantasy about her parents: the 'daughter' in the man or woman has not found a solution in homosexuality, maternity, or a career. To 'her' femininity really seems to equal the gap indicated by castration or, in Joan Rivière's words, it is enacted as 'a masquerade' to cover it. She is good at this but it cannot satisfy.

In the 1920s some important developments took place culminating on the one hand in ego psychology and on the other in object-relations theory, both Kleinian and non-Kleinian. There was a series of important and unresolved disagreements about the nature of female sexuality, but my point here is that despite an insistence on the problem, the question of femininity ceases to be what motivates the theoretical constructions. I propose to single out a few trends within Melanie Klein's work to indicate the implications of this.

In deciphering phantasy, Freud heard the child in his adult patients. Klein worked with children and found the infant in their phantasies. But there is a difference: the child and infant merge in Klein's way of thinking – their phantasies cope with the inner and outer realities in the present. For Freud, too, through his notion of the repetition compulsion, the child is alive in the adult's present. But for Freud the present always contains a construction of the past: the subject from birth to death is first and foremost, indeed, entirely, an historical subject, nothing other than what he makes of him or herself. This sense of history is not there in Klein's theory nor in her practice. Right until the end of his life, Freud's theory emphasised the analytic task of reconstruction of a history; Klein's highlighted interpretation and the analysis of the transference experience in which the task is to understand (largely through projection and introjection) what is being communicated between two people within the analytical session. Experience of psychic mechanism elicits the story which is no longer a tale told, but something revealed, discovered in process.

Where phantasy to Freud was the story – conscious or unconscious – that the subject tells about himself, for Klein it is the mental representation of the instinct and, simultaneously, a capacity to deal with inner and outer worlds. It joins instinct to object: primitively the oral drive phantasises an object; a breast or some substitute that can be sucked, for instance, a penis. And in turn, the object alters the inner ego; what is taken in from outside transforms the inside:

> The analysis of early projective and introjective object relation-
> ships revealed phantasies of objects introjected into the ego from
> earliest infancy, starting with the ideal of the persecutory breast.

> To begin with part-objects were introjected, like the breast and, later, the penis; then whole objects like the mother, the father, the parental couples.[23]

The boy and the girl have both the same and different drives: where their biology is different, their urges must differ. For Klein, the instinct is biological; for Freud it is 'our main mythology'. The boy and girl have the same objects. In Klein's theory, the object they first take in is predominantly part of the mother, then the whole mother; this gives them both in Klein's theory a 'primary femininity'. There is a shift of emphasis which, I believe, is crucial. For Klein, what you have got you transform by your phantasies and then take it in and it becomes you. For Freud, it is the attachment to what you have had to abandon that you take in. Freud's subject is constituted by filling the interstices where something is missing: one hallucinates, has delusions, tells stories. Klein's person becomes him or herself by taking in what is present. Psychically the mother in Freud's scheme is important when she goes away (the fort/da game), the penis when it is not there (penis-envy). Klein's concept of envy (interestingly enough also the bedrock of her theory and therapy) is for a mother who has everything.

For Klein the theory sets up a situation in which the ego phantasises directly out of its instincts and body feelings onto an object. Whereas Freud's 'body-ego' is always an homunculus standing on its head, for Klein, the objects (despite the accreted confusing phantasies) are, in essence, taken for what they are biologically and socially. The mother is a woman, feminine. The penis, even when inside the mother, is a masculine attribute. So, for instance, when the object of the oral phase moves from breast to penis, for the girl this becomes the heterosexual moment. The projecting penis is masculine where the breast is not. The gendered object gives meaning:

> For the little girl, this first oral turning to the penis is a hetero-sexual move paving the way to the genital situation and the wish

to incorporate the penis in her vagina. But at the same time it contributes to her homosexual trends in that . . . the oral desire is linked with incorporation and identification, and the wish to be fed by the penis is accompanied by a wish to possess a penis of her own.[24]

Freud listens to a story, constructs a myth. The unconscious shows they are only stories, myths. It is the gap, the point where the story vanishes, the subject disappears. (Ego psychologists believe the story is the whole truth and nothing but the truth – the story is all.) But, what we are witnessing in Klein's description is not the unconscious as another scene, that gap which has its own laws, but an unconscious that is filled, replete with a chaos of phantasmagoria, an unconscious as full as the external world seems to be. Her theory is about such an unconscious.

Perhaps I can give another analogy, tentative; a thought-in-flight. Freud's theory is a myth, a story of a story – the subject's narrative structuring of him or herself. It stops, it fails, it needs re-telling another way. Though a novelist writes of characters of different sexes, he or she never writes of anyone of no sex or in the middle of the dividing line – Virginia Woolf's *Orlando*, whose hero/heroine must change sides, highlights this. In Freudian theory, masculinity and femininity are only their difference from each other. Difference is articulated by something imagined to be missing. From the position of something missing, each sex can be imagined as having what the other has not. In essence this is what a novelist's story is all about.

But there is another literary analogy that could act as a possibility for theory. Not a myth, but a symbolist poem. This is what Klein's theory suggests. The wish to bite indicates the oral drive; the oral drive, aggression; aggression is Klein's (not Freud's) death drive. Physical impulse becomes a conception, the conception a theory. In a symbolist poem, the symbol shapes the product. The task is not to produce hypothetical lines around blurred fields of colour but to let the image produce its own shape. The poem, however, does not speak to sexual differentiation. As Adrienne Rich writes:

> If they ask me my identity
> what can I say but
> I am the androgyne
> I am the living mind
> you fail to describe
> In your dead language,
> the lost noun, the verb surviving
> only in the infinitive.

As far as femininity is concerned, we have moved from the hysteric whose femininity, being about nothing, had nothing she wanted, to the feminine boy and girl who, in imaginatively taking in their mother, have everything. But I believe there is a confusion in the conceptualisation here. This mother who has everything is not 'feminine'; she is complete. The poem is not, as many people including Klein in her theory of primary femininity argue, feminine, even if it partakes of the mother. Of course, the mother is where femininity in its positive filling in of a gap has landed and the association must retrospectively be made. But this poem and this mother are about notions of plenitude, fullness, completeness. Nothing is missing. The verb is in the infinitive. There is no 'I' nor 'other'. In the story sexual difference is symbolised around absence – the abandoned object cathexis, the envy of what is missing that once, imaginatively, was there. Here in the poem, the envy is for what is there and it is everything – milk, breast, faeces, babies, penises. What Klein is describing here is the raw material, the plenitude of objects and feelings which the story relies on when it comes to construct itself, to fill in its gaps. It is perhaps poetic justice that the hysteric who must repudiate her femininity which is about nothing comes to rest on a mother who has all. But we must allow the story to tell us something about the poem as well. In describing what he calls the deployment of sexuality in the nineteenth century Michel Foucault argues that there took place:

> A hysterization of women's bodies: a threefold process whereby

the feminine body was analyzed – qualified and disqualified – as being thoroughly saturated with sexuality; whereby it was integrated into the sphere of medical practices, by reason of a pathology intrinsic to it; whereby, finally, it was placed in organic communication with the social body (whose regulated fecundity it was supposed to ensure), the family space (of which it had to be a substantial and functional element), and the life of children (which it produced and had to guarantee, by virtue of a biologico-moral responsibility lasting through the entire period of the children's education): *the Mother, with her negative image of 'nervous woman', constituted the most visible form of this hysterization.* (My italics.)[25]

Motherhood purports to fill in the absence which femininity covers over and which hysteria tries not to acknowledge. From their positions along a continuum, motherhood and hysteria, to have or to have not, to be or not to be, constantly question each other.

Notes

All references to Freud's writings are to *The Standard Edition of the Complete Psychological Works of Sigmund Freud*, London, 1953—74. Each reference supplies the volume number and original publication date in addition to page number in the *Standard Edition*.

Part I: Feminism and the Question of Women

Women: The Longest Revolution

[1] Peter Townsend, *A Society for People*, In *Conviction*, ed. Norman Mackenzie (1958), pp. 119—20.

[2] August Bebel, *Die Frau und der Sozialismus* (1883), trans. H. B. Adams Walther, *Woman in the Past, Present and Future* (1885), p. 113.

[3] Charles Fourier, *Théorie des Quatre Mouvements*, in *Oeuvres Complètes* (1841) I, p. 195; cit. Karl Marx, *The Holy Family* (1845, trans. 1956), p. 259.

[4] Karl Marx, *Private Property and Communism* (1844), in *Early Writings*, trans. T. B. Bottomore (1963), p. 154.

[5] Karl Marx, *The German Ideology* (1845—46, trans. 1965), pp. 192—3.

[6] Karl Marx, *Capital* 1867. ed. 1961, I, p. 490.

[7] Friedrich Engels, *The Origin of the Family, Private Property and the State* (1884), in Marx-Engels, *Selected Works* (1962) 11, p. 225.

[8] *ibid.* p. 311.

[9] *ibid.* p. 233.

[10] August Bebel, *op. cit,* p. 7.

[11] V. I. Lenin, *The Tasks of the Proletariat* in *Our Revolution* (1917), in *Collected Works*, XXIV, p. 70.

[12] Simone de Beauvoir, *Force of Circumstance* (1965), p. 192.

[13] See Louis Althusser, *Contradiction et Surdétermination* in *Pour Marx* (1965). Althusser advances the notion of a complex totality in which each

314

independent sector has its own autonomous reality but each of which is ultimately, but only ultimately, determined by the economic. This complex totality means that no contradiction in society is ever simple. As each sector can move at a different pace, the synthesis of the different time-scales in the total social structure means that sometimes contradictions cancel each other out and sometimes they reinforce one another. To describe this complexity, Althusser uses the Freudian term 'overdetermination'. The phrase *'unité de rupture'* (mentioned below) refers to the moment when the contradictions so reinforce one another as to coalesce into the conditions for a revolutionary change.

[14] Apologists who make out that housework, though time-consuming, is light and relatively enjoyable, are refusing to acknowledge the null and degrading routine it entails. Lenin commented crisply, 'You all know that even when women have full rights, they still remain factually down-trodden because all housework is left to them. In most cases housework is the most unproductive, the most barbarous and the most arduous work a woman can do. It is exceptionally petty and does not include anything that would in any way promote the development of the woman'. (*Collected Works*, XXX, p. 43). Today it has been calculated in Sweden that 2,340 million hours a year are spent by women in housework compared with 1,290 million hours in industry. The Chase Manhattan Bank estimated a woman's overall working hours as averaging 99.6 per week.

[15] Karl Marx, *Capital*, p. 394.

[16] 'The African woman experiences a three-fold servitude: through forced marriage; through her dowry and polygamy, which increases the leisure time of men and simultaneously their social prestige; and finally through the very unequal division of labour.' René Dumont: *L'Afrique Noire est Mal Partie* (1962), p. 210.

[17] Karl Marx, *Precapitalist Economic Formations*, *op. cit*, p. 87.

[18] Friedrich Engels, *op. cit.*, II, pp. 233, 311.

[19] Karl Marx, *Capital*, I, p. 394.

[20] Viola Klein, *Working Wives*, Institute of Personnel Management Occasional Papers, No. 15 (1960), p. 13.

[21] Maternity is *the* distinctive feature on which both sexes base their hopes: for oppression or liberation. The notion of woman's potential superiority on account of her procreative function reaches the absurd in Margherita Repetto: *Maternità e Famiglia, Condizioni per la Libertà della Donna, Rivista Trimestrale* 11—12 (1964) but it is found even in Evelyne Sullerot: *Demain les Femmes* (1965).

[22] Philippe Ariès in *Centuries of Childhood* (1962) shows that though the family may in some form always have existed it was often submerged under more forceful structures. In fact, according to Ariès it has only acquired its present significance with the advent of industrialisation.

[23] J. A. Froude, *Nemesis of Faith* (1849), p. 103.

[24] Karl Marx, *Chapitre de Marriage. Oeuvres Complètes*(ed. Molitor),*Oeuvres Philosophiques*, I, p. 25.

[25] Karl Marx, *Private Property and Communism*, p. 153.

[26] Karl Wittfogel, *Oriental Despotism* (1957), p. 116.

[27] Friedrich Engels, *op. cit*, II, p. 224.

[28] Lawrence Stone, *The Crisis of the Aristocracy* (1965), pp. 663—4.

[29] Simone de Beauvoir, *La Marche Longue* (1957), trans. *The Long March* (1958), p. 141.

[30] Keith Thomas, *Women and the Civil War Sects, Past and Present*, No. 13 (1958), p. 43.

[31] Albert Ellis, *The Folklore of Sex*, in *The Family and the Sexual Revolution* ed. E. M. Schur (1964), p. 35.

[32] Claude Lévi-Strauss, *The Family*, in *Man, Culture and Society*, ed. H. L. Shapiro (1956), p. 274.

[33] Margaret Mead, *Sex and Temperament*, in *The Family and The Sexual Revolution, op. cit.*, pp. 207—8.

[34] Talcott Parsons and Robert F. Bales, *Family, Socialization and Interaction Process* (1956), p. 313. 'The instrumental-expressive distinction we interpret as essentially the differentiation of function, and hence of relative influence, in terms of 'external' vs. 'internal' functions of the system. The area of instrumental function concerns relations of the system to its situation outside the system, to meeting the adaptive conditions of its maintenance of equilibrium, and 'instrumentally' establishing the desired relations to *external* goal-objects. The expressive area concerns the 'internal' affairs of the system, the maintenance of integrative relations between the members, and regulation of the patterns and tension levels of its component units' (*ibid.*, p. 47).

[35] One of Parsons' main theoretical innovations is his contention that what the child strives to internalise will vary with the content of the reciprocal role relationships in which he is a participant. R. D. Laing, in *Family and Individual Structure* (1966) contends that a child may internalise an entire system – i.e. 'the family'.

[36] Talcott Parsons, *The Social System* (1952), p. 227.

[37] John Bowlby, cit. Bruno Bettelheim, *Does Communal Education Work? The Case of the Kibbutz*, in *The Family and the Sexual Revolution, op. cit*, p. 295.

[38] Betty Ann Countrywoman, in *Redbook* (June, 1960), cit. Betty Friedan, *The Feminine Mystique* (1963), p. 58.

[39] David Riesman, while correctly observing this, makes a rather vain criticism of it: 'There has been a tendency in current social research influenced as it is by psychoanalysis, to over-emphasize and over-generalize the importance of very early childhood in character formation. . . It is increasingly recognized, however, that character may change greatly after this early period. . . Cultures differ widely not only in their timing of the various steps in character formation but also in the agents they rely on at each step.' *The Lonely Crowd* (1950), pp. 38—9.

[40] Bruno Bettelheim, *Does Communal Education Work? The Case of the Kibbutz*, p. 303. From *The Family and Social Revolution, op. cit.*

[41] Jean Baby: *Un Monde Meilleur* (1964), p. 99.

[42] *Sotsialisticheskaya Zakonnost* (1939. No. 2), cit. N. Timasheff, *The Attempt to Abolish the Family in Russia*, in *The Family*, ed. N. W. Bell and E. F. Vogel (1960), p. 59.

[43] See Louis Althusser, *op. cit.* See note 13.

[44] Parsons and Bales, *op. cit*, p. 15n.

[45] Jean Baby records the results of an enquiry carried out into attitudes to

marriage, contraception and abortion of 3,191 women in Czechoslovakia in 1959: 80 per cent of the women had limited sexual satisfaction because of fear of conception. *Op. cit.* p. 82n.

[46] See Berger and Kellner, *Marriage and the Construction of Reality, Diogenes* (Summer 1964) for analyses of marriage and parenthood 'nomic-building' structure.

[47] Parsons and Bales, *op. cit.*, pp. 9—10.

[48] Riesman, *op. cit.*, p. 154.

[49] Marcuse offers the prospect of a leisure society produced by automation and the consequent shift from a Promethean to an Orphic ethos (eroticism over work-effort); and sees in this the true liberation of sexual energy for its own aesthetic end. Though he illustrates the difference (*Eros and Civilization*, 1955), this notion is too close to images of primitive societies dominated by the aura of maternal relaxation: '. . . satisfaction . . . would be *without toil* – that is, without the rule of alienated labour over the human existence. Under primitive conditions, alienation has *not yet* arisen because of the primitive character of the needs themselves, the rudimentary (personal or sexual) character of the division of labour, and the absence of an institutionalised hierarchical specialisation of functions. Under the "ideal" conditions of mature industrial civilisation, alienation would be completed by general automatisation of labour, reduction of labour time to a minimum, and exchangeability of functions, . . . the reduction of the working day to a point where the mere quantum of labour time no longer arrests human development is the first prerequisite for freedom.' (*ibid.*, p. 138). Against the consumer use of sex illustrated by Riesman, Marcuse poses the necessity for equal distribution of leisure, and hence the 'regression to a lower standard of life'; a new set of values ('gratification of the basic human needs, the freedom from guilt and fear . . . ') against an automated-TV culture. This is premature.

[50] Clara Zetkin, *Reminiscences of Lenin* (1925, trans. 1929), pp. 52—3.

[51] (See Ben Brewster, *Introduction to Lukács on Bukharin, New Left Review* No. 39, p. 25.) The capitalist mode of production separates the family from its earlier immediate association with the economy, and this marginality is unaffected directly by the transformation of the relations of production from private to public ownership in the transition to a socialist society. As the essence of woman's contemporary problem derives from this marginality, for this problem, *but for this problem only*, the distinction between industrial and preindustrial societies is the significant one. Categories meaningful for one element of the social totality may well be irrelevant or even pernicious if extended to the whole of historical development. Similar arguments, but principally lack of space in a short article, must excuse the total neglect of problems arising from class distinctions in the functions and status of women.

[52] Karl Marx, *Private Property and Communism*, p. 153.

[53] Karl Marx, *Precapitalist Economic Formations*, p. 85.

Women and Equality

[1] Anna Coote and Tess Gill, *Women's Rights: A Practical Guide*, 1974, pp. 15—16.
[2] *ibid.*, p. 21.
[3] *ibid.*, p. 16.
[4] Franz Neumann, 'The Concept of Political Freedom' in *The Democratic and the Authoritarian State*, Glencoe (New York), 1964, p. 167.
[5] *ibid.*, pp. 167—8.
[6] Quoted in R. H. Tawney, *Equality*, 1964, p. 48.
[7] Mary Astell, *Reflections upon Marriage*, London, 1700 (no pagination).
[8] *ibid.*
[9] Anon, . *An Essay in the Defence of the Female Sex*, London, 1696.
[10] *ibid.*, p. 17.
[11] Margaret Lucas, Duchess of Newcastle, 'Female Orations' in *Orations of Divers Sorts*, London 1662, pp. 225—6.
[12] Astell, *op. cit.*
[13] Lucas, *op. cit.*
[14] Astell, *op. cit.*
[15] Caritat, Marquis de Condorcet, 'Sur l'admission des Femmes au droit de Cité', 1790, quoted in Claire Tomalin, *The Life and Death of Mary Wollstonecraft*, 1974, p. 104.
[16] Mary Wollstonecraft, A *Vindication of the Rights of Woman*, 1792, 1970, p. 238.
[17] *ibid.*, p. 63.
[18] *ibid.*, p. 25.
[19] *ibid.*, p. 18.
[20] John Stuart Mill, *The Subjection of Women*, 1869, 1970, p. 238.
[21] *ibid.*, p. 230.
[22] *ibid.*, p. 259.
[23] *ibid.*, p. 259.
[24] *ibid.*, p. 316.
[25] *ibid.*, p. 219.
[26] *ibid.*, pp. 234—5.
[27] Arthur Young quoted in Tawney, *op. cit.*, p. 94.
[28] From the hymn 'All things bright and beautiful'.

Aspects of Feminism

1: What is Feminism?

[1] Freud, *Standard Edition*, IX, 1908, pp. 211—12.
[2] Judith K. Brown, 'A Note on the Division of Labour by Sex', The *American Anthropologist*, 72, 1970, p. 1075.

2: Feminism as a Political Movement

[1] Mao Tse-Tung, 'On Contradiction', 1937. *Selected Readings from the Works of Mao Tse-Tung*, Foreign Languages Press, Peking, 1967, p. 94.

[2] *ibid*. pp. 99—100.
[3] Marilyn Arthur, 'Early Greece: The Origins of the Western Attitudes Toward Women', *Arethusa*, 6, No. 1, Spring 1973, pp. 23—4.
[4] *ibid*. pp. 36—7.
[5] For this analysis of seventeenth-century feminists, see the subsequent publication of Hilda Smith's *Reason's Disciples*, 1982.
[6] Chaucer, 'The Wife of Bath's Tale', *The Canterbury Tales*.

3: Romantic Love

[1] Shulamith Firestone, *The Dialectic of Sex*, 1971, p. 142.
[2] *ibid*. p. 166.
[3] Denis de Rougemont, *Love in the Western World*, 1940, 1956, p. 17.

4: Feminism and Femininity at the Turn of the Century

[1] Ilza Veith, *Hysteria: The History of a Disease*. 1965, p. 47.
[2] 'Matrimony' in *Lady's Amaranth*, December 1839.
[3] Samuel Miller, A Sermon preached on 13 March 1808 for the Benefit of the Society Instituted in the City of New York, for the Relief of Poor Widows with Small Children.
[4] Henrik Ibsen, Notes written in Rome, 19 September, 1878.
[5] Edward Aveling, quoted in Tsuzaki, *The Life of Eleanor Marx*, 1967, p. 161.
[6] Elizabeth Hardwick, *Seduction and Betrayal: Women and Literature*, 1974, p. 46.

Part II: The Novel: Women and Children

The Ordeal of Richard Feverel: A *Sentimental Education*

[1] Meredith made a number of omissions and a few very brief additions for the edition of 1878. Most importantly he reduced the first five chapters to two and omitted details of Mrs Grandison's upbringing of her daughter. He thus shifted the novel away from its earlier stress on education, 'the system' and the Ordeal. As these are precisely the aspects that interest me, I have used the 1859 ed., reprinted by the Modern Library, New York, 1950, throughout. Critical reaction in 1859 tried to unravel the meaning of the novel by overconcentrating on the 'system'; it was doubtless partially in response to this that Meredith underplayed it in the second edition. The second edition is generally felt to be more coherent, but also more elliptical and enigmatic.
[2] *The Times'* critic wrote that this is 'a catastrophe in defiance of poetical justice

– this is neither the ancient nor the true method'. This opinion is reiterated by later critics, e.g. J. Moffatt, *George Meredith: a Primer to His Novels*, 1909.

[3] E.g. J. W. Beach, *The Comic Spirit of George Meredith*, 1911, calls it a '*comédie manquée*' in which the comic idea is somewhat obscure and the tragic interest takes over, making it 'something nobler than comedy'.

[4] Joyce completed for Meredith his work of building up an internal 'conversation' within literature by quoting the above aphorism in *Ulysses*, 1960, p. 255.

[5] Sir Austin's stress on 'pure' blood and his visits to doctors to discover the physical condition of the families of Richard's prospective bride certainly suggest that the Apple-Disease is VD. 'What terrible light [Dr] Bairam had thrown on some of [those families]! Heavens! in what a state was the blood of this Empire. . . .

Before commencing his campaign, he called on two ancient intimates, Lord Heddon, and his distant cousin, Darley Absworthy, both Members of Parliament, useful men, though gouty, who had sown in their time a fine crop of Wild Oats, and advocated the advantage of doing so, seeing that they did not fancy themselves the worse for it. He found one with an imbecile son, and the other with consumptive daughters. . . Both . . . spoke of the marriage of their offspring as a matter of course, "And if I were not a coward," Sir Austin confessed to himself, "I should stand forth and forbid the banns! This universal ignorance of the inevitable consequence of Sin is frightful . . . ,"' etc. (pp. 178—80).

Reference to VD was prevalent in pornographic fiction (see Marcus, *The Other Victorians*, 1969, p. 238).

If an obvious reference to VD was Meredith's intention, it makes this an even more extraordinary novel for a period in which there was a fairly rigid distinction between 'high' and 'low' literature – the treatment of sexuality being one of the main demarcation lines between the two.

[6] It is this sort of passage – which, strangely, he omits – that justifies Lindsay's claim that Meredith is inserting a politically radical message into his novel. Unfortunately, I cannot go along with his political redefinition of 'egotism', though much of his analysis is pertinent. J. Lindsay, *George Meredith: His Life and Work*, 1956.

[7] This is conveyed in a most striking passage in which they eat nine eggs for breakfast. The amount of eating in this novel, which has as one of its main themes the efforts of an upper-class family to sublimate sexuality, is extraordinary; it is actual and metaphorical, e.g.: 'So, without a suspicion of folly in his acts, or fear of results, Richard strolled into Kensington Gardens, breakfasting on the foreshadow of his great joy, now with a vision of his bride, now of the new life opening to him' (p. 332).

[8] John Henry Smith, in *Hiding the Skeleton*, Lincoln, 1966, traces through Meredith's intricate structure of blood, heart and spirit.

[9] This conclusion was suggested earlier by the cypress tree – another omen of Fate: the fourteen-year-old Richard sees this pointing at him as it did at his ancestor, Sir Pylcher, before he died in a duel.

[10] There is, of course, an uneasy similarity in the backgrounds of Richard's mother and bride: Lucy is the orphan daughter of a naval lieutenant.

[11] M. E. Mackay, *Meredith et La France*, Paris, 1937, has an excellent chapter on

Meredith and Molière; unfortunately, she makes no further use of his observations on Rousseau.

[12] This is according to W. H. Hudson, in *Rousseau and Naturalism in Life and Thought*, Edinburgh, 1903.

[13] Although personally convinced of the association, I feel some hesitation in asserting the parallel, not only because of the lack of direct evidence, but also because I have found only one critic in French, German or English who makes an explicit connection. This may well be oversight on my part. The critic is Sencourt, who writes: '*Richard Feverel* was a new *Emile*. But unlike *Emile*, he was to prove the excellence of the education according to nature, by showing the tragedy of education according to a system.' (R. Sencourt, *The Life of George Meredith*, 1929, p. 63.) And that is all. To suggest that Meredith is using Rousseau is not to deny that he was referring to the theories of Spencer and Mazzini, for instance. Quite the contrary.

[14] James McCarthy, *Westminster Review*, July 1864, pp. 31—2, in series 'Novels with a Purpose'.

What Maisie Knew: *Portrait of the Artist as a Young Girl*

[1] *The Notebooks of Henry James*, ed. F. O. Mathiessen and K. B. Murdock, New York, 1947.

[2] *ibid.*, p. 258.

[3] *The Art of the Novel*, ed. R. P. Blackmur, New York, 1934, p. 27 (my italics).

[4] R. D. Laing, 'Family and Interpersonal Structures' in P. Lomas (ed.), *The Predicament of the Family*, 1967, p. 122.

[5] *Harmsworth Encyclopaedia*, vol. 1, p. 730.

[6] Maisie's reactions confirm her wish to be left alone. Mrs Beale tells Maisie that Ida has given up her own daughter – Sir Claude is to: '"Take the whole bother and burden of you and never let her hear of you again. It's a regular signed contract." "Why that's lovely of her!" Maisie cried' (p. 211).

[7] Maisie also foresaw for her departing mother 'madness and desolation' (p. 159).

[8] D. Winnicott, 'Mirror-Role of Mother and Family' in Lomas, *op. cit.*, p. 298.

[9] Preface to *What Maisie Knew*.

[10] F. R. Leavis, '*What Maisie Knew*, A Disagreement', in M. Bewley, *The Complex Fate*, 1952, p. 131.

[11] This ingestive technique is made evident a number of times, where Maisie and Mrs Wix become one body: 'Shrink together as they might they couldn't help, Maisie felt, being a very large lumpish image of what Mrs Wix required of [Sir Claude's] slim fineness' (p. 81).

[12] Mathiessen and Murdock, *op. cit.*, p. 239.

Moll Flanders: *The Rise of Capitalist Woman*

[1] Arnold Kettle, 'Moll Flanders', in *Of Books and Humankind*, ed. John Butt, 1964.

[2] E. P. Thompson, *Whigs and Hunters*, 1975, p. 197.
[3] Thompson, *op. cit.*, p. 194.
[4] Gerald Howson, *Thief-taker General: The Rise and Fall of Jonathan Wild*, 1970.
[5] Gerald Howson, 'Who was Moll Flanders?', *The Times Literary Supplement*, 18 January 1968.
[6] Thompson, *op. cit.*, p. 195.
[7] Quoted in *Defoe*, ed. Pat Rogers, 1972.
[8] Ian Watt, *The Rise of the Novel*, 1957.
[9] Christopher Hill, 'Clarissa Harlowe and Her Times', in *Essays in Criticism*, vol. v, 1955, p. 333. See also Christopher Hill, *The Century of Revolution*, 1961.
[10] Quoted in James Sutherland, *Daniel Defoe: A Critical Study*, 1971.

Part III: Psychoanalysis: Child Development and the Question of Femininity

On Freud and the Distinction Between the Sexes

[1] Sigmund Freud, Letter to Karl Abraham, 21 July 1925. In *The Psychoanalytic Dialogue: the Letters of Sigmund Freud and Karl Abraham: 1907—1926*, edited by Hilda C. Abraham and Ernst L. Freud, trans. by Bernard Marsh and Hilda C. Abraham, 1965, p. 391.
[2] *ibid.*, 3 December 1924, p. 377.
[3] Letter 75 to Wilhelm Fliess, 14 November 1897. Freud, *Standard Edition*, I, 1897, p. 270.
[4] Freud, *Standard Edition*, VII, 1905, pp. 219—20.
[5] Freud, *Standard Edition*, XXI, 1930, pp. 105—6.
[6] Freud, *Standard Edition*, XIX, 1925, p. 257.
[7] *ibid.*, p. 256.

Psychoanalysis: A Humanist Humanity or a Linguistic Science?

[1] Lionel Trilling, *The Liberal Imagination*, 1961, p. 57.
[2] T. Vanggaard, *International Journal of Psycho-Analysis*, 56, Part 4, 1975, p. 493.
[3] Jean Laplanche and J-B. Pontalis, 'Fantasy and the Origins of Sexuality', *International Journal of Psycho-Analysis*, 49, Part 1, 1968, p. 17.
[4] *ibid.*, p. 16.
[5] Jean Laplanche and J-B. Pontalis, *The Language of Psycho-Analysis*, 1973, p. 318.

Freud and Lacan: Psychoanalytic Theories of Sexual Difference

[1] It is important to keep psychoanalytic object-relations theory distinct from psychological or sociological accounts to which it might bear some superficial resemblance. The 'object' in question is, of course, the human object; but, more importantly, it is its *internalisation* by the subject that is the issue at stake. It is never only an actual object but also always the fantasies of it, that shape it as an internal image for the subject. Object-relations theory originated as an attempt to shift psychoanalysis away from a one-person to a two-person theory stressing that there is always a relationship between at least two people. In object-relations theory the object is active in relation to the subject who is formed in complex interaction with it. This contrasts with Lacan's account of the object.

[2] Freud, *Standard Edition*, XXII, 1933, p. 116.

[3] Freud, *Standard Edition*, XI, 1912, pp. 188—9.

[4] Freud, *Standard Edition*, XXIII, 1937, p. 252.

[5] Freud, *Standard Edition*, VII, 1905, p. 56.

[6] Freud, *Standard Edition*, IX, 1906/7, p. 33.

[7] Freud, *Standard Edition*, XIV, 1915, p. 177.

[8] Freud, *Standard Edition*, XX, 1925, p. 37.

[9] This difference was to be taken further by other writers, most notably by Ernest Jones, who in arguing against the specificity of phallic castration and for the general fear of an extinction of sexual desire, coined the term *aphanisis* to cover his idea. This notion is not developed in Abraham's work but it did, however, set a future trend. Lacan returns to it, arguing that Jones so nearly hit the mark that his failure is the more grotesque for his near insight. To Lacan, *aphanisis* relates to the essential division of the subject whereas, he writes, Jones 'mistook it for something rather absurd, the fear of seeing desire disappear. Now *aphanisis* is to be situated in a more radical way at the level at which the subject manifests himself in this movement I describe as lethal. In a quite different way, I have called this movement the *fading* of the subject.''The subject appears on the one side as meaning and on the other as *fading* – disappearance.' '*Le Séminaire*, XI', 1964, Paris, 1973, pp. 189, 199. Trans. by Sheridan, *The Four Fundamental Concepts of Psycho-Analysis*, 1977, pp. 207—8, 218.

[10] Freud, 1935, 1971, p. 329.

[11] Auguste Stärke, *International Journal of Psycho-Analysis* 2, 1921, p. 180.

[12] Freud, *Standard Edition*, X, 1909, p. 8, n. 2, 1923.

[13] Freud, 1935, 1971. Letter to Carl Müller-Braunschweig (1935), published as 'Freud and Female Sexuality: a previously unpublished letter', *Psychiatry*, 1971, pp. 328—9.

[14] Freud, *Standard Edition*, XXII, 1933, p. 119.

[15] *ibid.*, p. 117.

[16] *ibid.*, p. 119.

[17] *ibid.*, p. 124.

[18] *ibid.*, p. 122.

Psychoanalysis and Child Development

[1] Victoria Hamilton, *Narcissus and Oedipus*, 1982, p. 4.
[2] *ibid.*, p. 32.
[3] *ibid.*, p. 245.
[4] Freud, *Standard Edition*, XVII, p. 138.
[5] D. W. Winnicott, *Therapeutic Consultations in Child Psychiatry*, 1971, p. 8.
[6] Melanie Klein, *Collected Works*, 1975, I, p. 144.
[7] Hamilton, *op. cit.*, pp. 17—18.
[8] Freud, *Standard Edition*, XVI, 1917, p. 457.
[9] Freud, *Standard Edition*, V, 1900 [1919] p. 373.
[10] Freud, *Standard Edition*, XIV, 1914, p. 50.

The Question of Femininity and the Theory of Psychoanalysis

[1] Freud, *Standard Edition*, XXIII, 1937, p. 252.
[2] Freud, *Standard Edition*, XXII, 1933, p. 79.
[3] *ibid.*, p. 211.
[4] Freud, *Standard Edition*, XII, 1911, pp. 78—9.
[5] Freud, *Standard Edition*, XXIII, 1937, p. 268.
[6] Freud, *Standard Edition*, I, 1893 [1888—1893], p. 160.
[7] Stephen Heath, *The Sexual Fix*, 1982, p. 38.
[8] Freud, *Standard Edition*, I, 1897, pp. 244—5.
[9] Quoted in Heath, *op. cit.*, p. 38.
[10] Quoted in Jean Strouse, *Alice James*, 1980, p. 118.
[11] *ibid.*, p. IX.
[12] Freud, *Standard Edition*, I, 1956 [1886], p. 12.
[13] Quoted in Heath, *op. cit.*, p. 46.
[14] Freud, *Standard Edition*, I, 1888, p. 51.
[15] *ibid.*, p. 228.
[16] Freud, *Standard Edition*, II, 1893—1895, p. 122.
[17] Freud, *Standard Edition*, I, 1897, p. 265.
[18] Freud, *Standard Edition*, II, 1893—1895, p. 123.
[19] Freud, *Standard Edition*, I, 1897, p. 251.
[20] *ibid.*, p. 271.
[21] Freud, *Standard Edition*, IX, 1908, pp. 211—12.
[22] Freud, *Standard Edition*, V, 1900, p. 357.
[23] Hanna Segal, *Introduction to the Work of Melanie Klein*, 1964, p. 8.
[24] *ibid.*, p. 97.

Index

abortion, 32, 44, 58, 210, 211
Abraham, Karl, 221, 223, 224, 225,
  227, 229, 265–7
activity and passivity, 226–7, 302, 308
Adler, Alfred, 234, 304, 305
adolescence, 42; *see also* puberty
adoption, 31, 279, 285
adultery, 105, 107, 108, 162, 165,
  179, 209–10
Africa, women's role in, 28
aggression, 226, 234, 235, 284, 311
agriculture, women in, 27, 28, 83
*Air of Reality: New Essays on Henry
  James* (ed. Goode), 171
Alceste (in *Le Misanthrope*), 165
Alexander, Franz, 265, 268
Algeria, women in, 17
Althusser, Louis, 18, 249
America *see* United States
American Anthropologist, 82, 88
Amerindians, 80, 214–5
'Analysis Terminable and
  Interminable' (Freud), 304
'anarchic carnival' *see* disruption
ancient world, societies in the, 19, 27,
  35, 36, 64, 96–102, 116
Andreas, 188
Andreas-Salomé, Lou, 265
androgyny, 103, 308
animals, 81, 82, 84, 85–6, 142, 226,
  227, 260
Anna O, Freud's case-study of, 303

Anne, Princess, 90
anthropology, 21, 23, 39, 77, 82–91,
  263
anus, 224
anxiety *see* separation anxiety
aphanisis, 270; *see also* sexual drive
'Apple Disease' (in *The Ordeal of
  Richard Feverel*), 155, 158
Arapesh men and women, 80
'Architecture of Hysteria, The'
  (Freud), 304
Aristotle, 64, 115
Astell, Mary, 63–4, 66, 67, 68
Athens, 93–102
attachment behaviour, 278
auto-eroticism, 110
automation, and the employment of
  women, 29–30, 45
Aveling, Edward, 122, 123

Baby, Jean, 43, 47
Balint, Michael, 252, 282
Bateson, P.P.G., 284
Bath, Wife of, 98–9
Beale, Mrs. (Miss Overmore) (in *What
  Maisie Knew*), 172, 176–180,
  186–88, 192, 193
Bebel, August, 20, 24, 27
behaviour, 21, 48, 69, 82–3, 92;
  attachment, 278; infant, 278, 308
Benson, Heavy (in *The Ordeal of
  Richard Feverel*), 147, 148, 157–8

About the Author

JULIET MITCHELL was born in New Zealand in 1940, but was raised in England from the age of four. After studying English literature at Oxford as an undergraduate and graduate student, she lectured on the subject at colleges in England and abroad. She has been a visiting professor at a number of American universities, including, most recently, Yale. She also trained as a psychoanalyst, and now practices in London, where she lives with her husband and daughter. She is the author of *Woman's Estate* and *Psychoanalysis and Feminism*, and is currently at work on three books: a selection from the writings of Melanie Klein; a book on psychoanalysis and the question of femininity; and a collection of essays, *Why Feminism?* which she is editing with Ann Oakley.